One Witch Had to Do It

One Witch Had to Do It

by

Hank Caruthers

Strategic Book Publishing and Rights Co.

Strategic Book Publishing and Rights Co.
12620 FM 1960, Suite A4-507
Houston TX 77065
www.sbpra.com

ISBN: 978-1-62212-965-2

TABLE OF CONTENTS

CHAPTER ONE

THE START

London Bridge past the English Village

I always led an extreme but magickal kind of life so it was difficult to decide where to start this book. Let's start in Laughlin, Nevada, where I was working a very dissatisfying job that was having a negative impact on my personality. I knew at the time this was happening and I was practicing a little self-help exercise on my walk to work every day.

It went something like this, here is a small tree (palm tree, most of what they have in Laughlin) and this small tree is me. Next to it is a larger tree that is me growing in a more positive way. Lastly there is a very tall tree that will be me when I can use my skills and have my attitude directed all in a more positive way. The unusual part of this was how hard it was to concentrate with all the noise coming from the birds. Even when I got to work and stood outside, the birds continued their squawking; it seemed directed at me.

This kept up day after day until I felt I had to learn what the birds were saying. I went to the local library to first learn what kind of birds were talking to me and what their characteristics could teach me about what they were trying to communicate.

Now I communicate quite well with cats, spiders and insects, and pretty well with dogs, horses, and snakes. So I was confident the birds were going to be just another species added to my list.

In my studies of 'the old religion of Italy' I read that birds were considered the messengers of the divine since they were the only creatures who flew to the heavens and back to Earth again. However I thought I would gain the same kind of knowledge I got from the other animals; the wisdom of nature.

In the library I learned the most abundant birds making the most noise were not crows like the local people I asked told me, but grackles. One of their characteristics was being able to make the sounds of other birds. They enjoyed making sounds so much, I started calling them gackles since they gackled all day long. I was also seeing one type of dove; there are only two types in the area.

I didn't go by what a lot of the metaphysical books said about animals, but found that my own observations worked much better for me. For example, most told a dozen characteristics of dragonflies, however, I learned from firsthand experience.

Camping one time outside Reno at the pond on Peavine Mountain, me, my two youngest children, and my buddy Stu were invaded by bees. Stu was trying to tan the inside of his arms and got stung on his armpit. My kids climbed in my van to get away from the bees, I lit a cigarette and used the smoke to keep the bees off me while Stu got in the pond to pack mud on his bee sting.

All of a sudden a group of dragonflies showed up and went right after the bees. I stood there amazed as this dragonfly-bee war went on until there were only dragonflies left. The dragonflies protected us that day.

From that day on, seeing a dragonfly meant that I was protected. There were many times when things could very easily have gone bad but a dragonfly showed up and the situation went way better than expected. I checked the books and never saw one that credited dragonflies with protection.

I began observing the birds. One of the first I noticed was a hummingbird outside the sliding glass door of my apartment in Laughlin. Directly off my patio there was a bush with flowers that the hummingbird was feeding on and two trees (not palms) on either side of the bush.

On the second day of observation some other birds flew in and perched in the closest tree. I watched as the hummingbird attacked those birds that were three times his size. He chased them out of that tree and when they landed in the furthest tree, he attacked again until they left the area. I found a protector in the bird world. I saw him chase away other birds that day. I never saw another bird land in the trees after that day.

Supporting the patio cover, I had a chain with bells hung on it that stretched from post to post. One morning I saw the hummingbird perched on the chain looking at me. It gave me the impression I was protected that day. I went off to work and it was one of the few days I would consider good at that job.

It developed into a pattern. If the hummingbird was perched on the chain in the morning I had a good day at work. If the hummingbird was on the chain when I got home from work I would not get called in for any emergencies in the middle of the night. There were plenty of those; that's one of the things that made that job so bad.

On the weekend I liked to go to a casino in Laughlin to kill a couple of hours playing twenty dollars on penny slots. One Saturday money was really tight. The way I figured it, I didn't even have the twenty dollars to lose but I was bored and had some time before the stores would open to buy the things I had to get.

While trying to decide to go or not, I happened to glance out the patio door and there sat the hummingbird. I walked over to the door that was partly open with the screen door closed. The hummingbird stayed on the chain.

I asked the hummingbird, "So you're saying it's okay to go to the casino?"

The hummingbird made the little chirping sound that hummingbirds make but in that I heard, "It's okay."

I went to the casino and won twenty dollars. Not a big win, but I had enough money to do the things I had to do plus an extra twenty to have fun with. Things still go well when a hummingbird looks at me.

The only thing I understood from the grackles was 'move'. It seemed to make a lot of sense because I hated the job and was really bored with the small town life. I started saving money, getting fewer tattoo sessions, buying fewer CD's and DVD's, and making fewer visits to the casino. They stopped cashing my paychecks anyway, which made me open a bank account.

I was already only spending twenty dollars on food a week and eating once a day because the depression from the job made me lose my appetite. I usually had to force myself to eat because I was rarely hungry. I called it extreme living-only eating enough to stay alive. I kept an eye on my weight and every time I got in the one twenty pound range, and was not on call, I tried to eat all weekend, though it was a bunch of one dollar cheeseburgers or fifty cent tacos.

I was happy with the way the bank account was growing and was considering whether to move back to Reno or try Las Vegas. It was about that time I heard one of the strangest sounds I have ever noticed. I distinctly heard on my way to work the caw of a crow. I turned to see the crow but the only bird there was a dove. I knew the sound came from there and as the dove looked at me again it made the caw of a crow. This had me thinking for a few days.

A dove was the symbol of peace, and a crow to me, meant the symbol of rebirth. How did a rebirth of peace fit into my life? What in the world did this have to do with me? Then I got the call. It was my half-sister.

My mother, who was suffering from Alzheimer's, took a turn for the worse and the doctors were only giving her another week to live. The first thing I did the next morning was look for that hummingbird but he was nowhere to be seen. That's when I knew this was all too real and my mother was dying. I went to work that day and the birds seemed strangely quiet. When I got to work I told my boss what was happening with my mother and that I might have to leave for Houston very soon.

He checked with the corporate office and I had no vacation time but had four sick days I could use. The company would not give any time off for a death in the family and that made me hate them even more (I didn't use the word hate lightly).

All day I did not get much work done but instead just thought of what my options were. In talking to my half-sister over the past few months I knew my mother was down to the mental capacity of a three year old and could not recognize anyone she didn't see every day. No matter how much I wanted to see her alive, with only four days I would not be able to stay for the funeral. If I waited for her to pass I could at least be there for the family.

I would have a thousand dollars saved with my paycheck Friday that might get me to Houston and back. But with only four days off I would have to drive twenty hours straight to get there for the funeral. By the end of the workday I had my plan.

I didn't hear from my half-sister that night but thought all night about my mother; the good times we had and all that she gave me by the way she raised me. She always had a way of making the everyday things fun. One of my favorites was swapping the letters around in names. The Handy Food Mart became the Mandy Hood Fart. We went Raskin Bobbins for ice cream, and drank a lot of Poctor Depper.

Before I went to driving school my mother took me out and showed me how to race, control a skid, diamond a corner and drafting. Mom used to race stock cars. She always encouraged me to be independent, "Go out and play anywhere you want. Just be home when the streetlights come on."

I don't know if she realized that's what gave me the guts to hitchhike halfway across the country at seventeen or why I rarely kept in touch with the family. But I think she understood I was my own man.

It was all thanks to my mother.

I went to work the next day feeling a little better and asked my co-worker if he would take the pager when I left. We worked out a time when I would take it for him and I actually got some work done that day. For a moment that day, since I had not heard from my half-sister, I thought maybe the doctors were wrong. Perhaps she got better and would be okay. I knew I was only hoping for the best.

When I got home from work I had dinner and waited by the phone. My half-sister called. She said Mom was in and out of consciousness, they had her on oxygen, there was a no resuscitation order she signed before she got sick, and she insisted on being cremated.

My half-sister also complained about my full-blooded sister refusing to see our mother to remember her the way she was. All the responsibility was falling on my half-sister for not only our mother but also for her dad, my step-father. I reassured her that if I was there I would do all I could to help, but as it was, I only had four days. I told her the rest of my plan. She said I could stay with her when I got to Houston. We hung up and I felt like this was it, I should start packing or something, when my full-blooded sister called; guilty conscious or something. She asked if I heard what was going on and I told her I was talking to the other sister. This sister started defending herself about her decision to not see our mother in the condition she was in. I tried to stay neutral.

She finished her defense then I told her about my plan. When she heard I had a thousand dollars saved she said I barely had any money and she would talk to our step-father. I got off the phone with her feeling insulted. That thousand dollars was a lot to me. Not to mention what I was going through to have that much.

The next day I informed my boss that things were not going well and I would have to leave on the weekend or the beginning of the next week. That was another real hard day to work.

My half-sister called that night saying she and my step-father stayed at the nursing home all night and that day, she just got home. Mom had not regained consciousness, and the doctors were saying the oxygen was the only thing keeping her alive. My half-sister was going to get some sleep and go back to the nursing home. I told her to let me know if anything happened and I would jump in my truck and head straight there.

The next day at work I kept my phone in my hand and had a feeling of impending doom all day but got no call.

At home that night I was surprised to hear from my full-blooded sister. She gave me the run down on all the flights they could have got for me with layovers that would take as much time as driving. She then told me our step-father paid for a non-stop round trip from Las Vegas to Houston leaving early Saturday morning. What a relief, but I didn't know if the timing was right. I figured I wasn't in a position to debate when I should leave so I would just go with the flow and see what happened.

I went to work Friday and filled out the paperwork to take the first four days off the next week. I handed off the pager and didn't get much work done for thinking about the trip ahead of me. I got home that night and started packing.

When I finished packing I broke out the atlas to look at my route to the airport. I noticed that Las Vegas was laid out a lot like Reno. It started me thinking about moving again. I lived in Reno for over thirty years. If Las Vegas was that similar I wouldn't have any trouble finding my way around if I moved there. The next morning driving into Las Vegas, I got on a six lane highway and felt like I was home since I hadn't driven on a real highway since I left Reno.

I got to the airport really early so the wait there seemed to take forever. I was so anxious to see my family after twenty-five years the flight seemed to take forever too. My full-blooded sister and her husband picked me up at the airport. They asked if I wanted to do anything and I said, "Shopping." It was really hard to find anything cool in Laughlin.

We went to a mall in Houston and I got a pair of shoes with skulls on them that fit. It was always one or the other in Laughlin. Shoes with skulls that didn't fit (I had a pair of those) or shoes that fit with no skulls. Yes I have a thing for skulls; they represent the higher state of mind.

We went to their house after shopping and started talking. That's when I found out why she didn't think my thousand dollars was very much. She saved over thirty thousand before she lost her job. When we were driving through Houston I noticed a lot of construction crews working and building going on.

I asked, "Don't they know there is a recession going on?"

Their reply was, "Not here, only the oil business is hurting." That's why she was out of work. After a while and a lot of idle chit chat, my half-sister called. They took me to her house. My full-blooded sister never wanted kids and married a man our parent's age. My half-sister and I had much more in common. She at least had two children who were grown now as were my four children. She went through a divorce as I had, but I have grandchildren. We at least kept up with the kids over the years.

I had a picture of her son in his Halloween costume hung in my trailer in Reno. I think my jaw hit the floor when I saw him. He was twice as big as me. We had a lot of catching up to do that night but we didn't stay up too late because again she was at the nursing home. Mom was still not conscious and they were talking about cutting the oxygen off.

Sunday I watched the NASCAR race with my nephew while my half-sister went to the nursing home. They did shut the oxygen off so she and her father stayed with Mom until she passed away that night. It was a quite night.

I got up the next morning, made up the couch I was sleeping on, and went outside for a cigarette. I lit the cigarette and got about three puffs off it when I felt the overwhelming presence of my mother.

Once again in my studies of "the old religion of Italy" I learned how to communicate with spirits. I got practical experience at graveyards in Northern Nevada doing graveside counseling in Virginia City, speaking with guardians of graveyards in Reno and in Gold Hill with a paranormal group. I even investigated other sites with this group and had success calling up spirits. I knew my mother was there.

I asked her if she was okay and she said, "I feel alone, terribly alone. I didn't expect this."

I asked, "Is there anything I can do for you?"

She replied, "I will feel everyone's love at the memorial service; that will help." Then she left.

In a way it was like any other time I communicated with spirits but there was something inside me that made me want to run inside and wake everyone up to tell them what just happened.

As I finished my cigarette I thought they really don't understand my abilities and I don't think they will believe this happened. I chose not to mention it again and have never told anyone until now writing this book. Looking back at it I still wonder if this didn't start everything you are about to read. The rest of the day went pretty normal. My half-sister checked her computer for jobs for me. Seeing how much work was going on in Houston had me adding it to the possible places to move. There were no toolmaker jobs which was not surprising.

I spent most of my life working my way up to this very skilled and precision oriented position only to see the invention of EDM machines that can cut hardened tool steel to within ten thousandths of an inch. That is what tool makers do, except we had to make the piece five thousandths over size, harden the tool steel, then grind it to size. The EDM machines were faster and as good as the best toolmaker. We were looking at machinist jobs which would be a step down for me, but there were plenty of those.

We had to meet with the funeral home about the obituary and to finalize the memorial service arrangements. After we finished that, we went shopping. My nephew needed a jacket for the memorial service. I barely put a dent in the four hundred dollars I took with me on the shoes and a hat that had spiders with skull heads on it. The hat was perfect for me because spiders are one of my totem animals and my right arm is tattooed with spiders in webs.

While they found the right coat, I found one hoody with skulls on it and a purple hoody too. You couldn't get those in Laughlin.

After shopping we drove by the place where the memorial service would be held; a church. That's when it hit me, I studied the "old religion." By common myth one of two things would happen, I would burst into flames, or the church would burst into flames. As we talked that night and finished our catching up all thoughts of the church thing disappeared and we got a good night's sleep.

The next morning I awoke with that church thing on my mind again. I remembered what my mother said. If she appeared at the memorial I would not be the only one who noticed but I would be the only one prepared for it. Between me and Mom we might be able to blow the doors off that church, so to speak.

After breakfast we started getting ready for the memorial. I was in a West Coast state of mind when I packed. My nicest shirt was a silk looking flame-shirt, how appropriate, and a nice pair of jeans. I wore the shoes and hat I wore on the flight to Houston, the skulls weren't as noticeable.

We got to the church early as did some others. My half-sister introduced me to some friends my mother made after I left at seventeen, and to the nurses who took care of Mom. That happened inside the church and to my surprise neither one of us burst into flames but so far I was wearing the brightest clothes.

I did tell someone dressed in black that I'm not mourning her death, I was celebrating her life. I kept going outside for a cigarette, but was actually looking for my mother who I could not sense anywhere. Then my step-father showed up.

We had our differences when I was growing up but a while back he told one of my daughters it was time to forget the past. I never did. Although I know I learned some valuable things from him.

My half-sister came outside to remind me to thank him for flying me to Houston and back. I agreed that was the least I could do. He was inside the church saying his helloes to everyone.

I was with my nephew by my step-father's brand new Escalade. I said, "We should get him some twenty sixes then he could be really big pimpin'."

We laughed and walked away. My step-father came outside to get something out of the Escalade. I waved at him. He called me over and told me to climb in. I got in and before I could say anything he said he was sorry we hadn't got together to talk. Then I got my chance.

With as much of I-am-my-own-man as I could, I said, "I want to thank you for flying me out here, but I would have gotten here one way or another."

As I looked into his eyes, I could see not only the sadness of losing my mother but a certain amount of wisdom he had gained.

He said, "That's alright. I can see you've lived a hard life."

We got out and he went back to greeting people, which left me standing outside the Escalade thinking, damn, do I look that bad? I walked away lighting one more cigarette while I looked for Mom.

I went back into the church and was reintroduced to my mother's friends that I hadn't seen in almost forty years. Most of them remembered me except one lady. It took everything I had not to say, well I will never forget your daughter but that's a whole other story in itself. The service began and I left my hat on in defiance.

They made a DVD using the pictures from my mother's life. The only real baby pictures were of me. My full-blooded sister's baby pictures were lost in a fire and I can only think that because my half-sister was in control of the pictures, she didn't want hers in it.

I did get to see the DVD before the memorial. On one of the trips out we swung by and picked it up. My half-sister wanted me to see it before the service so I wouldn't break down during the memorial. I teared up a little the first time and a little less at the memorial.

It was amazing to hear about all the things they did after I left home. I guess I was holding them back from world-traveling while I lived with them. Now I see why my step-father thought I lived a hard life. His was so easy gallivanting all over the world while I was working on a career in Reno that wouldn't last. That's alright. I could never dislike the man again after what I saw in his eyes.

The preacher went through his sermon with me glaring at him the whole time. Even as they prayed I saw him look up at me. I stared a hole right through him. When it was all over I rushed outside to position myself so he would have to walk by me. He said his niceties at the door then headed down the sidewalk towards me. I was ready. He was going to get an earful like he'd never had before.

He ducked his head and rushed by me without saying a word. He must have guessed I knew he was lying to the people. I chuckled just loud enough for him to hear. As the crowd came out, I saw my favorite aunt and uncle and their daughter. I went over to talk to them. We talked until my half-sister came out and said we were all going to my step-father's house.

When we got to his house my half-sister was telling me how she's had to make her dad some healthy meals to keep in the fridge because without our mother around he'd lost his will to live and would just pick up fried chicken take-out if he got hungry. That one struck a bell with me. I realized that was half my problem. What was I living for?

My kids were grown but I had to move away from them because I felt like I was raising one daughter's kids and one son wouldn't work because he could get money from me. Between asking myself, what am I living for? And do you know how long it's been since I've been able to buy fried chicken? It really had me going. Of course that was added to the fact my mother didn't show up at the memorial. My mind was whirling. With those things bothering me I spent most of the time at my step-father's outside smoking.

Two cute girls showed up and my nephew brought them outside by the koi pond. They sat down at the table where I was smoking. I was bothered with what was going on and now my vacation was almost over. I had to go back to that job and Laughlin.

I couldn't remember all that was said, but one of the girls did say, "You're a Wiccan. You know you shouldn't be smoking."

The next day I thought about what I wanted to say; what I didn't have the presence of mind to say then, "Little girl, when you have lived the life I have, you will smoke twice as much and hate every minute of it."

I talked to my favorite uncle a lot. He was a welder and knew about the toolmaker thing and what it was like for me working for a living; not what my step-father and his friends thought of as work. He even said he understood what I was going through because his health was getting bad and he couldn't go to work to weld as much as he wanted to. He also said for him any kind of work around the house didn't seem right and it was driving him crazy. Wow, one person in the world who understood me. I don't know if it helped, but it did make me feel better.

The next day my half-sister had to work so my full-blooded sister came to get me. It was for the day, before I had to go to the airport. I asked if we could go and see my favorite aunt, uncle, and their daughter. It was in the last neighborhood I lived in before I left.

We made the little tour of my old stomping grounds, and sad to say, it changed my mind about moving back to Houston. They showed me how Houston had grown so much that the line from ZZ Top, "out in the sticks down highway six," was just no longer true like when I was growing up there. There were no "sticks" left.

They said, "Houston has grown south all the way to Galveston." I needed nature and open spaces. Houston doesn't have them anymore. At least there were some in Laughlin, but Don Laughlin owns it all and there were no trespassing signs everywhere.

The old neighborhood where the rich people lived was kind of run down too. The houses were still good. They were well built and expensive when I was growing up, but a lot of the common areas were not kept up. The two eighteen-hole golf courses were down to one nine-hole practice course. Even the family jewelry store that was once a big expansive place on Post Oak was reduced to mostly watch repair in a local strip mall.

My aunt and cousin were still making the most of it. I was proud of my cousin, the way she worked with her life long battle with Cerebral Palsy. She knew that business (jewelery and watch repair) inside out and was very helpful to the customers I saw her with. How could I ask myself what I was living for, with her shining example right in front of me? I was living to make my life the best it could be. I just had to get out of Laughlin.

We went to lunch at a little restaurant in the strip mall. I made new observations with my mind clear.

I used to be the black sheep of the family but when my full-blooded sister married a man much older than herself and they decided not to have any children, the family looked at her as the black sheep. It all happened without me knowing about it.

Sitting there at lunch I saw my aunt talk to them like none of the things that were going on even existed. I had seen my half-sister's animosity towards them about seeing my Mom and sharing the pictures. She gave me a ton of pictures of my childhood and my full-blooded sister said she did not get any. She wasn't even sure she would get a copy of the memorial DVD.

No one at the service really talked to them. They just quietly came in and just as quietly left. Even at my step-father's afterwards everyone was stand-offish towards them except my favorite aunt and uncle. Seeing the way my aunt treated them at lunch made me realize why they were my favorite relatives.

They were such down to earth people they wished no ill to anyone. Another secret of life revealed in one afternoon. I gave my full-blooded sister all the pictures I had of her and the copies I had of both of us. I know my aunt was once the black sheep of the family as was I, so it was kind of funny that all of us off-color sheep were having lunch together.

After lunch they took me to the airport.

On the flight back all I could think about was what it would take for me to move out of Laughlin. Las Vegas looked even better when I got back. On the drive back to Laughlin I tried to imagine myself starting over in Las Vegas.

Getting home, I unpacked and went to sleep without eating. The next day I did laundry, bought my usual chicken, bread, and soda then texted my kids to let them know I was back. I was dreading going back to work the next day so I kept checking the bank book and the calendar trying to figure out how soon I could leave.

The next day on the walk to work I picked up another word from the grackles. They were saying, "Just move, move, just move."

Back at work nothing had changed. There was too much to do and no time to do it all. I got the pager back and thought it couldn't be that bad because there was only one day of work this week. But, I got called in for another water leak that put me farther behind.

When people moved out we had to fix their apartment to look brand new, but with all the water leaks and problems in the units that were being lived in, there was no time left to prepare a vacant unit. Two steps forward and about twenty back. I was getting way too close to the breaking point.

I started saving money like crazy. I was not going to the casino, not buying CD's or DVD's and not even getting tattooed. My income tax refund came in which was a complete surprise! My ex-wife left me with a huge bill with the IRS that I paid on for years and they always kept my refund. I guess there was a time limit on it. The refund was the size of a two-week paycheck which had me pushing three thousand dollars. From my perspective, I had a lot saved. I set a goal of five thousand and then I would move. Then my oldest daughter called.

She was living in Bellflower, a suburb of Los Angeles. She said she would have a chance to come visit me. One stipulation though, we had to go to Lake Havasu where she used to live. I agreed. I had not seen it though it was not far from Laughlin. The day after we talked the first time, inside my apartment, I heard a grackle say, "Havasu."

Over the next few weeks we finalized our plans for her visit and we both saved as much money as we could. The grackles were being very insistent. Every day I heard, "Havasu, Lake Havasu. Move to Lake Havasu."

I wasn't leaving it totally up to the birds. I was getting the Las Vegas paper and looking for jobs. It seemed the only thing in the paper I could do in Las Vegas was for a company that I had already worked for in Reno. With them I waited a year and a half for my first review and they gave me the maximum raise, thirty five cents. I told them, "That is a cost of living raise and you should just lay me off." They did. I don't know if they would hire me back but I knew I did not want to go back to work for them.

We got the plan for my daughter's visit all set and I made sure it was a weekend that I was not on call. The closest she could get by bus to Laughlin was Las Vegas. I looked forward to driving to Las Vegas again, but apologized I could not get any more time off work since I used it all to go to Houston. I was really excited about her visit because I was saving so much money I wasn't getting out to have fun, not that I thought there was much fun to be had in the area.

Finally the day came. She took off work early Friday to catch the bus and I had to work all day, but I didn't let anything bother me that day. The grackles still kept saying, "Move to Lake Havasu."

I drove to Las Vegas that night and had an easy time finding the bus depot. It was as easy as finding the airport. I knew I would love to live in Las Vegas. I always left early to go anywhere in case something happens so I was very early to pick her up. I noticed the Freemont Experience was only a couple of blocks from the bus depot so I went to check it out.

I found a few of my favorite penny machines and lost fifteen dollars. I said, "That's Vegas!" and went back to the bus depot. Las Vegas is notoriously tight. I still think it's better to play in Reno. Even Laughlin isn't as tight as Las Vegas. I could still live there, tight casinos would be just another challenge for me to conquer.

When my daughter walked through the doors of the bus depot I think she was as happy to see me as I was to see her. We had a kind of kindred spirit thing going on. I don't think any two people can understand each other any better than we do. Out of my four children she is the most like me. She was living in Los Angeles while her family lived in Reno. That was only the start to how we were alike, but throw in the tattoo deal and you can really see how she is like me.

We did a lot of talking on the drive to Laughlin, all about her bus ride and how excited she was to show me Lake Havasu.

17

When we got to my apartment I showed her my mom's memorial DVD then we got some rest. I didn't tell her what the birds were saying though I knew she would believe me. The next morning we just had coffee then got in the truck and headed for Lake Havasu. The drive was interesting. I had been all through Bullhead City and most of Fort Mohave but never past that. It's a beautiful part of the Arizona desert. It reminded me of driving from Reno to Pyramid Lake. You would expect to see a large body of water at the crest of every hill. Then we saw the lake. The excitement was building.

She had me take the first road in Lake Havasu City, London Bridge Road. As we turned on to it I got a feeling I'd had before. Some roads have a magickal quality to them, perhaps they fall on ley lines of the Earth, I don't know but I sure feel it. Highway Six in Houston, Highway One Sixty Five in Louisiana and White Rock Road outside Sacramento, all have the same feel as London Bridge Road.

The first stop we made was at a nature reserve park. We had the same sort of thing in Reno; signs telling you about the wildlife and plants in the area. After hiking almost to the end of the paved pathway we came to two hills.

We climbed up the first one and back down again with me echoing her as a little kid, "Are we there yet?"

She said, "Just to the top of the next hill." So we climbed again.

At the top she said, "If you sit up here and meditate, all you can see is the lake and it feels like water is all around you." As she sat down she said, "Every time I needed a dose of Nature I would come up here." She took her turn then I took mine and she was right.

We went back to the truck feeling refreshed and continued down London Bridge Road. Passing the hotels I saw the Golden Corral and knew where I wanted to go for lunch. Around a bend in the road we came to the parking lot of the English Village. We parked and went in through the ornate iron gate.

We passed the visitors center and the fountain that wasn't working. Then we could see it; the famous London Bridge. I could tell by the architecture that it was old but very well built.

My daughter grabbed me and said, "Come on Dad you have to see this shop."

It was the first one we came to, fixed up like a castle in the front. I was trying to see everything as she opened the door. The owner was outside and I guess I hesitated a second for all my looking. The owner said, "It's a little different but don't be afraid."

I scoffed at that and held up my right hand with the big pentacle tattoo on it as I said, "Oh I'm not afraid."

He had a lot of cool stuff in there. It was not quite a metaphysical store (I used to work in one), but there was some skull stuff, some dragon stuff and incense. Then I saw the swords.

"You have really good prices on these swords," I told the owner since I used to sell them for over two hundred dollars. All of his were under two hundred. One I liked was marked at sixty five dollars and I said I would take it. He sold it to me for fifty dollars.

He also tried to sell us on his tour of the London Bridge, but I said we were only staying the day and I would come back in a month to take the tour. It was the beginning of spring break so there were a lot of people there closer to my daughter's age as we walked through the Village with sword in hand.

There were several comments about the guy with the sword as we went from shop to shop and along the lake-side. After we made the rounds of the English Village we drove around the city and visited a boat shop where my daughter used to work. She asked about getting her job back and I bought a tank top to make it look good. They were not hiring at the moment she was told. She wanted to move to Lake Havasu more than I did. We then checked another job possibility, but they were closed.

We drove by where she used to live; she didn't want to stop. I sensed they did not part on good terms. Then we went to Golden

Corral for lunch. The food wasn't bad and we ate our money's worth, but it wasn't everything their commercials said it would be.

We headed back to Laughlin. On the way, she asked me what I thought of Lake Havasu. I told her I thought the store where I got the sword was cool and I would definitely go back. She said she knew I would like it.

We got back to my apartment in Laughlin and I dug out all the pictures my half-sister gave me. My daughter got to see my whole childhood in those pictures.

Dinnertime came and I said there was a casino with a ten dollar seafood buffet. She said, "Let's go."

In the casino we played some first. She won five dollars, I lost ten. Then we seriously pigged-out on seafood. We were so stuffed we barely talked when we got back to the apartment, opting to sleep off the big meal.

The next day was uneventful. We drove back to Las Vegas and got her back on the bus. We were both sad she was leaving. We had never gotten to spend time together like that even when she was a kid. We both tried but something always got in the way.

On the way back I was wishing I had worked in a casino in Reno so I would have some kind of chance of a job in Las Vegas. I got back to Laughlin in money-saving mode. I had only spent one hundred fifty dollars on my daughter's visit, but I planned on going back to that shop in Lake Havasu. The next month was hard. Work and home were about the only places I went. Things were not all that bad at home. Doing laundry was one of my favorite things. There was an old guy that always did his laundry at the same time I did. We started talking one day and I found out he was a wealth of information on Laughlin.

He did not belong to any of the organizations that were available in Laughlin. They wanted the town to be a retirement place. The organizations were run by wealthy retirees who were not very receptive of the wants and needs of the seniors on fixed incomes. I heard the same from seniors in the low income apartments I worked at.

The man also knew of the building practices in the area which was the very problem I was having at my job. They kept trying to sell him houses but he knew how poorly they were built. He was very happy to stay in the apartments we lived in. His life stories were fascinating. He was a painter. They displayed his art at the library and I went to see it. He was really good and I was happy I took the time to get to know him.

While sitting at home that month, I came up with a plan. I had done tarot readings at the meta-physical store in Reno. I told everyone that my tarot test was one hundred readings in one night with one deck (one of the hardest decks to read). Usually adding that's when I learned I need more decks. After that night I was allowed to work in the store.

I did a few benefit reading sessions for free and really enjoyed it. I made a sandwich board sign with free tarot readings on it and after the store closed I used the sign to offer free readings on Halloween at the tattoo parlor. I might be able to help that store in Lake Havasu by doing free readings there.

It was sort of a meta-physical shop and it seemed to me the owner would be open to it. I had my sign still and a small table with screw-in legs I called the portable altar. I could use my camping chair but still needed chairs for my customers. A new quest!

I should explain that one. It was always easy to find just the right thing at just the right price in the big city. In the Laughlin-Bullhead area it was a real challenge. I would go on a quest.

When I got my apartment in Laughlin I had only a couple of nightstands and a cot to sleep on. All I had at the motel I worked at for six years was a bed. I wanted a couch. It's just me so it had to be manly, no flowers, and I only wanted to spend one hundred dollars. Quest on!

I went to Bullhead and stopped for gas. While pumping the gas I looked up and saw a discount furniture store. When I finished putting gas in the truck I drove across the street. I saw a couple of futons out front for ninety nine dollars but I wanted a real couch.

I walked inside and the first couch was nice but four hundred dollars. The next couch was six hundred, the next eight hundred, then twelve hundred, then sixteen hundred. I turned and started for the door when the salesman asked if he could help me. I told him I was looking for a couch but they were over my price range.

He said, "Come with me to the warehouse. I've got a return in perfect condition I can let you have for eighty dollars."

In the warehouse sat one couch with a brown and black plaid pattern and no stains or wear. Quest over!

I handed the man eighty dollars and they loaded it in the back of my truck. I even got back to my apartment in time to catch my upstairs neighbor outside and he gave me a hand getting it into the apartment.

That neighbor turned out to be a good friend too, although he and his wife worked in Las Vegas ninety three miles away and spent most of their time commuting. He was able to show me the only land Don Laughlin didn't own and I was able to ride my mountain board there. He videotaped the first time.

Then I needed a coffee table to go in front of the couch and once again I only had one hundred dollars to spend. Quest on!

That night I thought about what I wanted in a coffee table. It must be wide as I'd be doing a lot of stuff on it. It needed to be as long as the couch to fill the space and cool, like it was one of a kind.

I got up the next morning to start the quest but one of my tires was almost flat. Well that's why I got Big O tires. They fix their flats free and there was a Big O store on the far side of Bullhead. I limped the truck down the street to the gas station and filled the tire up. Then I headed for Big O without making any stops so the tire would not go flat. When I got to Big O they said they couldn't get to me for about an hour because they were so busy. I would have to hang out there. I figured, no problem, I've got all day to work on the quest.

There was a little hamburger joint across the street I had wanted to try, so I walked across Highway Ninety Five and got a cheeseburger. As I was eating the cheeseburger in front of Big O, using a stack of tires as a table, I started looking around and saw a used furniture store in a little strip mall behind Big O. After the cheeseburger I went over to the furniture store.

When I went in I saw a lot of nice furniture, dressers and chairs but only the nightstands seemed to be in my price range. After walking around the whole store I thought I should get back to the quest and find the section for coffee tables. What I found was four coffee tables stacked on top of each other.

The top one was one hundred sixty five dollars and the next two were also over a hundred dollars. I got to the bottom one and as I shifted the stack of wooden tables to get a look I saw a blue marble top. It looked about four foot wide and I could see a wrought iron base.

I started searching for a price tag and could see the glue spot where one had been but was no longer there. Then I found a price tag lying on the back side of blue marble top that said eighty dollars. I asked the lady behind the counter if that was the price of the table. She came over and looked.

I showed her the glue spot and where I left the eighty dollar price tag. She picked it up and said, "Let me call the owner." When she got off the phone she told me the owner said she could give it to me for eighty dollars! I said, "Now the real question will be can I pick it up."

Together we unstacked the tables. The bottom table was about a foot shorter than my couch but everything else was perfect. It looked like it weighed five hundred pounds but I tested the weight with one hand and it was light. I picked it up to bring it to the counter by the door and I could see it was wood with a blue marble laminate over it. I paid the lady and carried the table to the truck. With a big smile on my face I loaded it in. Quest over before they could fix my tire!

There were other quests too, a desk, end table, and TV stand, all under twenty dollars each. I found a new but discounted TV.

It was a lot of fun finding them. Back to the chairs; I found the perfect ones at K-Mart but they were twenty dollars each so I got two instead of four.

Friday I handed off the pager feeling good about an adventure the next day. I got extra money at the bank in case everything worked out right. Then I could get a room and spend the night in Lake Havasu.

Heading out the next morning I was very excited that so many unknowns lay before me; the kind of extreme thing I love. Of course I got there early so I stayed on Highway Ninety Five into Lake Havasu City. I stopped at the Classic Burger and had a great cheeseburger that was half the price and twice as good as the place in Bullhead. I went on to the English Village. The owner was at the store.

I bought a vampire skull ashtray I would never use that way. While paying for that I asked him if he would like me to drum up some customers by doing free tarot readings. He said sure. I said I would put this in my truck and get my set-up. I think he was impressed by how prepared I was.

I set up the table and chairs well away from the door but still under the shade of the castle awning in front. I put a nice cover over the table then set out my bag of cards (fourteen decks) and put up the sign. When I finished, the owner sat down across from me and said I should do his reading first. I did and he said, "Very good," and went back into his store. Then it started.

Spring break was still going on and I had the only free thing in the Village. Not even an hour later I had a line of people waiting for readings. Each reading I did was giving me at least a five dollar tip. It was a marathon at first then I got a break and lit a cigarette as I started clearing cards.

When beginning a tarot reading I shuffle the cards putting that person's energy or their questions into the cards. With each build up of energy the cards actually get harder to push together. After the reading that person's energy is still trapped within those cards and a reading with them on someone else would not work. I learned that in my tarot test.

I carry so many decks so I can set them aside and do another reading until I can go back to clear them by doing a very loose shuffle trying to pass air between every card. When they are all cleared of energy they will act like normal cards.

While I was doing that, the owner brought out a girl saying since you bought something you get a free tarot reading. I asked her if she could wait a couple of minutes until I finished and she said she would. I finished the cards before I finished my cigarette so I got up and checked out the newspaper articles that were on the front window of the store. About all I got to read was that the owner's name was Gary and he had been a paranormal investigator for thirty five years.

I went back to the cards and that turned into another three hour tarot marathon before I got a break. This time I lit a cigarette and went to buy a soda. When I came back Gary was outside having a cigarette. I told him I had been the psychic in a paranormal group. He said he had been looking for a psychic for his group.

He asked if I was going on the tour that night and I asked how much it was. He said I would not have to pay. I said I would love to check it out. Some people came up and asked about the readings so I went back to work. I stayed somewhat busy until six o'clock with only enough time between readings to clear a few decks of cards.

At six o'clock I was clearing the last two decks when Gary came out and locked his store. He asked how I did and I stood up to pull the money I was getting as tips out of my pocket. I counted it and told him I made fifty dollars. I began to break down my set-up and he asked me if I was still coming back for the tour. I said I would but I need to get a room for the night then I would be back. I got everything back in the truck, he waited while I did. Then we said we would see each other in a little while and we left.

I went back down London Bridge Road to the Motel 6 and got a room. A nice young guy working the counter gave me a room with a view of the lake. I asked him how hard it was getting a job in Lake Havasu. He said, "Once you're here it's not too hard."

I went up to my room and collapsed on the bed; that was a lot of readings. Laying there for a couple of minutes I realized how thirsty I was so I went to the soda machine and got one. Back in the room I opened the soda and took a drink then figured I should try to get a shower in before the tour. I checked the bathroom and there was no soap. I decided on a cigarette instead. So after the soda and smoke I went back to the Village for the tour.

Gary was already there with some other people. A few more showed up and we started. I won't cover the tour here as most of this book takes place during the tour but on this tour, as I told Gary that night, I didn't feel much anywhere but the other side of the bridge where we started back; above the passage door.

I got that same sick to my stomach feeling most psychics get in a high activity area. It went away before we got to the center of the bridge. After the tour I went back to the motel and feeling a little hungry I got a candy bar and another soda. In the room I had those and one more cigarette then got a good night's sleep.

I woke up with the sun the next morning and opened the window for my morning smoke. I wanted to see my view of the lake but the vacant lot next door seemed to catch my eye. When I looked at the lot there was a rabbit looking back at me. As clear as day I could hear that rabbit's voice. He said, "Watch me." Then he hopped about five feet and looked at me again. That time I heard, "Do you understand?"

I asked, "You want me move?"

The rabbit hopped away and I said to myself, oh great, now I have to add rabbits to the list. I had a better feeling about Lake Havasu after making some money so I wasn't saying no to moving there.

I drove back to Laughlin that day feeling pretty good although I knew I would be going back to work the next day. The next weekend I went back to Lake Havasu. I bought a pair of dragon bookends and two skull flags. I set up to do tarot again but spring break was winding down and I only made twenty five dollars. It goes that way doing tarot. In Reno, some days I made nothing and one day I made three hundred dollars. I went back to Laughlin that night.

Two weeks on call and I was pulling my hair out. We had unfinished patches all over the property and they were hounding us for more finished units. Our new manager had all she could take and was quitting. I threatened to walk several times. I hung on until I had it all figured out.

When I got off the pager I'd drive down to Havasu and talk to Gary. I could come back to work Monday and give my two week notice. By the end of that time I would have five thousand dollars. My next trip to Lake Havasu would have a big purpose.

I should mention that during those two weeks, not just the grackles were saying move to Lake Havasu but doves, pigoens and sparrows were saying it too. I walked to work going, I know, I know. By the time I got off the pager I was a wreck. The drive to Havasu helped calm me down.

I went to Gary's shop in the Village and asked him if I could do the tarot thing full time. He said I could. I told him I was going to quit my job and had money saved up. But I would have to find a place to live. He said he had a room at his house he would rent to me for four hundred a month with free utilities. We had it set for June first. I went back to Laughlin ready to do it.

Monday I went into the manager's office and said, "I think I will join you. I'm giving my two week notice."

She said she needed it in writing on an employee action form so I filled one out. She then sent it to the corporate office. By Wednesday they said that they did not want me to stay the two weeks and let me go that day. I was not going to make it to five thousand dollars but had plenty of time to get moved. I still had to wait for my final check. I took the first load to Lake Havasu Friday. I went to the Village and did some tarot readings that day.

I told Gary I would pay the first month in advance if I could start bringing stuff over before the first. He agreed and at the end of the day he showed the way to his house. I unloaded my truck and saw my room for the first time. I drove back to Laughlin knowing I would not need all my furniture.

I made several trips to Lake Havasu the next week but spent my nights in Laughlin. By the next Friday I had everything I could take in Lake Havasu. I spent the night in Havasu. The next day I went back to Laughlin to get rid of the furniture I could not take. I was sad to junk my couch, but to keep the power bill down I never used the air conditioner. My place stayed about ninety degrees and I sweated a lot on that couch. My old TV, desk and chair I took to the apartments I used to work at thinking some low income person could use them. I then handed in the keys at my apartments.

I had already closed my bank account and paid the first month's rent to Gary. I still had four thousand one hundred dollars, so on the way to Lake Havasu I stopped at the Avi casino where I always went for cigarettes and got two cartons. Then I went in to the casino and played my favorite machine for the last time. As I left the casino it was like saying good bye to my native state. I got to Reno in 1975 and was going to live in Arizona in 2009. It was sad. A lot of unknowns lay before me.

CHAPTER TWO

THE ME TOUR

From the fountain looking out the front gate

My first week in Havasu was quite an adventure. Finding my morning coffee was the first order of business. I tried Jack In The Box but felt like I should be able to get coffee for under a dollar. So I found the McDonald's and they gave me a senior discount. Spring break had ended so the Village was a lot less crowded. Gary said most of the business would come from tour boats. Most of my readings seemed to be locals who heard there was something free in the Village. I did five readings the first day and made eight dollars. I already planned on eating two dollar cheeseburgers each day to save money. After work I went to the McDonald's then went back for the tour.

For this tour I didn't try all the psychic stuff. I just listened to Gary and learned all the interesting facts about the London Bridge. I also learned that Gary's two older boys, who took turns helping with the tour, were like ghost magnets. I could feel the spirits were afraid of me but very attracted to Zach and Micah. At the end of the first week I got an idea.

Zach would take a hundred pictures on the tour to catch a few spirits. I could let him use my camera which only took six pictures. He would have to sense the spirits while I did what I used to do with the other paranormal group, pull the spirits out. I asked Gary if it would be okay to do that and he told us to go ahead.

Before the tour, Zach and I went over to the Pub where I could sense there were spirits inside. I sat in front of the doors while Zach sat off to the right of me. I started doing a tarot reading concentrating on the spirits inside the Pub. Every time I felt the spirits I could see the flash of the camera. Zach was doing great.

I got a wild story out of the cards that told of a man who loved his wife so much he kept her body after she died. The time period felt like the 1800s. When he finally died they were together again and stayed in the London Bridge. With the help of a dark spirit they were able to move over to the Pub. The dark spirit was their protector. He had always been a fighter. That night when we got the pictures on Gary's computer we saw an orb with a man and woman's face and a dark spirit looking out the window.

During the second week, one of Gary's friends got an EVP (electronic voice phenomenon) that said, "Help me my feet are broken." They asked me what this meant. As they told me about it I could see an older lady jumping off the bridge but not landing head first as most of the people who ended their suffering from illness had done. She landed feet first breaking them and ending up in the water dying from hypothermia.

30

Gary said, "That was good on your part, but just because you say it, doesn't make it true. If you have it on an EVP then everyone would have to believe it." That really got me thinking. If I could pull them out of where they were hiding, then it should be pretty easy for me to get EVP's.

With my competitive spirit I'll get the best EVP's Gary has ever heard. I went over to the Radio Shack and picked up a forty dollar digital recorder. I still felt the spirits were scared of me so I would have to stay just far enough from Zach or Micah to pick up what the spirits around them were saying. This first tour with the recorder I called the Me Tour, for the best EVP we got. I let Zach take the recorder at first. He turned it on near the entrance gate and immediately got, "We protect him."

Gary was talking about the lamppost when a voice asked, "Can you hear me?" Then a car drove by.

Next was something strange. It said, "We shoulda be insane."

This was followed by, "Got coffee brewin' in my room."

My experience told me these were spirits. They say random things so they will not be noticed in recordings.

After that I got, "The party has just begun."

Then the question, "Does Hank know we're right here?"

Then the answer, "Maybe."

I was amazed to find this now. I didn't think they said my name for a few more tours. Zach picked up Gary talking about the phone booth. We started our walk down to the water's edge and we got a voice saying, "Keep up." Later, "Finish tour." We heard, "Hank was here," before we reached Gary's store.

I always stayed at the back of the tour so as not to be in anybody's way when they were taking pictures. Past Gary's store, The Dungeon, a female voice said, "I know."

Psychically I picked it up as, "I know who you are." But a male voice came in when I analyzed it and said, "It's not who you think."

A clear male voice said, "If I'm up here." But then it changed to another worldly sound as it said, "Then don't get there."

They seemed to be establishing where each should be as they said, "You need to back up right here." A female interjected, "Yeah ... So we can hear this some."

She then asked, "Am I talking now?"

Past The Dungeon and the restrooms we got to The Jersey Grill Restaurant. There we got one of the male voices saying, "I could poof poof right in right here."

The estimated speed of spirit energy is two thousand miles per hour. I have experienced how quickly they can travel to other parts of their world. Funny that they should refer to it as poof poof.

Then a female played on that as she said, "Siete poo." Once again trying to cover up what they said. A voice came in after that and said, "And we think it's right." But the voice changed for, "Don't you?"

Some of these voices could possibly be those of people but they were coming in at the same volume as the obvious spirit voices as with, "Get by you."

Then immediately after that, "He stalled a rocket."

That could be one of those random things they say. They talk a lot about their abilities, however. I say the next thing when I tell Zach to give me the recorder because I saw he had a nervous habit of rubbing his finger over the microphone.

I got a good example of how spirits use sounds to make words as through the sound of a passing vehicle we hear, "You wait for me."

Then a male voice said out of sound, "Just tell me we got it."

A female voice finished with, "Got it there."

I found a lot of one spirit finishing another's sentence on the EVP's in these tours.

We are still walking when a female voice said, "Let's speed up."

A male announced, "I get these three peaks at." He is cut off with, "How do I get through these people?"

A female said, "I will get up here." This is the second reference to being at a higher vantage point that can only be done by spirits. We are on a walkway and no one is climbing.

A male asked, "Can you hear me?" It's not Gary's voice.

It is interesting to note that Gary is talking a short distance away but the recorder is not picking him up. We only pick up these voices that don't seem to be the people listening to Gary's facts about the bridge.

A female voice came in saying, "I think we're going to the bathroom right here."

On one tour I almost called it the bathroom and bucket tour. Read on to find out why bathrooms would be so important to spirits.

She then said something that could not be made out but a male voice said, "Except when break in this tomorrow."

He followed with, "That's gonna take the three bucket."

We found the meaning of bucket on this tour.

After a, "Hi there," that I believed to be a person passing by, I got, "What are you getting here?" It was in a very spooky chopped up voice.

I can't tell who said, "Did I ever tell you about that?"

Followed by, "It's fine."

Then a female stated, "Inside this it is."

I could just make out, "We had to see him up to there," with an echoing sound. It sounded like they're following me when I thought they were afraid of me. A clearer male voice said, "We see about him." This was the first example of spirits interacting with human speech that I had when a voice said, "I'm still waiting for." This was just before Gary said, "Historical information on the bridge."

I got, "Hank," from a female.

A male finished with, "Is a wild one."

I guess I was kind of wild. You could just make out the female saying, "We've got to hurt him."

This was not surprising. There is a Down On Hank Tour. They said things to push me in a certain direction, remember the birds.

A clicking voice said, "We could do it for fun." And sometimes I thought they were. "It's about TV," was next. It was hard to nail down the meaning of that one.

I usually watched too much TV to get much done but Gary and I were both annoyed by the antics of the paranormal investigators on TV and I expected the spirits were are also. A male voice said, "We're gonna get an onboard." I took that as permission to be with me all the time.

A female stated, "We have all been here before."

A male remarked, "You got to look at everything."

A combination of voices asked, "Did you ever pump?"

A voice came back with, "I told you that."

Followed by a female asking, "How do you know?"

It sounded like a voice almost singing, "It's bugging me a lot."

I could barely make out, "And you will see."

It got clearer for, "First of all."

Again a real faint beginning with a strong ending, when they asked, "Is that all we need to get?"

A male warned, "They'll probably call here." And then, "The back you called up."

A female then replied, "Don't know if you do that."

Another said, "Hank will bump bump."

Did this give the impression they were talking about sex? They were.

After a little silence, one of the females said, "We want that bathroom."

A male ordered, "Not you for Hank."

He then said, "I guess we could call right here if that's a home. After that we go back to Hank. I still have these fears. We were going to White Castle through here."

It was amazing to get any references to old London. That side of the bridge was on the White Castle side. But what was the fear, all the disease or Jack the Ripper?

A voice said, "Been here before."

A male voice advised, "You will be seeing what you got going on the market."

A female started with, "You'll be."

A male finished with, "the Sun God."

The female added, "You'll be what's his name."

The male said, "Bahidrak." I could not find anything about that name.

A very high pitched voice remarked, "Now how absurd," and, "There's even more flowers."

A male stated, "It's simple to geek with a top gun right here."

Another male asked, "Are you going to get anything?" Then he said, "Then we will talk like him."

The high pitched voice came back and ordered, "Be a serious one." Then, "You gonna watch me move or what?"

Okay, she was moving into the bathroom. That brought up some questions, but the most important, was moving what?

The male started, "I believe that he at least."

A female interrupted with, "That he warm up."

All the years of working in low income housing did leave me with a cold outlook on life.

The male replied, "People stuff."

The high voice asked, "You're doing what?"

The male answered, "It's there."

"A ba-ba," comes after that.

A male remarked, "I'm glad you tell me when it's flat."

Then the high voice said, "I just said bucket."

A male voice was saying, "I just said," in time with the high voice.

Well she didn't say fuck it. They did substitute bucket a lot.

The high voice said, "What that for was it."

They didn't always get their phrasing right.

A male said, "Your fault," twice.

A female ordered, "Stay here for a moment."

A male voice pointed out, "That's where you screwed it up right here."

This was one of the times they gave hints that they scripted most of what they said.

The female replied, "I doubt if you feel about pick up."

That's either about my pick up truck or picking up the conversation with things they wanted to say.

Someone said, "Your cord."

Then there were a few seconds of no talking.

A male voice barely came in with, "Go big."

The high voice advised, "Don't worry about it."

A male started, "We forgot."

A female finished with, "Your head under that thing."

There were wise cracks and we were not even on the bridge yet.

The male directed, "We will be back in your copy later."

Was this a reference to some script they had?

Another male remarked, "It appears quite gnarly."

Don't forget they were people once and they use the language they used when they were alive.

A female stated, "A job I can get fifty."

A male voice said, halfway through what she said, "That's plenty."

"Or more," came after the female voice.

That may sound like people discussing work but there is something the spirits get also. Read on to find out more.

A male voice pointed out, "When you leave there's no place for you."

Another male voice added, "This has got to be different than, than what you're, what you're used to."

A male voice asked, "You did before?"

The female answered, "Fuck Hank."

A male voice disagreed, "It's not what you did."

We started walking up the stairs to the bridge and the spirits grew quiet. Gary talked about the steps leading up to London Bridge and about the chipped corners of the bridge. As we climb the stairs only Gary speaks. There was something different on those stairs and I could feel it. This was one of the places I wanted to understand all the energies here that made it so different.

Gary talked about the video at the museum. We climbed again. As we neared the top a female voice said, "You have no idea what you're talking about."

I was picking up children at the bottom of the stairs. At street level I got a male voice asking, "Are you all now being good?"

Then another male replied, "Now I can move again the next time."

Both were talking about what was on those stairs.

I faintly got a female saying, "I can help you."

Then a male remarked, "Nice to get in front of the people people."

What sounded like the same voice announced, "People on the bridge already."

It grew quiet again except for passing traffic and Gary telling of Mr. McCullough and Mr. Wood standing by their statues at the beginning of the bridge.

As we began our walk on the bridge, Gary gave its dimensions.

Crossing the bridge I got, "Hank is stupid, he win it."

One of them asked, "Both?"

The answer came next as, "He could win both if he wanted."

I got a laugh and then, "He will probably get a million."

A female stated, "You can't see him."

One of the males said, "He's dumb."

We were about in the middle of the bridge when the female sang the last part of, "Hank will go for a California girl."

A male said, "Greek," at the same time as California.

After that I got a whispered, "Hank right here."

The female told them, "I'm the one who thinks a positive way for Hank."

She then started, "If London Bridge."

A male finished with, "Is getting ready."

If they scripted this whole thing the ghosts of London Bridge were learning their lines.

A voice with an accent replied, "We're too busy to look."

A female pointed out, "Up here he quit it," and, "Hank quit."

When a male voice remarked, "He's not dead yet."

Another male suggested, "Let's check."

Then the female started, "The wing." We lost the rest in noise.

I know now she was referring to the wing book.

A male then said, "I can't believe you want to," and in a whispering hollow voice, "believe Hank."

The female confirmed, "Yes you can believe."

One of the males started, "We're hoping."

The voice changed for, "We cheated a weasel."

Psychically I felt there was more on the end of that.

A male replied, "It will fish."

When a female said, "Hank." It was so clear I could hear it before I got good at analyzing EVP's.

A very quiet voice asked, "Did you hear?" It became clearer and louder for, "What I did," and, "What I did today."

The female remarked, "You told me already. So we can get started. Hank is getting ready to tell me, Hank."

A male faintly stated, "I can't wait to hear what he says to me."

Another male said, "I get the poetry."

The female offered, "That's part of Hank."

Yes I do write poetry.

The female also suggested, "Let them climb up," and, "Does anyone know how to stand?"

Then there were disrupted voices. It was almost a pattern of missing sound.

38

A male commented, "Anyway, anyway I've gone here before."

Before usually means when they were alive.

Again the female said, "Hank," and, "the secret."

A male finished with, "Is everywhere."

He also added, "You didn't know it was Hank," and in a ghostly whisper, "You thought better Hank."

The female replied, "He would like it better if we have it," and, "Only if he wanted to."

She also started, "You'll get."

It was not clear but I got a male voice saying very ghost like, "Rid of Hank."

I'm glad I didn't hear that one early on.

The female remarked, "I bet you did that before."

Then he replied, "It's a gift."

A ghost voice was one of his abilities.

There is more disrupted sound and I only got, "You'll have to burn over Yeowseth."

It cleared up and a male asked, "Did they offer me another one?" I brushed something against the recorder.

Another male stated, "I know who you went to in that room."

He also asked, "Di are you back on foot?"

The female started, "Now you."

A male jumped in with, "Woke you up."

A male then pointed out, "That's what you wanted."

A car drove by drowning out the rest. I shut the recorder off because there were more cars coming.

I restarted the recorder on the other end of the bridge and got, "This is ahead of me."

A male asked, "Who you fuckin'?"

Another added, "You're fuckin' now," and, "That's a fine favor."

The female replied, "For him."

A male remarked, "I can't cut you too short."

She came back with, "You're so short."

Even short had another meaning in their world.

The male then replied, "It's nothing."

I turned the recorder off as we waited for the traffic to pass.

We crossed the street and I turned the recorder back on at the top of the stairs.

First I got, "If this is what you'll Hanky get."

Then he started, "Hank."

Another voice added, "Your buddy."

The female finished, "Real maintenance."

The parking lot for the Heat Night Club was just below the passage door. Here I picked up, "I ordered Nestea."

There was background noise from the outdoor bar. However the clanging of glasses stopped for, "How does it took you?"

The female announced, "We got here right."

She also suggested, "You'll need this."

Then a voice asked, "What'd you dream about?"

She replied, "If only for a few days," and a strange, "I'll get it wicket."

A male stated, "It's true while I go pee," and, "If that's where Hank will meet me."

I guess if you wanted contact with people, the bathroom would be a good option.

A male offered, "We can keep from getting here."

Another male announced, "Hank is in here."

The other male confessed, "I might stop him."

We were at the stairs by the passage door below where I felt spirit energy on the first tour. I didn't and still don't understand the next one, "Hank thirty cups down here."

A male started, "The judge is."

Another asked, "Can you see?"

We got, "We might be."

Zach reached the passage door and asked, "Hello, is anybody in there?"

A real strong, "Me," came back.

We first heard this that night after the tour with the recorder plugged into an amplifier. It was so clear we heard it listening to the tour without being separated. Behind Zach was a male saying, "He can't even get along with Hank."

He added, "Let's get exactly what I'll receive from here."

Zach asked, "If anybody's in there can you please knock like this?" He knocked on the passage door four times.

While Zach talked one of them asked, "What do you get to take from being here?"

A male then replied, "I'm convinced he won't get anybody."

A voice, which could possibly be from the bar, but sounded the same as what we heard so far said, "Anyway he got back here drinking."

I don't drink alcohol.

A male directed, "Don't worry about him what we're supposed to do."

Zach asked, "Huh?"

A female stated, "He loves you."

Zach asked, "Please say again?"

A male replied, "We went forty fifty miles. He's a broken hero."

That was a fine example of what I felt was pick up. He was supposed to say forty or fifty miles and he wanted to describe me as a broken hero. I felt that way sometimes.

A male confessed, "I know you will lose doctor."

Another male read out loud, "That's three zero nine."

A male pointed out, "He'll never wish you were here."

A male also requested, "I want to leave this stuff."

A female remarked, "I don't see why we have to do this."

Again Zach asked, "Hello is anybody in there?"

A female replied, "Even after I talked to you this morning."

She added, "I guess you and Cindy," and, "Aren't she beautiful."

That made it sound like a spirit.

She then stated, "I'll take you."

A male asked, "Do they bite hard?"

Another male remarked, "He said he had to goof my party."

The female revealed, "I will stop believe it," and, "I got a look at his room."

She then stated, "And you'll see two black orbs."

Their biggest concerns for me were my physical and mental health. I felt those were the dark spots in my room. Listening to spirits talk was not the best thing for my mental health.

A male claimed, "I was waiting for that," and, "We have to use what we get."

Another male suggested, "He'll get used to it."

One of the males remarked, "And you looked at all your favorite parts of people."

Remember she moved into the bathroom.

He also added, "You gotta be better before we can fix it."

She replied, "We all proved we could get."

I felt 'the job done' would be next, but a male interrupted with, "What do people say things about this to others?"

Another male answered him with, "I do believe Stella and you believe her right."

The other male said, "You're the man."

A male replied, "It's not what he told ya."

In a very spooky voice another male asked, "Do you need to go rape somebody?"

An answer came with, "I'm here before he fucked you."

I turned the recorder off going back up the steps to the bridge.

I started the recorder at street level and got, "I've seen you."

Then it sounded like a female whispering, "Anyone will bleed."

A male asked, "How many dogs did you eat back in there?"

Then typical of spirits talking, one of the males replied, "If you tell me, you tell me you did it."

The female confessed, "I can't get you."

A male asked, "What do you think of Brianna?"

Another male stated, "You got goldfish."

Someone said, "Shut up."

I hoped it wasn't me but I thought it was Zach.

A male ordered, "Rest your bones."

Another male pointed out, "A penis is all he's got."

One male asked, "I suppose you like that huh?" and, "Then you can bump bump."

He also noticed, "You're not sitting with Hank."

An almost metallic voice replied, "You just don't get this."

A male said, "See what we have here," and he asked, "What do you think for Hanky?"

The answer came with a question when one of them whispered, "He's quite special, you get it?"

Another answered, "Yes I do."

A male guessed, "You must hate that."

The reply was, "It's short to be like that."

I would now define short as any outward sign of negativity.

A male stated, "You're making good progress with Hank."

Another said, "Hank won't believe that."

Yet another replied, "It's not meant for him to believe."

One of them directed, "You'll wait to get asked."

There were eight seconds of silence with a disrupted sound which seemed like a long time when analyzing this tour. I took out ten seconds of recording and got three to six EVP's out of every ten seconds. It was interesting he was making good progress with me.

This was the first time I recorded him to hear what he had to say. He must have been with me for a while. I saw times in my life when I was inspired to make myself more positive. It was always something jumping out at me like the self-help exercise in Chapter One.

The female started, "I think." This was followed by a disrupted sound.

She then said, "I didn't get this far monkey business," and, "Hank you, you with me?"

She added, "I know Hank would do it," and, "You'll see that I love him."

She started to say, "I could seriously," when the disrupted sound made the rest inaudible.

A strange combination of voices suggested, "You wanted something different."

A male pointed out, "You picked."

A female whispered, "Hank," and, "Escape." This was followed by two whistles.

I got a strange sound then a male saying, "Zacher busy."

It went to the disrupted sound.

The female remarked, "It's as simple, simple as it gets." I got, "Hank," again.

She added, "Hank doesn't even know."

A male boasted, "I'll be active."

She replied, "Just like me."

A male said, "I can't believe you're fuckin' Hank."

She stated, "Hank won't miss this one."

She asked, "How many days has it been?" Her sound was disrupted.

She then asked, "Aren't you begging?"

A male answered, "For that thing you got behind your leg."

She replied, "For you it isn't." There was more disruption.

A male remarked, "I'm investigating. Do you believe what Hank was saying?" The first part was disrupted.

Through a very broken disruption a male confessed, "I was in love with different people." The disruption cleared up for, "I wish I was involved in something." The disruption started again as he said, "Anything but his head."

It cleared up again when he added, "You can throw a bucket in."

The female replied, "That's not good."

It was very broken up but it sounded like he came back with, "Yes it is."

44

It was clearer as he asked, "You think he will succeed if he works?"

It broke up so badly at the end that it was hard to tell if he finished, "On it," or I picked that up psychically.

There was more disrupted sound and some time with no talking.

A male then suggested, "He might quit." He asked, "Do you believe in Hank?"

A female replied, "I still believe in Hank." She asked, "Any idea what Hank is?"

Next was a bark. Was it a dog? It did not sound like it came from a dog.

A male said, "He hasn't worked in anything yet."

The female repeated, "Yet."

By this time we made our way back over the bridge and down the stairs across the channel from the passage door. Gary talked the whole time but did not come through on the recorder.

For most of the tours I could tell where we were by what Gary said. This one seemed so different. Much of Gary was missing. We finally heard Gary say, "Just take a picture, take a picture right here."

A female boasted, "I would make it big."

A male remarked, "I can't get to Hank."

The female continued, "Hank can get big," and, "anyway through JC claims it."

A male suggested, "See if we can get to him."

The female finished, "I can't wait till he gets that big."

The male replied, "If he don't eat."

I accidentally turned the recorder off.

Turning the recorder back on, I got a female saying, "Y'all have a snake."

A male asked, "What's up, can I?"

At the same time a female asked, "What's the meaning?"

A female then exclaimed, "Watch out Hank!" as I nearly walked into the picnic table when I was checking the recorder. I saw it at the last minute.

A male remarked, "Accident victim."

Then he said, "He couldn't believe in himself if he wanted to."

A female started, "He is."

The male interrupted, "He won't be big."

The other male snapped back, "You don't get this," and, "He'd be dead tomorrow," then, "If we ask Hank."

The female asked, "What'd you say?"

Then there were three barks. It sure didn't sound like a dog.

After that the female asked, "What did you giggle?" and, "Is he short now?"

She also stated, "He went backwards in his life," and, "You didn't think he'd watch?"

A male asked, "Did much did he?" She suggested, "We gotta put meow."

A female confessed, "Now I gotta pee."

It could be a person, but with all the bathroom talk I couldn't be sure.

A male corrected, "You didn't see."

The female added, "Hank."

The male finished, "Anywhere."

She asked, "Can I go where I want?"

He replied, "Let me check that."

He then stated, "It has to be." Someone's child yells drowning him out. After that he added, "Direct view everything. Pay for me. I didn't know you were going."

That was the end of the tour. I turned the recorder off.

When we got home I plugged the recorder into one of my guitar amplifiers and listened to the tour. The Me EVP stood out the most. It got included in every tour after that. We picked up other bits and pieces that night and soon after I got my computer. Most of what we got did not have the same meaning as what you read here. That showed us why it was important to get what was being said all the way through.

Of course it was said that the more the spirits tell you the more questions you would have. From the start I thought they protected me. There was mention of listening to Gary. They were very interested in the facts and history of the London Bridge.

We had a female spirit so into sex she was residing in the restroom to check out penises. The male spirits were jealous that she had plans for me.

On one set of stairs something was keeping the spirits from talking while on another set of stairs the spirits were able to talk better. There was a lot of talk about me and if I get big or quit. Their opinion of me is questionable at best. This was quite a first recorded tour!

CHAPTER THREE

MICAH ON TOUR

The London Bridge footings on the White Castle side

The next tour we went on it was Micah's turn to help. Micah was a couple of years younger than Zach. There was a lot of build up about Zach and the Me EVP, which I sensed left Micah feeling less important. I was feeling more confident and was ready to ask some questions. I wanted Micah to be as much in the spotlight as Zach was, so this was Micah On Tour.

A male sounding similar to Gary said, "I waited for you guys."

Then another male at the same volume warned, "Then we will drop Hank's good part real quick."

The other male replied, "I didn't mean to get. I didn't forget. Bet you don't either." There was static.

He then added, "And we should feel closer," and, "Now we will get even when we get there."

A female asked, "Is that an answer?" She said, "I get this." Then, "What's so friendly?"

One of the males answered, "Hank deserves it."

She asked, "You think so?"

He replied, in a deep voice, "I don't think anymore there's hope," and, "Hank is helpless."

She said, "I thought you'd need this," and, "I don't think anyway."

Then asked, "You hate this don't you?"

He answered, "You go with Hank." He asked, "Ready to do this?"

He added, "Hank is a troubled man," and, "This is the money right here."

His voice changed when he said, "The money."

I didn't believe it was actual money, but a different form of payment.

He then suggested, "Let's go think about it." A car honked at the word think.

He also stated, "I'll think up here. If you look he's from Masta. You go on the tour tonight with Debbie. Hank will be there when you get there."

We got four seconds of silence and then he spoke, "I see why you want to get on it," and, "I'll wait till Hank stands up."

He started saying, "All we have."

The female finished with, "From his work."

Another female asked, "How'd he get that weird?"

The first female started to give an answer that I could barely pick up, "Basically what it is."

The other female announced, "I am queer for sure."

The first replied, "I can have Hank for sure."

Someone directed them, "Break a little bit."

Well so much for that pick up.

A male ordered, "Don't go play with this."

One of the females announced, "Hank is right here."

He warned, "Now you will have to pay for what you did," and, "All we need is for him to get." Then he finished, "Hank to get wind of that."

She replied, "I don't think he heard it."

She was right. I was still only picking the most obvious discrepancies for EVP's and getting small pieces of what was here.

A male said, "Let's see you waste it."

Someone asked, "How will he get that?"

The male answered, "That's a bold question," also, "And he drooled from in here."

Debbie asked, "Have you had it before? Hank gets back here."

The other female replied, "I can't even see him."

She added, "Wait for Hank," and, "I don't live with." Then a human laughs.

During the laugh I heard, "Dick lick." I didn't know if anyone else would.

A male asked, "What, what did he say to you in the bathroom?"

She answered, "Oh you've got to be kidding."

Another male remarked, "It pays, it pays to be Hank," then, "We both knew that," and, "Gotta find her."

The female announced, "I'm in love."

Debbie replied, "It's sad."

The female clarified, "I'm in love with Hank."

Debbie remarked, "Great."

Someone asked, "Are you?"

Then there was a strange metallic sound covering up what I psychically picked up as "Trying it?"

A male asked, "Are you going to miss? What you've been waiting for?"

Debbie asked, "Do you love Hank?"

A male asked, "Gonna miss me some too?"

Another male told him, "You'll just have to deal with it."

He then directed him, "Just go and bother Hank."

Debbie commented, "I don't believe we're doing this."

The other female repeated, "I'm in love with Hank."

A male asked, "How you like to go," then whispers, "With me?"

The other male guessed, "Bet she won't."

They replayed the scene again.

The female stated, "I do believe."

A male replied, "Don't believe it."

The female came back with, "I didn't think you did."

She asked, "You didn't use the book did ya?"

She added, "I need him some more," and, "It's no use you waste it."

He replied, "Nothing but Hank."

She remarked, "It's possible he's in."

He suggested, "Hank won't do anymore."

She confessed, "It's sexual. Anyone would do that. We're painting a picture."

I was in the privacy of my room but privacy did not mean anything to them. A male laughed and asked, "How you gonna get to Hank?"

She started, "But now Hank."

A male interrupted, "Hank he doesn't want to."

Then he added, "He want to be with her." This came through a clicking noise and it was difficult to tell if it was audible or if I picked it up psychically.

A male started a comment, "And on this."

The other male asked, "He played nickels right?"

The first male ordered, "Go down underneath the bridge."

The female asked, "Is it too late to go see Hank?"

Debbie stated, "And beauty is sacred."

A male asked, "Is he in love with you?" He added, "There's more to Hank than you see."

The female replied, "And you did. Answer Hank."

The male continued, "I believe that you would. Go to a people. And get something. I guess that can't be helped."

She asked, "Have you seen what I do?" and, "Can I go out of here today?"

He pointed out, "Eight hundred million kinds," and, "You can do it."

She remarked, "I'm not here to lose any sleep."

He asked, "You called me a zombie didn't you?" He told her, "I can just get up there."

She announced, "I can see Stacey."

He commented, "I won't go begging to come back here," and, "Do like Hank and do it yourself."

She asked, "What are you saying?"

He suggested, "Just be more like Hank. Is that what you're going to do? I don't think you love Hank. Hank is at the gate once more. If you wanted to. Be with Hank."

Debbie replied, "That's what's included." Then she said a second, "Included," that I only heard separated from the rest.

The male stated, "Hank doesn't know who the fuck is here."

The female admitted, "I don't know if he's sensitive to it."

He directed them, "We get through with Hank. Then get something to eat."

They don't actually eat. They were talking about it. People give off energy which spirits use and I have always been able to use that energy myself.

She commented, "But he is that important." Her voice changed as she said, "He is".

The male replied, "Over protecting him."

Another male asked, "What ya workin' on?"

She answered, "A two bit whore." Then she told the other male, "You'll give up on Hank. I don't care what you do. I don't care what you think."

The male admitted, "I'm just thinking on it."

52

She announced, "Hank won't be queer though."

He stated, "We got all these people working," and, "He's doin' it." That was said twice.

She suggested, "Maybe he will just do it someday."

He insisted, "A Wiccan won't do anything."

She asked, "Has he been? Has he been through here?"

The male asked, "Has he been through here before?"

A female laughed. Then the female from the bathroom asked, "Do you think he will wish for me?"

We walked from the gate towards the fountain. I left the recorder on. It was sitting with our other stuff on the fountain rim.

I got Gary in front of the griffin-like statues saying, "It's got a dragon's head on it."

A female confessed, "I can't really see that good." She asked, "Are you just fucking with me?"

She then announced, "There goes the pizza."

The male stated, "I'm searching for that thing."

She replied, "I searched everywhere believe it," and, "Let's get through this real quickly."

The male asked, "Guess what he bought?"

She answered, "I guess it's for his birthday present for you."

He replied, "Yeah but he has to go big."

Another male said, "Hank will be big."

The female remarked, "That's what we really need," and, "Anyway they put the bridge."

The newest male bragged, "I fathered some."

The female informed them, "I can see for tourin'."

The first male said, "That's as long as Hank been with us."

A female giggled.

He directed her, "You can walk with Hank and you."

He is cut off by a female asking, "Is he busy doing that?"

A female said, loud enough to be a person, "And down here where it's,"

A male interrupted with, "It's two fifty here."

A female started to ask, "Is this?"

A male cut her off with, "The new village yeah."

He added, "Shopping is what people do."

The female asked, "Who could that be?"

Then Gary said, "In the Pub area. I'd want to take some pictures up here."

A female asked very quietly, "Is there children?"

Gary said, "One night I was at the Pub. Those windows. One night I came through here and then. Appears a head. I just cleared back up a bit. Someone stepped up here before then they went right through here. Then he had to come kick you out."

Someone from the tour group asked, "What'd you hear?"

Gary started the story of the lamppost, "These are original lampposts from London. See that line there? Back in the old days you had to open up that trap door and light a candle, later kerosene, then propane. We got nine of them in the deal and this one has never been lit. It still has the gas regulator for propane."

Someone from the tour said, "Wow."

They then asked some questions about the lamppost which Gary answers. The whole time the spirits were quietly listening to Gary. He started talking about the phone booth when the clock tower chimed.

Gary gave the facts about the phone booth and what they were doing in London with them now. He then told about all the paranormal activity around the phone booth. I turned the recorder off.

Turning the recorder back on later at the bottom of the stairs going up to the bridge, I got, "Molly told me."

Gary told his stories on the steps during which I got a faint, "Just come on."

A male asked, "Did Hank hear the smart real question?"

A male remarked, "There's blood right behind your mother."

A female asked, "Are you kidding?"

A male ordered, "You will take the cans."

She replied, "It's not your business."

The first male stated, "I don't believe it. They are rue cancer mouses. He wasn't addicted at first. What you're supposed to do."

She asked, "What is accomplishment?"

He answered, "You'll just do conversation tomorrow," and, "You'll go fetchin' with me."

The other male remarked, "Lost in Hank's room."

Someone said, in a whispering voice, "Hank did it."

Then one of the males asked, "Did he shampoo?" and, "Is he talking?"

Someone else asked, "Is he clean?"

At the time I was showering every day but working all day then going on the tour.

A male whispered, "We can make him better than him anyway," and, asked, "Did we get what was in there?"

Gary then talked about the stairs.

A male said, "You got here," and asked, "Can you see?"

He directed the other male, "You go by him."

The other male replied, "Stacey got here."

Gary said, "At seven thirty I'll be leaving."

He goes on to talk about his foot injury and that the tour goes at a slow pace. That might be one reason I get so many EVP's.

A male ordered, "You shouldn't be over here."

Another male asked, "Did you put that Gopie in there?"

A Gopie is an overseeing spirit. My teachings said that there are guardians for every graveyard. A Gopie would be similar for an open place like the bridge. That is also on the stairs where the spirits could not talk and had to be good. It looks like they have to be respectful of the Gopie.

A male suggested, "You can be the smallest bird."

I knew there was something going on with the birds. The smallest would be a hummingbird. While Gary was talking about the tape at the museum on the stairs a male announced, "Hank is in there," and, "He held us up," referring to the Gopie.

A male ordered, "Take a classroom paper."

Another male replied, "That's fucked up."

He told the other male, "You don't need classroom paper."

Among paranormal investigators it is believed that beyond the light that you go to at your death, is a place where you learn to live in the spirit world. It seems like they even have classes on how to deal with people like me.

Gary continued his story about the Museum Tape.

A male suggested, "Give a couple of daggers to Hank."

Gary continued.

A male commented, "You do that. Got to see Julius Caesar around. You get to take some quacked ribs first. Then you bomb bomb the state."

It all sounded like Gary but Gary never said those things.

The male pointed out, "There's a big example," and, "Don't change the Heat Club like that."

Would that be the disrupted sound I experienced before?

He finished, "At least you'll get off here."

A female asked, "Will you be long?"

He answered, "Yes. One through five more years now. They touched me. Auger one hundred and thirty three feet here. There's no question you got to go. Before long when Hank leaves."

Gary then said, "And he says on the video tape that it was like the bridge was calling for its own atmosphere."

That was the last line of the story.

A lady with the group, only ladies were talking so far, said, "Ooooh."

At a much lower volume a male stated, "All these people don't look, look so happy."

A female spirit asked, "You would give us to a just a once a man."

A male remarked, "I surely don't believe your painting anymore."

Another male replied, "Hank looks like he's beat."

One of the other males stated, "You gave what you did a tour."

Another male said, "They're unbelievable."

56

One male announced, "Hank was in last year."

The female replied, "You can't hold Hank to it."

A male remarked, "I can't believe Hank answered you."

She boasted, "I got to go be with Hank."

A male warned, "Hank will see you when you do that."

Another male agreed, "Okay go to Hank if that's all that matters."

A male asked, "Does it matter to you?"

A car drove by almost drowning out the female saying, "If I go to Hank."

I turned the recorder off at street level because of the traffic.

Micah and I crossed the bridge with the tour but let them pass by the passage door before turning the recorder back on. Gary always said to turn the recorder on and wait before asking any questions. This was what happened.

The female asked, "Is that what that's for?"

A male replied, "I'm addicted to smoking."

The female said, real loud and clear, "Take me."

A male interrupted at their normal volume with, "but Hank's right here."

He added, "But Hank ain't over there."

Another male commented, "Appears you don't know Hank."

The other male remarked, "I copy that you don't know who Hank is."

One of the males stated, "I'm a doctor."

I started the questions by asking, "Is anyone here?"

A male said, "I guess now we'll hear about it."

The other male asked, "We're getting there but what do we do for now?"

The first male replied, "Give him an answer."

I then asked, "Can you tell me your name?"

The female asked, "Is it nice to be like Hank?" and, "I like Ha..." but the other male interrupted with, "Is that what you used to do?"

The first male answered, "Whatever you answer Hank."

The other male countered with, "We know what we're doing here."

Then I asked, "Can you tell me why you are here?"

One of the males replied, "I don't believe he asked that."

A man from the parking lot said, "Now you can start your vehicle."

A male spirit asked, "Do you believe what Hank just said?"

Another male warned, "Careful what you wish for."

One of them annouced, "I seen him a few days ago."

It sounded like a human male said, "We're at seven."

I asked, "Is there anybody here you can name?"

A male suggested, "Maybe he knows we're baby-sitting him."

No, I'm just psychic that way.

A male replied, "That would be quick if Hank we're like that."

Another male remarked, "Maybe he's down, maybe he's down there."

A kid yelled and a male accused someone, "You took it."

Micah asked, "Are you an astral being?"

A male replied, "I still don't believe it."

The female yelled, "Hey Hank we've been here."

A new female said, "I'm supposed to lien right here."

The other female invited her, "You go right ahead and lien here."

A lien is a place they go to gather energy. To lien is gathering energy. Being lien is giving off energy. I am not lien and it really bugs them that I can control my energy. I asked them about lien later.

Micah asked, "Do you like it here?"

A male answered, "It's easy."

Another male added, "I do, but it's better than anything you ever heard about anywhere."

One of the males asked, "Is Hank with you too?"

Another remarked, "I can't hear very well."

I believe it's a human who asked, "Is there a kitchen?"

Micah asked, "Would you rather be a ghost or alive?"

A male asked, "When do I get a second?"

Another male suggested, "Put your hands right here a second."

The female admitted, "That's Ike told me," in a childlike voice. She asked, "Did he ask about me?" She stated, "I want to tell you all something. You trust people don't you?"

A male answered, "I think good people."

The female asked, "Is that true beyond belief?" and, "You'll be like."

The male interrupted, "I don't know anything," and, "I don't think he's here." Then, "He's working to me."

She replied, "Just a little bit."

He warned, "If Hank hears that."

She stated, "I can see."

He admitted, "It is just easy to forecast people. Do you believe Hank? Crazy down there."

She answered, "I believe in Hank."

He remarked, "He goes uptown today. He went up with me. I wasn't doing anything. It was a bit of information."

She informed him, "I'll take care of it." and, "I think you can."

She then added, "There's a chance he'll hear it."

He ordered, "That goes with me."

She replied, "Easy," real loud and clear.

Gary said, "That creepy door."

The female spirit remarked, "I've seen it."

A lady on the tour said, "And now."

Gary repeated, "That creepy door."

A male spirit stated, "Being good."

A lady somewhere, possible the Heat, said, "In sell is that door." and, "How are they supposed to hear you shut the door late."

It sounds like a spirit who remarked, "Okay you're finished here."

Gary started talking but as he said, "Fly" the female spirit said, "They took that fly off the ground."

With her childlike voice she added, "He's helping me out."

A male warned, "They leave this house."

Gary said, "The bridge came in ten thousand pieces."

The female spirit remarked, "We knew that."

Gary said, "The bridge was very nice about."

Interrupting, a female stated, "He called me."

A male interjected, "Except for Hank," during, "He called me."

Gary continued with, "They marked each piece with wax."

A lady with the tour group laughed.

Gary and a lady were talking and a male spirit whispered over them, "We want Hank."

The male spirit asked, "What'd you leave for?"

While Gary was talking, the female spirit yelled, "I see some light in Hank."

We had a dog sound on the last tour now we had the female spirit going, "Meow," while Gary was talking.

The male spirit asked, "He noticed us yet?"

Gary said, "The Lord Mayor of London actually came to Lake Havasu with the original plans Sir John Rainey had drawn up."

After Gary's story of how the bridge was put together, the male spirit asked, "Will you say that to Hank?" It had a very soft ending.

Gary said, "You're dipping into specific storage and there was really good stuff in there."

The female spirit stated, "We all do this."

Gary finished talking about what used to be stored in the bridge and started the next story. When Gary paused the male spirit replied, "It's okay."

At Gary's next pause the female announced, "He's still with me."

Gary continued.

The next pause the male remarked, "I may see you."

The female cried, "Hank should be here," and, "I can't get to him."

Gary said one line and paused.

The female demanded, "Hanky here."

The male replied, "I can't see him." He asked, "Is Hank a steady off?"

The female came with, "That's on you," at the same time.

Gary finished talking about the passage door and we went up to the street where I turned the recorder off.

I turned the recorder back on at the stairs at the other end of the bridge picking up Gary telling about the two spirits seen on those steps.

At a pause the female said, "Hank."

Gary continued but I picked up a commercial I guess from a radio. Gary told the story of the lion. At another pause in the story, the female suggested, "Bring her."

While Gary was talking, a faint female voice commented, "I can't see if Hank is back. And once a man. On witches."

Gary continued with his story and the female pointed out, "You're on the book," while Gary was talking. Gary finished that story with a few comments from the ladies on the tour.

Walking to the spot for the last story, the female spirit guessed, "I don't think Hank is coming."

Gary asked a question of the people on the tour and after their answer there was a pause.

A female spirit remarked, "I think better times are coming."

The male spirit replied, "At least I'll be happy then."

Gary and the tour continued, but while they were looking at a spot on the bridge a female announced, "It's up here."

The male added, "Where Hank would be."

The female replied, "You're kidding."

He then stated, "This is where he'll be. It's true I got the paper. What do you think for an answer? Everybody should meet each other."

The female remarked, "I don't want to but I'll have to enjoy it," and, "Hank won't be staying here tonight."

The people on the tour started talking amongst themselves. At a pause in the conversation, the male warned, "I told you about Hank," and, "Do you like weed?"

I was using it for shamanistic purposes.

Gary and the tour group talked. During a lull in the conversation, the male spirit remarked, "He is, he is the worst of Hank."

Gary was talking and the female spirit commented, right behind him, "Hank is old as crap."

A long period of silence went by and the male spirit suggested, "Maybe he's the self exploding types."

The female asked, "You know about that?"

He replied, "That's him smoking."

He then stated, "This just fuckin'," and, "You gotta peak through this."

The female remarked, "Later."

Gary said, "Olaf the Viking."

I turned the recorder off.

This was an informative tour that brought up more questions. If they get lien from people's energy, what about cemeteries? There was more evidence that this was scripted out, so how much was fiction?

We see there are positions like Gopie, how structured is their world and what other positions are there? They were in the birds. Were they in the other animals?

Apparently their teacher came to give them some help with the sound. But how were they changing it? They were doing this because I was supposed to go to the bridge after I died. But when will that be and what will I be doing? When will they start answering my questions? How much more can I get them to reveal?

CHAPTER FOUR

THE GEORGE TOUR

Britney getting a picture of an orb

The day of the next tour a couple came into the store for a reading. It was George and his girlfriend. They were very interested in the paranormal and said they had an annoying spirit in George's house. We talked about the psychic course I was giving because they wanted to communicate with spirits. They agreed to go on the tour to see how we did our paranormal investigation. I called this one the George Tour.

When George showed up for the tour he brought his sister Britney. We started recording at the lamppost. First I got Gary talking. From a distance I heard what sounded like a female spirit saying, "He's here."

When Gary stopped talking, a male spirit suggested, "Let's go get him," and, "I think we're on to Hank."

The female spirit we heard before asked, "We got rid of him?"

Another female spirit loudly replied, "Break the ice."

Gary said, "Formally over there on that door right there."

After the next line in Gary's story the male spirit commented, "That's a devil man."

Gary continued his story about a dark spirit.

Gary said, "We quickly step out of the way."

The male spirit remarked, at a much lower volume, "We have already."

Gary started the lamppost story. At the first pause the male spirit stated, "You can have it."

At the end of Gary's next line he said, "A hundred years old, okay."

At the same time the male spirit asked, "What is old?"

The female spirit informed them, "You'll help me later," and, "I'm with Hank."

Gary carried on the lamppost story but at a pause the female spirit remarked, "You got it." Gary continued and she added, "Now I have it," while Gary was talking.

Gary had just finished the lamppost story when the clock tower chimed; it drowned everything out.

On the way to the phone booth one of the male spirits announced, "Hank is there." He added, "If we ever get to it."

The female spirit was saying, "There," when he said, "To it."

Then the female spirit replied, "I have it." The male spirit warned, "You better."

During the phone booth story the female spirit ordered, "You will be Hank." At the next pause in the story she started, "We got."

The male spirit finished, "It."

At the next break in the story the male spirit commented, "It's so pathetic."

Another male spirit asked, "Is that true?"

The male spirit replied, "Definitely with Hank."

The female spirit started, "Beat," and the male spirit completes, "Hank over."

Gary asked, "Do you know what EVP's are?"

The male spirit remarked, "I will see," at the same time the female spirit asked, "You will?"

Gary said, "Electronic Voice Phenomenon."

The other female spirit warned, "And watch yourself."

Gary said, "That's where you take a tape recorder and actually try to record the voices of the dead. It works very well."

The male spirit replied, "I know what it is."

Gary said, "It is our best evidence to date of life after death."

The male spirit added, "It will be nice."

Gary said, "One of the girls on my paranormal investigation team came over here."

The male spirit started, "Hank."

Gary said, "And."

The female spirit finished, "Need help?"

Gary continues his story but at a pause the female spirit was saying, "If you told me." While Gary was talking she remarked, "You'll see about Hank," and, "I could be like you with that hat."

As Gary paused the male spirit ordered, "Do you know what I'm saying, move Hank."

Gary talked again but at his next break in the story the female spirit asked, "Now what'd you say?" However her voice changed for, "You say."

Gary continued and the female spirit announced, in her childlike voice, "That's Hank."

Another female spirit remarked, "I get two more," just before Gary said, "And two days before that we're on the tour." He went on to finish his story.

The female spirit, in her childlike voice, stated, "I'm supposed to get this." She then sang, "Can you call?" and spoke, "I can get there." She almost sang, "It's your hang-up."

The other female spirit asked, "Don't you have a pencil?"

The first female spirit directed her, "Get with Hank," and, "You got wax."

Gary started telling about the clock tower. At the first pause in the story the male spirit commented, "I should steal some," and, "I know you would."

At the next pause the female spirit demanded, "Hank will be with me."

George said, "Call big Hank." George was the only person in any of the tour groups who said my name.

Gary said, "Yeah," and at a much lower volume the female spirit replied, "But he's with me."

Gary said, "They got a plaque in there that says."

The female spirit remarked, "Anyway."

Gary went on to say the next line but at the end of it some spirit started, "I need to tell you."

Gary said the last line and George said, "Oh yeah."

The female spirit asked, "Can you see him?"

Gary said, "You know the missed bump," at the same time the female spirit replied, "No I know Hank." She then started to say, by herself, "In there used to be."

Gary and the tour group talked a little. At a break in the conversation the female spirit asked, "Did you see his money?"

At the next pause the male spirit asked, "Can you see Hank?"

Gary went on to say, "In 1959 they actually figured out."

The female spirit remarked, "Hank."

Gary continued, "That the London Bridge was sinking into the River Thymes to the tune of a quarter inch a year." Gary went on with the story of how they decided to get rid of the bridge when a strange metallic voice came in with, "He's a misfit," over the top of Gary.

The male spirit asked, "Where is he?" as Gary paused.

Gary said another line and the female spirit asked, "What did you test me for?"

The male spirit ordered, "Stay here," before Gary talks again. He then asked, "Can you see Hank?" while Gary was talking.

At a pause some spirit uttered, "I like birds," in a strange way.

Gary went on but the female spirit announced, "I think I can see Hank," while he was talking.

The male spirit asked, "You think you can?" while Gary told how the bridge was bought.

The female spirit started, "He wants," and the male spirit interrupted with, "I knew it," all at a short pause.

At the next pause the female spirit asked, "Can you see him?" and while Gary was talking she replied, "I hate they have it." I thought that would be the book.

The male spirit told them, "Hank plays with it," while Gary was talking. Some spirit commented, "Hank like this," with Gary still talking. Behind Gary the female spirit instructed them, "He's on like that." They must have been talking about the recorder.

The female spirit announced, "We're on."

Behind Gary we heard the female spirit say, "Go ahead and answer he can't be home." She then told them, "He's a idiot."

The male spirit remarked, "It's in your head," while Gary was talking.

At a pause another male spirit commented, "I'm preparing for next year again."

The male spirit informed them, "He can't believe in anything," and asked, "Have you seen Hank yet?"

Gary started another story but as he was saying, "Sir John Rainey," the female spirit replied, "You got it. At least you got it."

Gary paused and the male spirit agreed, "That's right."

Gary started talking again and the female spirit said, "I think we got it. Now we can because we got this. You said it wouldn't make it. We got you Hank." Gary paused and she announced, "There's Hank." Then she whispered, "Hank."

Gary started telling how the bridge was in the Guinness Book of World Records on the walk to the water. While Gary was talking the female spirit replied, "I could get home." Gary paused and she continued, "When I like to." When she said, "To," it got stretched out and shifted up and down like what you would expect to hear from a ghost.

Gary started another story and behind him some spirit suggested, "We take him." Gary paused and the male spirit stated, "It's already done." Another female spirit agreed, "Okay." The other male spirit asked, "Are we taking him too?"

The other female almost sang, "We break men," and the other male confessed, "I do it."

The first female spirit informed them, "You can take him you read it."

The other male spirit admitted, "I didn't read it." It was not the book because the wing book didn't show words.

The other female spirit asked, "Did you ask about that?"

While Gary was talking the female spirit loud and clear spoke, "Haven't seen it. Hank went into there." Behind Gary she remarked, "And now he's miserable," with an electronic noise at the end.

One of the spirits annouced, "I see it."

The female spirit told them, "You wouldn't get that there."

The spirit that spoke before replied, "That was a lucky man."

The female spirit admitted, "And we're not here."

We reached the water and Fred was playing his clarinet while Gary talked.

The female spirit annouced, "And we'll get dinner now." When she said that we could not hear Fred playing but after she said it, Gary and Fred continued. The next one I thought I heard was the female spirit saying, "Hank wants to come to the bridge," but Fred was playing note for note with the female spirit and Gary was talking in time with it all.

The other female spirit asked, "When will he move?" Then, "Look at that," in a strange way.

The female spirit informed them, "We've seen that before," and one of the spirits replied, "Aww," at the end.

68

The female spirit began singing, "At every moment you. You never got back to me," while Gary was talking. She sang, "I kill you too much," and whispered, "Hank." She continued singing, "For my heart." Fred joined the song on his clarinet but no one ever sang with Fred.

The female spirit spoke, "Get upstairs right and now goodbye," in front of Gary talking.

Gary talked and Fred was not playing when the female spirit asked, "And can you hear us Hank?" in a whispering voice. From behind Gary she also asked, "Was it something I said?"

The male spirit asked, "You know Britney?"

The female spirit started, "Can," then sang, "We do that?" She spoke, "It gets better," and a very strange voice replied, "We have it now," behind Gary. She commented, "I need something," and sang, "You think you got it all?"

A male spirit from earlier asked, "I did, can I answer?"

The female spirit sang, "Will you get more of that?" when we get to the stairs from the water's edge.

The female spirit eerily sang while another female spirit called out, "Agnes come see us underneath the bridge." The whole EVP has a creepy feel and no one sang at the bridge.

Fred started playing behind us but we don't hear him or anyone else when the female spirit suggested, "Hank you can do anything." Less clearly she replied, "You think it's easy."

The other female spirit asked, "Is Chris there?" and, "Is here?" while Gary was talking.

The female spirit uttered, "Hank," then Gary began, "Before I figured out I was the tour guide and I could stop where ever I want."

The male spirit agreed, "We are the same."

Gary said, "Take a rest right."

The female spirit added, "Going with him." She asked, "Where you going?" and announced, "He's gone." She then asked, "Have you seen Hank before?"

The male spirit asked, "Don't you have nothing to say?"

The other male spirit replied, "No it'd be like Hank's tour."

Gary said a line and the female spirit remarked, "I can get it." She continued, "He wants to stop," while Gary gave the next line. Then she finished, "Upstairs yeah you'll bust him."

Some spirit suggested, "You'll miss."

The female spirit added, "The jack of all trades he knows."

A male spirit commented, "Payment," in a metallic voice that made it sound like pavement.

Next we heard singing, Fred playing, then more singing and out of that the female spirit announced, "Here they come."

The other female spirit disagreed, "Nope operator."

The male spirit remarked, "He'll make a story with me." He went on, "These people can't do. Can't do anything."

The female spirit ordered, "Get up here." She then sang, "And you can have a story now," as Gary set up the next story. She continued to sing, "About what you did in Havasu and you have to try to." There was another line to the song that I could not make out over Gary but she didn't finish anyway. She stopped to say, "You get right there."

Gary was telling about the Museum Tape when he said, "He looked down and there's no bridge."

The female spirit replied, "There's a bridge here."

Another female spirit agreed, "That's a big, it's fair."

The female spirit stated, "That's all you'll see," but her voice changed for see.

The other male spirit requested, "You got to do that to me," with Fred playing.

The female spirit sang, "I got him out to work on it. Ta-da-da-da. That's all Hank is going to get."

The other male spirit replied, "I'll take it."

The other female spirit remarked, "He'd like that."

The female spirit almost sang, "I got my," but her voice changed for what I thought was, "pay." She did sing, "It got to be like that."

The male spirit asked, "Did you wash through that pump?"

The female spirit sang, "Like yesterday and the answer." She said, "Given," and whispered, "To Hank."

The male spirit asked, "Did you get close enough to do what I did?"

They both commented, "Hank," but the female spirit continued to sing, "You'll never work with me," with a car driving by and it could still be heard. The only other EVP I got there at street level was, "Hank," when no cars were passing and Gary was not talking.

I turned the recorder off before we walked across the bridge. I turned it back on at the passage door after I explained to George how to ask questions.

As soon as I turned it on the male spirit asked, "What are you doing Hank?"

The female spirit asked, "Why does it matter to ask?"

As I told George, "Just ask any questions about that," the female instructed behind me, "Just ask."

I asked, "Is anyone here?"

The female spirit answered, "We've always been here Hank."

The other male spirit added, "We all answer him."

I asked, "Can you tell us your name?"

The other female spirit annouced, "He asked some more," while another female spirit who should be Agnes repeated, "Your name," behind that.

The female spirit asked, "What did he say then?"

The male spirit asked, "He didn't ask that did he?" while Agnes confirmed, "Yes that's what he did," behind him.

The female spirit sang, "I can't eat," and the other female spirit replied, "I might answer Hank."

I asked, "You got anything you want to tell us?"

The other male spirit answered, "I gave up to ring home."

Agnes accused, "He did a copy."

The other female spirit came in with, "I got him right here."

The female spirit asked, "Is that what you want to say about that?" and she replied, "Next day you won't be on it."

I asked, "Are you a ghost or an astral being?"

The female spirit refused, "I won't give an answer," and sang, "I'll sing to you."

The other female spirit asked, "Is it multiplication?"

The female spirit suggested, "It's your turn."

I asked, "Have you always been at this bridge?"

The female spirit asked, "Hank what'd you say to me?"

The other female spirit informed her, "And you will be answering this one."

Agnes asked, "What'd he say to you?"

I asked, "Do you move away from the bridge?"

The other female spirit answered, "That's a simple for asking." She asked, "So you want us to take this question he asked us?"

The female spirit guessed, "I believe he's all done."

The other female spirit confirmed, "Okay."

I said, "Thank you for talking to us."

The female spirit replied, "It's nothing."

I turned the recorder off. I turned the recorder back on when we were on the stairs on the other side of the bridge. Gary was telling the lion story.

Behind Gary I could barely make out the other female spirit as she asked, "Is that what you want?" She remarked, "It's easy to tell. If I like him. I think." The rest got drowned out by Gary.

At the end of Gary's line we could hear the female spirit say, "Hank will work."

As Gary said, "Got her by the throat man, okay," the other female spirit denied, "We're not the one."

The male spirit advised, "You don't have to feed on that one."

The other female spirit commented, "It's not like Hank. Can go get that bump."

The female spirit told them, "And that's what Hank asked us the other day."

The male spirit replied, "I am spaceless."

Gary continued the lion story almost to the end when the female spirit repeated, "That's what Hank said."

Gary said, "She got an orb with a lion's face in it."

The female spirit stated, "He wants to know that from me."

Gary finished the lion story with, "You check those out on our website."

The female spirit added, "Or get more from Hank."

We walked to the last spot on the bridge and the female spirit commented, "I think they're through with it. That's what he says at the end of the tour. We could get help from you. That's what you could do for me Hank. All of these must be with you, cause you're such a misfit," but she had help with the word such.

Gary talked for a while and at a pause the female spirit started, "If you."

The male spirit finished, "Want to."

Gary went on describing a ghost picture and at a break in that story the female spirit replied, "Thanks Hank."

Gary asked the tour group, "Do you see anything on my bridge?"

The female spirit answered, "Just Hank."

George asked, "Where?"

Gary said, "Over here."

The female spirit stated, "I can see him."

The male spirit drawn out remarked, "If you wanted the bridge cleaned by him."

The female spirit suggested, "I'll get Hank."

Gary asked, "Anybody got a camera?"

The male spirit directed her, "Make your move."

Gary said, "Take a picture right here."

While the tour was taking pictures the female spirit ordered, "Go with Hank for this time."

The male spirit added, "We want him here."

The female spirit replied, "I can't say."

Gary asked, "Got a camera? Who's got a camera?"

The male spirit repeated, "Make your move."

The female spirit asked, "Did we leave something on it?"

The male spirit remarked, "Basically we respect him."

Didn't they just call me a misfit?

The female spirit spoke at the same time, "With money Hank."

The male spirit started, "All that Hank does," and the female spirit finished with "Is smoke."

We all talked a little about what's on the bridge but at a break in the conversation the male spirit asked, "Are you looking for Hank?"

Gary tells more about what's on the bridge during which the female spirit stated, "I'll be in Hank's room." While Gary was still talking she remarked behind him, "I got his room backwards. I just can't get used to him. He wants some."

The male spirit replied behind Gary, "It doesn't matter what Hank wants, it's what we got."

The female spirit asked, "Can we do what I see wrong?"

The male spirit answered, "Hank does," and then added, "He's obviously not coming here. He can just a pick."

A man on the tour said, "There's something wrong with his camera."

Gary said, "Oh Hank."

The man said, "He's got a bad lens on it." I really got upset when he said that about the pictures of orbs that I had gotten. He was trying to say I wasn't getting pictures of ghosts. It's one thing to not believe what you can see with your own eyes but quite another to call me a liar. My camera took pictures without ghosts too.

The female spirit asked, "What's the matter Hank?" Right before I said, "No," biting my lip. She replied, "I won't talk to you in fear."

The male spirit advised, "He wasn't talking to you."

The female spirit stated, "We have to get out of here."

Gary and the tour group talked a little but when they finished the female spirit started to say, "He never waits."

Gary cut her off with, "He took pictures of himself and they weren't like that. That was the night before."

The female spirit commented, "We'll never make it. I couldn't get no pants more to Hank anyway."

The male spirit disagreed, "Yes you can."

The other female spirit added, "If you wanted to."

Gary said another line about the spot on the bridge.

The male spirit remarked, "I guess that's the touring."

Gary continued talking but the singing started again with the female spirit going, "May I touch you?"

Gary said a line with no singing. Behind his next line the female spirit sang, "And would you like that."

The other male spirit replied, "You're touring right," as the female spirit sang, "We're going Hank."

The male spirit began to say, "Nothing," as she continued to sing, "For you know. You won't be close enough." She then told me, "I can help you. If you can't do that." She started to fade as she added, "I trust in you." She came back to say, "I'm waiting on Hank. They're busy Hank," with Gary talking in the background. She then stated, "If Hank wants to do that to me. I could go with Hank."

The other female spirit asked, "Is he in the bathroom?" and, "Do you love Hank?"

The first female spirit replied, "If I give it to him."

The other female spirit remarked, very clear, "Nag him," and asked, "Is he living friendly?" behind Gary's talking. She asked, "Does he acquire that I'm talking to you?"

The female spirit answered, "I've got to go to the bathroom," and asked, "Where is he?"

The male spirit stated, "Hank is a Wicca witches," and, "He can't play with his Dallas fable." My Wicca teacher was from Dallas. We had a strong Wiccan community in Reno and I felt much better with like minded individuals.

The female spirit asked, "Can you hear my voice?" and admitted, "I only get that one right."

The male spirit added, "Insecurity on top of that." He then stated, "So people could think you continue on faking," with the female spirit pointing out, "I am right here on top of him," at the same time.

The female spirit asked, "You don't think I'd be leaving without Hank do you?" while Gary was saying, "They were thinking posies out of the garden without the magick would actually."

Gary said, "Exactly what's wrong with them," but it was like a hollow metallic voice was saying it with him. If that was not strange enough, they said it again.

The female spirit replied, "We're going from here to over there."

Gary and the tour talked a little more and the female spirit asked, "Are you ready Hank?"

Gary said, "Olaf the Viking."

The female spirit stated, "Now we can leave Hank."

I turned the recorder off.

CHAPTER FIVE

THE CHERYL TOUR

Sensing a spirit behind me, I turn and take a picture

The tours were going very well. We got another one with me ready to try new ways to communicate with the spirits. It was very rare to have the spirits communicating with the people on the tour but it seemed to happen on this tour. I called this one the Cheryl Tour for what happened at the phone booth.

I thought I would try some questions first since I was getting some answers. I started at the pub doors where I asked, "Is anyone here?"

There was silence until a childlike voice replied, "It's a bottle, let it go."

I went over to the phone booth and asked, "Are you over here?"

The childlike voice answered, "Almost." After a moment the female spirit, the same one that was talking to me, stated, "Here goes something."

The male spirit that always seems to be with her remarked, "We're here."

I asked, "Can you tell me your name?"

The female spirit said faintly, "I don't believe it's been a year."

The childlike voice admitted, "I'm not supposed to talk to him."

I barely picked up the male spirit asking, "What would you say anyway?"

I asked, "Have you been here long?"

The childlike voice stated, "We talked to him," and, "We talked to him before."

Another female spirit asked, "Was it here?"

I asked, "Is this where you want to be?"

The childlike voice announced, "There goes Hank again," and, "I think that he can hear me."

I asked, "Was anyone removed from here so you could be here?"

The female spirit replied, "You won't believe the answer."

The male spirit asked, "He wouldn't believe what?"

The female spirit answered, "I just got to wait for him."

I stopped the recorder and joined the tour who gathered at the fountain. I turned the recorder back on with Gary talking about the fountain.

At a pause the female spirit confirmed, "I think you can Hank."

Gary started talking about the ghost shows on television and explained about EMF meters.

I took the recorder still running over to the phone booth and sat it on the ground at the back right corner pointed towards the fountain.

After I rejoined the tour, the recorder picked up the male spirit asking, "Is that what Hank brought from home?" There was a brush against the microphone.

There was some silence then the recorder got Gary finishing about EMF meters and how they only pick up interruptions in the electromagnetic field. He compared that to what we were doing with the EVP's.

Along with traffic noise the recorder picked up the male spirit stating, "All he's got is a temper. You're supposed to be with Hank. You think I'm the only asshole."

The female spirit replied, "I think I'll go with Hank."

The male spirit commented, "Hank will come back here."

The female spirit suggested, "I'll take him back."

Another male spirit admitted, "I would like that with you."

The male spirit announced, "Hank is in," chopped up.

The female spirit came back with, "I'll just be with Hank," and, "Let's go easy with Hank okay."

The male spirit warned, "Hank will be back in a moment. Now let's dig. It's much less common than food. The very best possibility of him also. That's an example of this thing."

The other female spirit agreed, "That's a clear thing." It was not very clear to anyone else. I still couldn't be sure of what they were talking about. It may have been for communication.

The male spirit informed them, "I know Christine went. And you'll see her later."

Another male spirit announced, "Dave's up here. I like you some."

The male spirit explained, "That's exactly what we're trying we're trying to do for Hank." The second "we're trying," came without the slightest pause. He then stated, "Hank worked for twenty four years. Before he started screwing with batteries. He works magick but what for. I just told you what everybody." The traffic noise comes back as he spoke, "We've got to get going for Christine."

The other male spirit confirmed, "I know what to do. I just call Hank an asshole."

The first male spirit replied, "You're all helping Hank. I can't go in the pub. They won't leave a fucked up measure. Hank wants to be here."

A female spirit jumped in with, "I need a fucking break."

The other male spirit stated, "This is where they watch the Beasley Cup from. Back in the USA."

The clock tower rang drowning out all sounds. After twenty seconds of chiming some spirit remarked, "This is good," in a chopped up way.

Another male spirit in static started, "It's a New Year's Eve."

A female spirit interrupted with, "Jack is here."

The other male spirit suggested, "Let's go back home."

The first male spirit ordered, "Copy this. Give Hank the extreme."

Jack told him, "I can measure him."

The male spirit stated, "Hank is not too great. Hank really don't look too good. Have you be done this? The one down by the river wants to come. Are you busy before?"

The other female spirit asked, "Can he live through this? Hank will come in. I believe in Hank some."

The recorder, still sitting by the phone booth, picked up the tour at the lamppost. Gary told the whole lamppost story without any extra voices.

We walked over to the phone booth and Gary said, "And these right here; these are original telephone boxes from London and if you never felt this thing you really ought to feel it. It's made out of solid iron, okay, it would take a crane to pick it up. They actually tell me they're putting them into landscapes and things like that in people's back yards."

A person on the tour asked, "What's that?"

Gary said, "About three or four months ago a couple came over from London."

A child on the tour asked, "Mom, what's that?"

Gary said, "I don't know."

The little girl said, "It's a red thing."

Gary said, "See that, that thing is a tape recorder. Don't step on it. Hank did you leave your tape recorder over here, this one is." He picked it up and showed it to me.

I replied, "Yeah."

The mother of the child apologized, "Sorry I touched it."

Gary said, "That's okay," and laughed. He went on, "As they told me, these people were making showers out of these things back in your house."

The mother of the child asked her daughter, "Are you using the phone?" while Gary was talking.

Gary continued, "This one's about fifty years old. We get a lot of activity around the phone booth."

The mother asked, "What's her name?" again while Gary was talking.

Gary said, "We get high EMF readings."

The little girl said, "Cheryl."

Gary said, "One of the girls was on my team was over here."

The little girl said, "That's magick."

Gary said, "She was actually doing EVP's. She asked can anybody tell us your name?"

A female spirit came in behind Gary saying, "I know about that."

Gary said, "Two distinct voices come back."

That female spirit stated, "I can't like you."

Gary continued, "One said her name was Marsha, and the other one said, hello there my name is Cheryl."

The mother of the child gasped and cried out, "I just said that."

Gary asked, "You said what?"

The mom answered, "It... well you'll hear it on the little EVP."

Gary asked, "What's said?"

The mother replied, "It says Cheryl."

Gary laughed and asked, "You said that?"

The mom swore, "I promise you."

Gary said, "I believe you, oh I believe it, that one."

She asked, "Whose recorder's that?"

Gary continued the phone booth stories while the mom tried to get her daughter to stay with her and carried on about the Cheryl incident. When we finished at the phone booth I picked the recorder up and turned it off.

I turned the recorder back on while we walked to the water. A male spirit remarked, "EVP's really paint pictures."

The other female spirit agreed, "Oh you could say that. I can't believe he just had that idea."

That male spirit whispered, "I am now freaking him," as Gary began to speak.

When Gary paused, the other female spirit asked, "Can you fix the bucket-bucket?"

Gary continued telling about what was received with the bridge.

At another break, the female spirit in her childlike voice asked, "Have you seen ghosts?"

The male spirit related, "He just always wanted to see you."

Gary started talking again but at the next pause the male spirit asked, "Are you with Hank?"

Gary gave more facts about the bridge.

At another pause, the male spirit complained, "We will never get to Hank."

The female spirit admitted, "I need to see him."

The other male spirit stated, "Well at least you can't see Hank."

I got a combination of voices saying, "Beats me right there."

The female spirit confessed, "But I love being in love. Hank do you want to be with us? Hank can't take this."

The male spirit asked, "Does Hank seem to be that good? Not the penis he woke up with."

The other male spirit told them, "I can take Hank." The word Hank was emphasized. He finished, "To the parking lot. Where he has his truck."

Another male spirit admitted, "We can't believe in Hank."

The female spirit yelled, "Get Hank!"

The male spirit added, "Get the wing book."

Some people walked by us talking and I said, "People talking," into the recorder. That was close to the water by the Hawaiian Ice shack.

As they got out of range I started to pick up Gary, but after his first word the female spirit told me, "We're here Hank."

Gary told about one of the people associated with the bridge.

A lady on the tour said, "Think how he felt."

At a much lower volume the other male spirit started, "I'm so happy that," and the other female spirit finished, without skipping a beat, "He's gone."

There was a little silence then the other female spirit stated, "I have one."

The other male spirit suggested, "We'll go eat."

The female spirit started, "We're supposed."

The male spirit finished, "Go eat except we're touring."

The other female spirit asked, "Can you go eat?"

The male spirit excused them, "It's not your fault. This is quite a bucket. I can bucket too far."

The other male spirit stated, "Hank can't come."

The male spirit spoke, at a much lower volume, "I think he'll do that Hank."

The female spirit replied, "I can take it," with a small dog bark at the end.

The male spirit added, "It's not the program."

Gary said, "This arch right here is called Dead Man's Hole," which put us coming away from the water crossing the pathway to get to the stairs.

The other female spirit announced, "There is someone in that hole."

Gary started explaining about Dead Man's Hole with, "And the reason they called it."

A female spirit we hadn't heard before cried, "He's a zombie."

I went over to the bottom of the stairs while Gary was talking under the arch and asked, "Is anyone here?" All I got was Gary telling his story. I said, "We are trying to record your voice," and still only got Gary coming through. I asked, "Can you hear us?"

Out of the silence came the faintest of voices as the Gopie replied, "Yes, I see you standing there."

I said, "We thank you," as the tour approached me.

The female spirit cried out, "Wait for me!"

The male spirit directed her, "Back up me," before Gary started talking again.

Gary passed me as he took his position on the stairs to tell about the bullet holes.

A spirit whispered in a human-like voice, "Come with me Hank."

It seemed to come out that way when they were trying really hard to make me hear them directly. I believed it was the female spirit who said it. She then asked in the same way, "Hank can you hear me?"

The tour group passed me with a child talking to his parents.

Before Gary spoke the female spirit stated, in her normal voice, "I could get back."

It got strange as someone said, "If you're Jewish," when Gary said that the bullet holes came from WWII.

Gary asked, "Is anyone Jewish?" which he usually asked on the other side of the bridge at the end of the tour.

Before a lady on the tour answered, "No," one of the female spirits stated, "I can't hear."

Gary continued with stories about the building of the bridge, Charles Dickens on the bridge, and the Museum Tape all without any spirit talk. I think they were worried about the Gopie on the

84

stairs but they didn't know when I had talked to the Gopie I was respectful which gained his favor.

When Gary finished the stories we began climbing the stairs. On the way the female spirit encouraged, "Go faster or go…go home." Because she was anxious to go eat?

I turned the recorder off at the top of the stairs.

I turned the recorder back on at the passage door. The tour was close by so I picked up Gary before I asked, "Is anyone here?"

The female spirit answered, "We're here," between Gary's words.

We could still hear Gary when I asked, "What is your name?"

The female spirit asked, "Guess what Hank just said? I don't know if it's serious. And does he hear? Just as scary as he are. That's Hank for ya."

My nickname is Scary Guy.

I asked, "Do you stay at the bridge or do you go around?"

It sounded like a combination of voices replied, "I can't hear him."

Another female spirit asked, "What's he smoking?"

A male spirit that sounded similar to Gary answered, "Exactly basically at the moment the bridge is home."

I asked, "Do you know you are dead?"

The male spirit remarked, "We told you the answer."

The female spirit asked, "Did he say something beautiful?" with Gary saying, "the bridge," in the middle.

The tour drowned out anything else they said before I asked, "Are you a ghost?" The female spirit answered, "He is," while the male spirit was saying, "A baritone."

The male spirit asked, "Did you like that?"

The female spirit called me, "Hank."

I finished, "Thank you for speaking to me."

All the spirits started talking just as the tour was talking nearby so nothing could be understood.

I then picked up the female spirit saying, "I did it for Hank," before I shut the recorder off.

I turned it back on at the top of the stairs on the other side of the bridge.

The tour was talking before the female spirit started, "He was."

The male spirit finished with, "Making a theory of maintenance." He then added, "If he wanted positive money. I'm positive."

A combination of two female spirit voices asked, "Can you go right after him?"

The male spirit answered, "Believable decision. That's my favorite sun room."

The female spirit boasted, "I am beautiful."

The other female spirit asked, "Did you see the penis on him?"

The female spirit answered, "Yes."

Gary said, "So in 1666."

The other female spirit announced, "Here I come."

Gary started telling one of the black plague stories when at his first pause the male spirit stated, "At seventeen he left." That was true, I hitch-hiked out West at seventeen.

Gary went into the Black Beard the pirate story. At his first pause the female spirit started, "But Hank."

Another male spirit finished with, "Beelzebub shopping."

The male spirit corrected, "Hiking."

The other one insisted, "Shopping."

Gary went on to tell three stories on the stairs without any other voices.

After the lion story I got the female spirit suggesting, "We should do that," with the other female spirit whispering, "Hank," on top of it.

We moved down the stairs with a little talk from the people on the tour.

When they finished talking the female spirit announced, "I want you people. All to be people. And all the people."

The other female spirit interrupted with, "I can't hear you like this."

The first female spirit replied, "Just use keyhole all the time."

Gary asked the tour group if they could see anything on the bridge. A lady answered him saying, "I can see some stuff."

The female spirit told me, "Thanks Hank."

The male spirit stated, "Everybody told you."

The female spirit started, "You need."

The male spirit finished, "To go big."

A car passed on the bridge above us. Out of that sound the female spirit started, "I can't get," and the male spirit finished, "To my room." She said, "Exactly."

Another male spirit directed them, "Both of you. Should go with him."

The male spirit that sounded like Gary ordered, "Pop off a monkey right there."

A male spirit looking at the book stated, "It's the same wife I see."

Another male spirit suggested, "You need these up here."

A male spirit bragged, "Got me eleven stories to make."

The other male spirit barely came in with, "He's not that strong."

The female spirit and the male spirit spoke together, "That's what you think."

Gary asked, "Do you see anything on the bridge?"

Various no's came from the tour group and Gary asked, "Who's got a camera?"

One of the little girls on the tour answered, "I do."

Gary came back with, "Okay who's got a camera taller than two foot." Everyone laughed.

While they were taking pictures the female spirit stated, "I believe Hank."

After Gary talked again the male spirit whispered, "Hank we're leaving."

The female spirit guessed, "I think you can for justice."

The tour talked about their pictures for a while then headed back to Gary's store. I stayed at the lion spot after they left and asked questions.

I asked, "Is anyone here?"

The female spirit answered, "I'm here."

The other female spirit suggested, "Let's see what he says."

I asked, "Can you tell me your name?"

The female spirit answered, "No."

I asked, "Do you know who I am?"

She replied, "Yes, you're Hank."

I turned the recorder off.

CHAPTER SIX

GEORGE'S GARAGE

With Christine touching my camera
I got orbs in the daytime

George and his girlfriend took my psychic course but had to go to Georgia before the last class. When they came back to Lake Havasu George stopped by the shop to tell me of their success at communicating with spirits on their vacation. They were doing so well I loaned George my talking board so they could learn the last class on their own. George retuned to ask for my help with a spirit causing problems. It was moving things and making noises in the middle of the night. There were other spirits there they wanted to keep. I told George I could take care of that.

Upon entering the house I could sense where the good spirits were. I started by clearing each room of negative energy. After that I searched for the problem spirit, finding it hiding in a wall between a bedroom and the hall. I thought I had brought black salt but when I opened it I found it to be a black ash of something I did not know. I thought of Dorothy Morrison's story of coloring a candle with a magic marker and said to myself, I can make this work. I banished that spirit from the house and felt it leave.

I sat with George and Britney and we talked about the messages they were getting. The main one was go to the garage. I decided each one of us would go to the garage with the recorder and ask questions. Britney went first. This is what happened.

She entered the garage and turned the recorder on. There were boxes and bags by the door she had to make her way past. When she was clear the male spirit suggested, "We could ask her," and, "I will make it." He asked, "What is Hank doing? Did he answer your problem?"

The female spirit answered, "We could get somewhere."

The male spirit said the following, "It's not him. I know where. And you get a turn. Your turn with Hank. What'd you do with that? Like you've been here. I will with her. This will be magick. Don't forget your stuff. We won't have to come back here. I used to smoke pot. Not like Hank does. Sooner or later. I overcame it. At least one of them. Did you forget everything? I've already been here."

The female spirit replied, "Hank," really strong and then, "Hank remembered."

The male spirit asked, "Are you going with Hank? I think she is going to say some…"

Britney cuts him off with, "Is anyone here with me?"

The male spirit asked, "Can you see me? Can you even hear me? Exactly what do I say to her?"

Britney asked, "Is there anything you want to say to me?"

The male spirit answered, "I just want to see Hank right now. Can you get Hank? I just can't wait for her any longer. Act mature if she loves me." That was really rare for him to make a joke but that was a good one. With the way the female spirit had acted about being in love with me she probably deserved it. He added, "Here we go again."

Britney asked, "Have you been here long?"

The female spirit suggested, "Say that we've been here. Like twenty-eight years."

The male spirit replied, "I don't think we could win. Could you please get Hank? Surely you can't have anything…"

Britney asked, "Are you here to be with me?"

The male spirit remarked, "I guess we win here. We came for Hank. When is Hank going to be here? I can't even. I just can't wait for Hank. I think we should go to him. I wish Hank would come out. You won't stand there and talk to me. You won't even go get Hank. I'm not going to wait for her to do something. I stayed careful with you."

The female spirit asked, "What would you like me to say?"

The male spirit answered, "I should get off this case," with a pause in the middle as he waited for a sound.

The female spirit told him, "It's not like that. You want me to stay?"

The male spirit replied, "Yes."

The female spirit ordered, "Then wait for her. You'll get a chance to talk to Hank."

The male spirit explained, "I just can't seem to wait for her anyway."

The female spirit asked, "Do you think Hank will come out soon?"

The male spirit answered, "I can talk to Hank anywhere. I cannot tell him this anywhere."

Britney turned the recorder off and came back to the kitchen. George took the recorder and went to the garage. He got past the stuff by the door then turned the recorder on.

The male spirit announced, "I can hear Hank."

George asked, "Is anybody in there?"

The male spirit answered, "Send Hank up here."

The female spirit repeated, "I can hear Hank."

The male spirit asked, "Can you see Darwin to pull it?"

The female spirit replied, "That's just so it."

The male spirit remarked, "I never saw like this."

George asked, "Is there anything you want to say?"

The female spirit asked, "Have you ever seen Hank here?"

The male spirit asked, "Why did you ask if Hank was still here?" Then stated, "This guy will be a much better man. I just know he will with Hank's help."

The female spirit added, "That'll be a beautiful day if he want it."

George asked, "Are you a human spirit?"

The male spirit replied, "I guess next will be Hank. You could slice the air in here. Get started."

George asked, "Am I where I should be?"

The male spirit answered, "There are ways to do that. Now go get Hank to come back here. I can understand peace right here. Is he in there?"

George asked, "Have you been inside?"

The male spirit remarked, "I'll give Hank some more. I just can't get over Hank. Hank can't write a book. I could get lost in there. Now we know Hank's in there."

George asked, "How long have you been here?"

The male spirit answered, "I think it's been long enough for Hank. I can work with Hank."

The female spirit demaded, "You won't treat Hank like that."

The male spirit replied, "Just get Hank and I'll feel better. What did I say anyway? I'll be standing right here."

George asked, "Can you follow anyone around?"

The male spirit answered, "That sure is creepy. I can't wait for Hank to get out here. You can't send Hank out here can you?"

George asked, "Are you guys almost done?"

The male spirit came back with, "I think that's it right here."

The female spirit ordered, Now you get Hank in here."

The male spirit replied, "Christine, you will be right here. It's everything we waited for."

George asked, "Is anyone down to share?"

The male spirit announced, "Hank will be right in."

Christine added, "And we'll see when Hank gets in here."

The male spirit remarked, "And I don't believe it."

Christine stated, "They never put him in. They don't put him with what the way's doing." George turned the recorder off and came back to the kitchen.

I took the recorder in the kitchen, stood up, and did a quick clearing and grounding of myself. We had been talking about energy and how I used it in magick. As soon as I opened the door to the garage I could sense who was in there. It was a relief to know I wasn't dealing with new spirits but what seemed like old friends.

I turned the recorder on past the boxes and the male spirit annouced, "Hank is in here."

I asked, "Should I show them how I get my power how you like the most?"

Christine replied, "And you'll make. You make fun of everything."

The male spirit told me, "Hank you need to step up here. Is this what you wanted Hank?"

Christine remarked, "Hank has never been here."

The male spirit admitted, "I go through those phases."

I asked, "Did you have to talk to them?"

The male spirit commented, "I think Hank looks better now."

Christine asked, "Do you wish something we can do? I have never been here. This will be us." There was a bang on the garage door then a clicking sound. Next it sounded like brushing against the recorder and a big set of clicks in a rhythmic pattern resembling the sound disruption. I had to call it the machine noise.

The male spirit confirmed, "Hank looks like he heard it."

Christine agreed, "I think he did."

There was more brushing sound that I would say is the machine shutting down. Read on to find out why I would know this.

Christine asked, "Is there anything else we can do Hank?"

I asked, "What's that?"

Christine asked, "Can you hear me talking?"

I tried again, "Hello, I'm Hank. Can you tell me your name?"

Christine answered, "Yes we know."

The male spirit started, "But."

Christine asked, "What is our name for?"

The male spirit replied, "It's a deal with Hank."

Christine gave in, "Oh, I guess okay. Then my name would be Christine."

The male spirit confessed, "My name is Chester Buccini."

I said, "I would also like to help Britney. Are you going to help Britney?"

Christine answered, "I can't get close enough to help her."

Chester stated, "We're not here about her Hank. Did you get your answer?"

Christine replied, "We still have work with Hank."

Chester asked, "What can we do to make a better Hank?"

I asked, "Can you tell me anything else about her?"

Chester asked, "What are we supposed to do? I'll give you something." He hit the garage door twice.

He then added, "I can't do anymore than that Hank. Can you give us an answer Hank?"

Christine asked, "Can you see him up there?"

Chester remarked, "We've been here two hours and twenty four minutes."

Christine replied, "I'll give him some," and again two wraps on the garage door.

Chester asked, "Is he done with me?"

I asked, "Can you tell me if you are an astral being?"

94

Chester repeated, "Astral being. Is that anything like it used to be? I don't think I can do this yet. Can you hear?" Then there was the sound of a whistle.

He asked, "And can you hear?" There were two raps on the door with two rebounds.

Christine remarked, "This is easy."

I asked, "What type of astral being would you be?"

Chester asked. "Can you see us right here? Can you hear this?" He hits the door once as he said the word this.

He asked, "And can you give us an answer?" Then came two whistle sounds.

Christine started, "Hank," still using the whistling sound and finished, "You wouldn't believe. That Hank that's enough."

I said, "Thank you for talking."

Chester asked, "Did he hear me?" and I shut the recorder off.

I went back in the kitchen and George and Britney asked what all the banging was about and I told them that it was the spirits from the bridge that I was dealing with.

George took me home and we plugged the recorder into the amplifier. We heard their voices but couldn't make out everything they said. Shortly after this I got the computer and headphones and worked on this short recording to know their names.

CHAPTER SEVEN

THE LA1DAY TOUR

A spirit hanging around Gary to hear the lamp post story

A news magazine from Los Angeles came to take the tour. I called this the LA1Day Tour. I started by placing the recorder at the phone booth.

First Chester gave his opinion, "I think Hank is still crazy."

Christine started, "I have to feel."

Chester stretched out, "Secure."

I thought it was Chester, but it sounded like a bird saying, "I believe that's right."

He then said normally between the birds, "Hank will never change. Does he not fear what people will think? He can't be cluttered. I can't tell you what he did to me before. I think we'll see our published book."

Talking like a bird he asked, "Which way the (bird sound) Hank?"

A male spirit commented, "Jazz is so twenty."

Chester told him, "Shut up. I thought you study."

Christine instructed, "Mean Hank."

Chester replied, "Be there after," and, "Can you hold it?"

Christine suggested, "Try to hold that."

Chester remarked, "It's not so heavy," and said in a strange voice, "I need it for Hank." In his normal voice he said, "We're always controlled."

Some spirit volunteered, "I could push."

In heavy bird talk Chester announced, "Hank will have hands on it tomorrow." In half speech and bird whistle he continued, "Wait till Hank gets here." Separated from the bird he finished, "You asked what part is that. It's made for him."

Another spirit replied, "Bucket up right here then."

Christine stated, "Hank will have book success."

Some spirit whispers, "Can you get the presets here?"

Chester asked, "Does?"

Christine added, "Hank."

Chester finished, "Clean up second." He went on to say, "But Hank wouldn't be here. That's it you got it. It's not their business."

Christine asked, "Does Hank want us here?"

Chester advised, "First of all you have to shut that."

Christine asked, "Did he?"

Some other spirit asked, "Did Hank go see that?"

Chester answered, "I guess he spots the circles here."

Christine replied, "That's alright."

Chester remarked, "Told you they would get upset at that. If Hank grows up."

Christine added, "A little bit. Hank went."

Chester finished, "Petered back home."

Another male spirit suggested, "Then you'll have to penalize him."

Chester came back with, "He has nothing left."

One of them, possibly Christine stated, "That's trouble."

Chester instructed, "And Hank sit up here with me. I can't weigh the man."

A female spirit commented, "I thought Frank was here."

Some spirit announced, "Hank's always visiting us."

Chester replied, "That doesn't prove a thing."

One of them asked, "That is impulse isn't it?"

Another spirit directed them, "Take it home."

Chester added, "You will talk. If you feel you have to drop it. If Hank's always visiting you here. Then what Hank felt."

Christine stated, "Hank loves me," as it went to a bird chirping.

Chester advised, "Careful you were talking to me what we have to drop today. Did he drop in on you? What is it about that? Same with people. That's a basketball. He's smoking too much. Did you like that?"

Strangely after that I got both what sounds like Gary and a whistling whisper saying, "Now my secret."

Then Gary's laughed without the whisper.

Some male spirit remarked, "That's more."

Christine added, "Like Hank."

Chester said, with the whisper from before, "I can't wait for Hank to be here."

A combination of voices spoke, "That's what I think."

Chester finished, "About Hank."

A bird chirped and I got a faint, "If that's what Hank wants," by Chester.

Another male spirit replied, "I don't think he's coming here."

Chester informed him, "That's what it's like outside."

Christine remarked, "It'll take a minute," with a sound possibly coming from a bird.

She added, "Beautiful," at the same time Chester was saying, "Drop this."

Chester then told Christine, "If you want to go to Albertsons go with him."

By this time I was trying to focus on being more healthy and stopping at the grocery store after I was finished at the Village.

Christine replied, "That's okay."

Chester said, "Hank will grab a sandwich."

One of them, possibly Chester, announced, "There's nothing to see over here."

I started picking up Gary and the tour when one of the spirits asked, "What's he saying?"

Christine started explaining, "That's what he had on his," and a bird finished, "Head."

Chester and Christine complained together, "Can't get the aooph."

Then a bird and Chester finished, "He got."

Chester stated, "It didn't work for anywhere. Hank will do the same old thing."

Christine suggested, "I will take Hank with me. Can he go to Albertsons with me?"

Chester remarked, "Hank is such an A-hole."

Christine added, "Let's see what Hank does," with a bird joining in. She then finished, "It works if you count on Hank," with the bird.

Chester replied, "I want to get him back here."

Christine said, "Hank waited." A bird whistled. She told him in partial bird talk, "We'll go out and see Hank."

Another female spirit commented, "Hank is not from around here."

A male spirit asked, "What's it like for him? I still feel guilty."

One of the spirits quietly instructed him, "You cannot do that."

He then remarked, "I bet you can't wait to get out of here."

Chester complained, "It's been miserable by Hank. He's not what you'd call an A-hole."

Christine replied, "At least you'll help me with him. Can I go with Hank?"

Chester stated, "And that what, what we have."

Christine asked, "Will you go back? Can you see for yourself?"

Again I heard Gary's laugh as he was telling how the Village used to be.

Chester ordered, "You have official duty."

Christine announced, "I can see more."

Chester added, "Give sixty days."

Christine came back with, "Give me some dope."

Chester asked, "What'd you say?"

One of the spirits complained, "He will bring his camera out there."

Another spirit asked, in a whispering voice, "Did you see what Hank's bringing?"

Chester stated, "He'll try to tape this. What's Milo doing here? What is Hank doing?"

A male spirit started, "He's been standing there for," and a female spirit finished, "Fifty years."

Another female spirit remarked, "Looks like recycle some stuff."

Christine announced, "He's right here."

With a motorcycle passing by Chester suggested, "Just wait till Hank gets over here. Can you see what's over there? That's what we get for helping Hank." With a bird's help he finished, "That's what we get if I do good."

Then again I got Gary laughing as the tour reached the lamppost and he started his story.

Christine gave a good strong, "Hank," while Gary was speaking.

A male spirit asked, "That's Hank?"

Chester asked, "Can you see who he's with?"

After some talk from the magazine guys Chester stated, "He's a pipe cleaner."

I got the feeling Christine was trying to defend me as she started, "Hank is."

Chester cut her off as he asked, "Is he?"

Chester added, "Then he will suffer."

Another spirit replied, "So will we."

They tried to make a bird sound but was not quite a bird.

Christine suggested, "If you like that," while another female spirit was saying, "If you like him."

Christine finished, "Get after it," as the other female spirit added, "Like Hank."

A female spirit commented, "It's a dumb ass."

Chester added, "And he has a board."

Gary started coming in even though he was at the lamppost for the last thirty seconds. He was telling the lamppost story and some people were talking. At the end of the story a female spirit asked, "Will you be nice to 'em?"

Gary and the tour arrived at the phone booth. As Gary started the stories about the phone booth, the clock tower chimed drowning him out. By the time we heard Gary again, he was talking about the pictures of apprehensions at the phone booth.

As he paused Christine announced, "I'm here for Hank," like she wanted the tour to hear.

At the end of the of the Marsha and Cheryl line, possibly only I could hear it, a bird chirped, "Hank."

I picked up the recorder and we started walking.

Right away Christine told me, "Hank I'm in the bathroom."

Chester stated, "I still see him. That's not supposed to happen. Everything I've been here is all."

Christine confessed, "Still I have to think. Back up will you. I'd die with Hank."

Chester asked, "Are you opposed to that?"

Christine answered, "That's what I got here. In the book."

Chester replied, "That's what people say about you."

Christine asked, "Is that how they are?"

Chester started, "If Hank has cancer."

Christine asked, "Is that all you think? I missed him in the bathroom."

Chester continued, "It's in the top of him. I've seen it."

Christine commented, "I care about Hank. I think."

Chester told her, "You have to help him. There are lots of things to tell him. There's Cathy."

All of a sudden Gary came back in giving some history of the bridge.

Chester broke in with, "We'll bring the bridge."

Another male spirit suggested, "Maybe Hank get into trouble."

Chester admitted, "Once we tried but he said that. He asked me. If both made it. No, I already fixed it. It's a big thing I couldn't even fix right."

I couldn't be sure what they were talking about. I almost got in trouble once in Lake Havasu but it didn't seem to fit this.

The other male spirit asked, "Did you ever get it fixed?"

Christine asked him, "Did you ever see Hank before?"

The other male spirit answered, "Since eighteen thirty seven."

Now they were talking about past life when the bridge was in London.

Christine added, "Hank could have been on top."

The other male spirit asked, "Is he on the bridge?"

Christine replied, "He's the one taping us." There was a lot of static and then really clearly she confessed, "I like him spanking that. Only at night."

Chester ordered, "Do business."

Christine came back with, "Not all the time."

The other male spirit stated, "Now we're getting somewhere. He's thirsty. I can hear that must be worse for Hank."

Christine told him, "It takes a bit."

Chester added, "He's got to try to quit smoking."

A female spirit remarked, "That was broken."

The other male spirit asked, "Can he bucket with me today?"

Christine answered, "And Hank won't be breathing."

The other male spirit replied, "Fuck."

Chester commented, "No doubt. Walk the tour like that."

Christine started to ask, "Do you think..."

Chester finished, "He's a positive role model?"

The other male spirit asked, "Can he get in trouble?"

The magazine guys came back in. I was sure they and Gary were talking as we walked.

After twenty seconds of them talking, the other male spirit came back in with, "If Hank can do that walking."

Christine replied, "Hank can do it."

The other male spirit stated, "I'm proud of Hank. Hank might give an answer."

Christine told him, "And then you're believing his answer."

Chester announced, "He's got a shortie in there."

I called part of an unfinished cigarette a shortie.

Gary and the tour came in again. After six seconds of the tour the sound was disrupted with Chester saying, "That's why we haven't been here," at a much lower volume.

The other male spirit commented, "These people look real good."

Chester directed them, "Just stop, take a look at that."

Christine replied, "Hank looks good. I guess I should just give this back to him. See I wanna go in here. Can you get off of it? How do you do this?"

The other male spirit suggested, "This one might."

Chester admitted, "I've never seen why you control that."

The other male spirit stated, "We made a difference."

Christine said, "Hank," with a different sound. She then announced, "Hank could hear that."

I was standing at the shaved ice shack while the magazine guys were by the water with Gary. I remembered turning to my left and behind me I heard a noise but nothing was there.

The other male spirit suggested, "Get the room."

Chester stated, "They are right there. It was very promising. Why would you step up advance way?"

The other male spirit added, "About that side step. They would sell my body in Arizona. It's worth the gamble though."

Chester said, "Apple," as a test and the machine made a noise. He then commented, "Well this thing is working."

Christine replied, "Weird."

The other male spirit told them, "Hank is awful wiped out," with the volume increasing on every word.

Chester related, "They're really poor when they do that."

The other male spirit remarked, "It's not fair."

Chester replied, "It's not the first time."

The other male spirit guessed, "I think Jack would take so long."

Chester asked, "Are you buying Britney?" I asked for her to have help.

He finished, "He's not gonna torch anything. Thousands of them."

The other male spirit stated, "Hank is broken."

Chester commented about me, "If you're gonna take some, take some."

The other male spirit told him, "They have a ferry down here now. And he will."

Chester added, "The very next port that they came."

That one was about cigarettes. A ferry went across the lake to the casino where there was an Indian smoke shop.

Christine announced, "I staple."

The other male spirit replied, "A lady can't build it."

Chester stated, "I'm very selectable."

The other male spirit suggested, "Make a movie about something odd."

Chester confided with him, "That was a secret. At first you don't believe anything he did. I love," then it went much lower in volume for, "To take pictures."

The other male spirit refused, "They can't take pictures of me."

Christine told him, "They're taking a picture of that."

Gary came in with a story by the water.

After Gary, Christine remarked, "I think it will last twenty."

Chester replied, "Make it quick. We won't be like that Hank."

The other male spirit announced, "He just loomed at me."

Christine let him know, "He always does things like that," with the sound chopped up. She commented, "That failed," clearly.

Chester stated, "You didn't have to stay until after the performance."

The other male spirit replied, "Oh well, it's six thirty seven."

Christine remarked, "Hank, whatever, Hank. Take me through."

Chester announced, "Another feat goes by," with Christine saying, "Then kick me," at the same time.

Chester said by himself, "The nineteenth of December."

The other male spirit asked, "Did he have some coffee in here? So he can go with me. Does Hank want to go with me?"

Chester admitted, "We don't know anything."

Christine stated, "Hank will fail."

Chester commented, "It didn't have to fail right in front of the lab."

The other male spirit asked, "Is this a boat shop?"

Chester started, "This."

Christine added, "Doesn't matter."

Chester finished, "Hank."

The other male spirit asked, "Is it true it matters to me?"

Chester answered, "It does."

The other male spirit asked, "Can I help you with something?"

Christine asked, "Can you get here?"

The other male spirit replied, "I just won't be in here."

Chester insisted, "Not with me."

Gary said, "When they first put the bridge up in London."

The other male spirit asked, "Will you go to Hank?"

Christine answered, "We'll get there."

Chester added, "It'll just be a moment. You'll just know how inside the break I am."

Christine stated, "You shouldn't be here."

Chester directed him, "You should be. On top of the clown."

The other male spirit suggested, "Even Mikey should."

As Gary and the tour started to come back in Chester started, "You will get in front of."

Christine finished, "Hank. Where's Hank?"

Gary came in with casual talk to the magazine guys.

Seven seconds later the other male spirit announced, "I see these still."

Christine replied, "That was good."

The tour came back in with Gary telling about the bullet holes on the Gopie's steps.

As Gary paused Christine commented, "I guess they need the customers."

Gary continued until he finished about the bullet holes and we climbed the stairs.

The tour got ahead of me and Christine said, "Hank."

Then other male spirit asked, "Will be in here?"

Chester ordered, "Don't break this thing."

The other male spirit suggested, "Hold that piece."

Then there was a slapping sound I got quite often and Christine announced, "Hank just heard."

Chester remarked, "These faces walking in a fucking fog."

The magazine guys were out partying in Lake Havasu the night before. The ones that could make it to the tour were hung over.

We stopped at the next spot on the stairs.

Gary started the Museum Tape story and Christine called behind him, "Come in here. He won't. Hank."

The other male spirit asked, "Did you see Hank?"

During the Museum Tape story Gary paused and I faintly picked up Chester saying, "I will take him."

At another pause the other male spirit remarked, "We've seen this before."

Gary finished the story and we climbed the stairs. I turned the recorder off.

While the tour was at the statues I went ahead across the bridge to the passage door to ask questions.

Turning the recorder back on I got the other male spirit asking, "What's he tape?"

Chester answered, "Is anybody here?"

I asked, "Is there anyone here?"

The other male spirit asked, "Can Hank hear?"

Chester replied, "He puts voices in there."

Christine announced quite loudly, "Anybody can say anything."

The other male spirit stated, "I can just stay here."

Chester agreed, "I think you're supposed to do that."

Christine started, "Hank," and a deep, "Will meet us here," followed.

I told them, "Talk to me."

Christine asked, "Is your paperwork down?"

Chester cut in with, "In any place."

Christine asked, "Is it down here?"

Chester announced, "We're going in here now Hank."

Christine admitted, "Hank led us to it. It's not here. Is there something here? I'm digging through everything. Hank your magick..."

Another female spirit yelled, "Shut up."

Chester commented, "Yet to give an answer."

The other male spirit replied, "I'm on it."

Chester remarked, "I can't get this in here."

Christine added, "Now we will make a difference."

The other male stated, "He didn't hear like you said he would."

Christine replied, "In the middle would it be. I can't say if you heard. If I should post."

I asked, "Do you stay at the bridge?"

Another female spirit asked, "Does he know that?"

Christine answered, "I can't get there."

The other female assured her, "I will cover for you."

Chester suggested, "Take him back through the scene."

Christine reminded him, "Hank can hear this."

The other female spirit started, "If you can see anything."

I asked, "Are you happy here?"

Then I placed the recorder down on a ledge by the passage door.

The other female spirit answered, "Of course I'm happy here. Why is he here?"

Christine replied, "Being here. Is what Hank is doing."

Chester advised, "Easy how you do it."

Christine commented, "That's Hank for you."

The other female spirit told her, "I can take on Hank."

The other male spirit offered, "I will get that."

Chester replied, "I don't need a thing."

Christine stated, "I can't find it."

Chester repeated, "Easy with Hank I told you. It should be here. I can't hear you."

The other male spirit remarked, "I can't hear either."

Chester asked, "Hank do you take so long?"

Christine sang, "Always," and said, "Patient."

Chester added, "Or he's thinking something."

Together the two other spirits spoke, "You know we're here."

Chester proclaimed, "We found it here."

Christine agreed, "I see it here."

Chester remarked, "Usually it's got to be somewhere."

In an echoing voice the other male spirit asked, "Can he read that?"

Christine answered, "And he's magickal."

The other male spirit asked, "But is he just people?"

The other female spirit suggested, "Maybe it's his magick. Can you hear that? Is he?"

Chester cut in with, "Look at that picture."

Christine read, "It says here we're working for Hank."

My guess was they found the paperwork. Apparently I hid it in the bridge behind the storage door. No wonder this had to be done in Lake Havasu.

Chester remarked, "You like this."

The other female spirit started to ask, "Did he have..."

Chester and Christine combined to say, "I don't know if that's it."

The other female spirit asked, "What do you do around here anyway?"

Chester replied, "I think it's just a miracle."

Christine yelled, "I found it here!"

Chester joked, "Easy bonehead."

The other male spirit asked, "Has he been here lately?"

Chester advised, "Hold that fear."

The other female spirit stated, "It proves you're handy."

Christine uttered, "I wish Hank was here."

The other female spirit announced, "Hank's here."

Chester warned, "You won't be seen. If you can hear something different. Hank is very in to it."

The other female spirit replied, "Here's an answer for you."

Chester stated, "Days till we could get through this Earth like that. If he asks too much of you."

The other female spirit informed Chester, "I got this down here," with a rhythmic clapping sound.

Chester asked, "Are you done already?"

The other female spirit requested, "Hank be an adult for me."

Chester added, "And he talks just like people."

The other female spirit stated, "It doesn't matter what he's saying. Hank's supposed to be here."

Chester remarked, "I don't believe it. We won't have to do this. And we want to."

Christine told him, "You give Hank the willies."

The other female spirit asked, "Can you see him there?"

The other male spirit asked, "How are you supposed to pick up Hank?"

Christine commented, "I don't believe this Hank."

The other male spirit replied, "He's in that room up in there."

Chester confirmed, "That's the one we went to. He's supposed to be here," with the sound breaking up.

The other female spirit stated, "I can answer."

Chester told her, "But he's not here. If you can see there's something over there."

Christine came back with, "He prefers it like that," and a car honked at the words like that.

The other female spirit announced, "I can't see anything from here."

Chester remarked, "It's not like him to get upset. And you can quit both for me. There's something in the air."

The other female spirit suggested, "Make it closer. He just about missed it."

The other male spirit added, "Make it fit...Make it fit both."

Christine stated, "Hank seems a little different. This is what he is. And he take Christmas spirit home."

Chester spoke, "It's all up to Hank. Speaking of wishes."

The other male asked, "He asked about me right?"

The other female spirit explained, "Hank needs better equipment. But let me show you something. Take him to the city. Hank put that fan up. You will never be here."

Chester said, "This is his source right here."

The other male spirit asked, "What did you find in Hank?"

Christine sang, "That's a poor man."

The other female spirit told them, "You should see this. You're disgusting Hank. I thought he knew everything."

Chester replied, "That was not in his room."

The other male spirit guessed, "I think it got too close to him."

Christine stated, "I've seen his penis in his bed."

Chester remarked, "He's not beating back there right here. Hank took his pants right here."

Christine suggested, "Cause he's hot."

She was right. I went in the back room of the shop and dropped my pants to try to cool off.

Chester said, "He's a flirt in here."

The other female spirit agreed, "He could be in here."

Christine asked, "Did you want to stay here?"

The other male spirit asked, "When's Hank supposed to be there? I see the people again."

The other female spirit suggested, "Wait for her to come and get here. I like the rest of you."

Christine told me, "Hank you're not supposed to. You should return," with part singing.

Chester asked, "Guess who's back here?"

Christine repeated, "You were asked return."

The other female spirit replied, "Behind the bush."

Christine remarked, "This is flatfooted. That's a zombie for you."

Chester agreed, "Yeah but you liked him first."

Christine asked, "What do you think we're doing here? Would you lay me down?Can you get close to me? And he's just a mad man. I think I'm better than him. I think he needs to change. Hank won't like what you're doing here. At least it hasn't happened."

Chester asked, "Have you got the main thing? I've been looking for you. What did Hank say?"

The other female spirit asked, "What should I ask him? He just likes to look at me."

Chester admitted, "I am for Hank."

The other female spirit announced, "I can't understand what he's saying."

Christine told her, "I get a strange idea. Wait for it."

The other female spirit suggested, "Little bacteria."

Christine added, "From Hank."

Chester commented, "He's into everything. Do you live here?"

The other female spirit replied, "Go with him," with her voice changing.

Chester ordered, "Right here is good."

The other female spirit confessed, "I fall to pieces," with her voice changing again.

Chester remarked, "He's the president."

Christine told them, "I just came with him through this. You will be in there."

The other female spirit stated, "He does maintenance here."

Christine suggested, "I would leave him here."

The other female spirit confirmed, "You'll be right here."

Christine directed, "You get to answer now."

Chester announced, "This is the break here for Hank."

The other female spirit called, "Hank get over here."

Chester repeated, "Hank get over here."

The other female spirit demanded, "Hank get over here and say something to me. To heck with him."

Chester remarked, "He'll get here."

Christine explained, "It's like Hank to be slow," with the sound breaking up. She then said clearly, "Get used to it."

The other male spirit exclaimed, "Get the fuck here."

Christine corrected, "Get the bucket back."

The other female spirit suggested, "Let me answer."

The other male spirit asked, "But is he going anywhere?"

The other female spirit commented, "Not so easy walking outside. He walked on past."

The other male spirit ordered, "Get the energy from him."

Christine replied, "I need to see."

The other female spirit called, "Get the heck over here."

The other male spirit stated, "We can go up here."

Chester remarked, "That's the end."

The other female spirit asked, "That was a bird that killed him?"

Christine asked, "When did he say he would get over here? I see now he's coming."

The other female spirit announced, "I see him," with the other male spirit saying, "I'm a doctor," at the same time.

Chester told her, "Bye, Sherry."

Sherry asked, "Should I ask, ask him?"

Some people walked by talking, then the other male spirit asked, "Who the heck was that?"

Chester admitted, "I could sound out right here," with a clapping noise.

The other male spirit replied, "Hank is broken."

Christine informed them, "Hank knows better than to do that."

Sherry begged, "Please tell me he's right here."

Chester remarked, "I think he's been partying today."

Christine asked, "But did you see him?"

Sherry pointed out, "That's the place I have for him."

I picked up some people talking, then Sherry asked, "Do you think normally Hank was here?"

Christine answered, "Normally Hank would be here."

Sherry replied, "I guess this is touring."

Christine stated, "I have the case."

Chester started to say, "We're doing..."

Sherry interrupted with, "Just leave me this or that."

Christine announced, "I can see him standing there."

Sherry ordered, "Don't feed that to me."

Chester added, "That's our story to stick with for now. Hank could do better."

Christine replied, "If he were with me."

Chester said, "I can still see Hank."

Sherry asked, "Is he right now going over here?"

Christine answered, "It doesn't look like he lost his thing."

That would be the recorder.

Sherry told them, "I'm on the edge of leaving."

Chester confirmed, "Hank's doing it. Now what's he saying?"

Sherry remarked, "If Hank delivered. I need some better foot."

Then there was some music with a dog bark.

Christine assured her, "Hank will do real fair."

The other male spirit asked, "How do you like Christine?"

Chester explained, "He smokes that just to feel good. It's just like the man who bumped free."

The other male spirit stated, "I know what he's doing."

Chester asked, "Did anybody get some fuel?"

Sherry confessed, "I didn't ask if you had."

Christine asked, "Is it black?"

Sherry asked, "What do you have to do with Hank? Ask her what to do with it."

Christine answered, "That's all he ever did."

Sherry measured me, "Hank is an eight forty eight."

Christine asked, "Did you leave with a tattoo?"

Sherry told her, "You ask an awful lot."

Christine replied, "That's the bridge we're going in after."

The other male spirit announced, "I think they're coming."

Sherry admitted, "I see he used to be useful."

Loud enough to be a person, a female something said, "Seventy eight for one."

Christine guessed, "It might happen."

The other male spirit stated, "I couldn't see anymore."

Christine ordered, "Just say what you hear."

Sherry said, as loud as a person, "We're supposed to take Hank here. I know it's exciting here."

Again loudly a male spirit announced, "We have junk right over here."

A new male spirit asked, "Did he tell the truth?"

Sherry answered, "He makes a truthful idiot."

Christine added, "That is the magick."

The new male spirit asked, "What are we supposed to use Hank for?"

Sherry replied, "Hank could be the new Erwin."

Christine reminded them, "Hank is still human."

Sherry admitted, "He is the spirit we're after."

Christine asked, "Did we peak?"

The other male spirit answered, "Almost did. At first run."

Sherry commented, "We were biking."

Chester pointed out, "That was in Mardi Gras."

Sherry asked, "Has he been to Mardi Gras?"

Chester told her, "That was years ago. He didn't send a post card. He needs a bucket. The worst bucket in proof reading. I can call him anything. He might just give up. Now can you feel it?"

Sherry added, "We won't get to use Hank there."

Christine came back with, "Hank knows better than that."

Sherry stated, "We're finished with Hank. There's a place for him here with me."

In a chopped up sound Christine asked, "You mean he can be the next Erwin?"

Chester ordered, "You will be the one to go with Hank." It was also chopped up.

It was clearer when he admitted, "He doesn't do what he's supposed to do. You will still take Hank?"

Sherry replied, "Bring him on if he thinks he's tough."

Chester asked, "Is that your answer?"

Christine told him, "You already know the answer."

Sherry started, "If you think that's weird."

Christine finished, "You'll take Hank for us."

Sherry asked, "Did you make this thing up?"

Gary started coming in and Christine announced, "That is him."

Sherry asked, "What's Hank doing?"

Gary talked a little about the bridge and Sherry asked, "Is that this bridge?"

Christine suggested, "Talk to Hank if you want."

Sherry asked, "What should he say?"

Chester answered, "That's a part of Hank. He won't break us here."

Sherry announed, "Here we go. Is Hank the last man?"

Chester guessed, "Maybe these people like him different."

Sherry confessed, "He's the best I have found."

The other male spirit complained, "I told you guys but you tried to ditch me."

Chester told them, "Anything you tell. The answer is right here. Pumping propane."

Sherry asked, "You hear that?"

Chester commented, "Death for Hank. I just shouldn't care about."

Sherry finished, "Helping."

Christine ordered, "Let's go Hank."

Sherry asked, "Do you think he heard it?"

Chester stated, "Hank will never ditch on me. What's Hank doing?"

Sherry and the other male spirit answered, "I think he has no idea."

Chester added, "And live across the street. If Hank had an ass full."

Christine suggested, "Wait for Hank," with a little help from the sound machine.

The other male spirit came back with, "Let's put him in hand cuffs."

Chester remarked, "He'll see his birthday."

Sherry confessed, "I've had it with all these people. It's the music too."

Chester asked, "Is Hank over there anymore?"

Sherry answered, "They won't move it."

Chester ordered Christine, "Dance with the leaves or something."

I've seen the dance with the leaves. Only a spirit could make the leaves move that way.

Christine replied, "Tell him we're naked."

Sherry asked, "Did he tell you something?"

Chester admitted, "I won't test him."

Sherry announced, "I hear the animal."

Chester asked, "Why is he looking at me?"

Christine answered, "He wants me. Ready Hank?"

Sherry commented, "A secret you bother me with."

The other male spirit gave a reading, "Fifteen fifty seven here."

Chester suggested, "I bet Mikey could go with Mikey."

Mikey stated, "Building up be it."

Chester instructed, "Opposites go here," and Christine offered, "I got it," at the same time.

Christine directed, "Do it here."

Some people yelled in the parking lot of The Heat.

Mikey asked, "Is somebody crying for me back there?"

Chester asked, "Can you repair the bicycle he rode?"

Sherry gave her opinion, "He's an animal."

Chester remarked, "You mean Hank won't sit on me. Just like a doctor can."

Mikey told them, "He said he would."

Chester started, "Hank goes."

Christine laughed, "Ha-ha-ha."

Chester finished, "Down here."

Mikey asked, "What will Hank do when he gets here?"

Christine answered, "He won't do anything like you think."

Chester added, "That's what we had for yesterday."

Mikey complained, "I don't get anything."

Chester stated, "And what he needed we couldn't hear. So we'll spend today on it. He won't even come here." And someone said, "Thank you," over him.

Mikey announced, "You're the man."

Sherry replied, "I can hear it."

Chester pointed out, "He has a way of doing it," with a lot of static.

Mikey asked, "Can you take me in there?"

Christine told him, "Easy does it."

Mikey suggested, "Hank would never leave us alone."

Chester instructed him, "Just wait for Hank to get here."

Mikey asked, "Does he have to quit smoking because we see cancer? I killed a man."

Sherry asked, "Where is he?"

Chester asked, "Can you tell me what he's doing?"

Sherry asked, "Is that absurd?"

Christine directed, "Take off him after," with Chester helping at the end.

Chester announced, "He's not supposed to be with Hank," with Christine's help.

Sherry pointed out, "If you're both the same."

Christine replied, "Yes Hank told me something." With enough volume to be human she then stated, "He likes to see shock man."

Chester asked, "What's Hank doing? I know Hank is fair game."

Mikey asked, "What are you saying?"

Chester told Sherry, "Hank will go with you. Big Red. If Hank would just get here."

Mikey started to say, "It's not fair what Hanky..."

Chester interrupted, "Got it here, hope that was long enough. Compare his light. What is Hank doing? But there's nothing anyway. This Daniel wasn't here either."

Sherry asked, "Who is he?"

Chester answered, "They just let anybody do that." Then a car honked.

Mikey asked, "Did you ever tell?"

Christine called me, "Hank."

Chester asked, "Think he can hear it?"

Mikey asked, "Has anybody seen Hank before?"

Another spirit came in and announced, "I've got business right here."

He needed to lien.

Mikey asked, "You think he's supposed to be quitting?"

Sherry replied, "Think we got it going today Mathew. Love what Hank's doing."

Chester commented, "Hank should be here already."

Sherry asked, "What's he saying?"

Chester stated, "Hank was in here. You're left hurting me. Most of Hank's thinking. Hank couldn't stand if he had to do it."

Christine said in my defense, "He does everything. Did you see the blisters on him? Where's Hank going to?"

Sherry remarked, "Never seen him before."

Chester suggested, "Guess he's gone tonight."

Christine started, "Maybe it's just..."

Chester finished, "Ten thirty."

It may have seemed hard to believe they would have any use for time on the other side, but my observations showed the movement of spirits away from the bridge at eight o'clock every night.

Sherry announced, "He's gone."

Christine admitted, "I can't get through this anyway."

Chester asked, "Did you ever see Hank when he did that? Even if Hank was here. Even if he did."

Sherry stated, "Hank's supposed to be here."

Mikey suggested, "Let me go see if Hank's in here."

Chester guessed, "Maybe he's back home again."

Mikey asked, "Can I go?"

Chester asked, "Is Hank here?"

Mikey answered, "We looked everywhere."

Sherry informed him, "Hank won't quite see ya."

Christine announced, "I found him."

Chester ordered, "You're not supposed to be here when Hank gets here."

Mikey added, "If he does anyway."

Chester asked, "What'd he say?"

Christine guessed, "Bet you did that thing to Hank. I should have told Hank at this spot." She sang, "That's all that Hank brought."

Sherry asked, "Has he ever been there before? I've had enough of this door."

Chester stated, "Hank's upstairs. Help him with that Sherry. Happy birthday to me Hank."

Christine replied, "If Hank would be up there."

Chester told them, "Hank wrote this bridge. On top of that he never."

Christine asked, "Did you ever drink soda? We're not in the basket Hank. Is Hank after..."

Chester interrupted with, "Hank just said locker thirty seven."

I didn't say it, but somehow it popped into my head and I thought it was weird.

Sherry commented, "And we look like mouths to them."

Chester remarked, "His ass is broken."

Christine said, "Thank you."

Chester announced, "Now he's going to sharpen stuff."

Sherry asked, "Is that your cigarette?"

Christine answered, "He doesn't like it."

Chester replied, "Automatically different. Hank will never trust again."

Sherry admitted, "I feel his pain."

Christine stated, "I see what he's saying."

Chester confessed, "We'd love to clean out your pipe."

Christine added, "Vacuum cleaner."

Sherry told them, "I can see Randi's worked with Hank before this."

Chester asked, "If you like Hank would you please take him?"

Sherry instructed, "Get off of there. If you can't hold it."

120

The spirit she was talking to replied, "It's not easy going everywhere."

Sherry commented, "Baby-sitting again."

The visiting spirit asked, "Is that fair?"

Chester suggested, "That was Hank, someone forgot to tell him that."

Christine disagreed, "Not with all our business here."

Chester stated, "Everyday he's just wrecking, he's got to live."

Christine replied, "He wants to live right now."

Sherry asked, "Is this where he has to do his homework?"

Christine called me, "Hank."

Chester added, "We're here. Let's see if he's seen us."

Christine told me, "Hank there's someone else here for you. Hank what are you doing? Hank you're messing up the picture."

Chester offered, "I will stay here with dick lick."

Sherry agreed, "Okay if that's the answer."

Christine guessed, "I think Hank is off today."

Chester remarked, "Hank is over."

Christine suggested, "If I just go up here. If Hank was a woman."

Chester continued, "With a beautiful figure."

Christine asked, "What is he doing? And as a woman."

Chester confessed, "We take Hank for granted. But Hank is guilty."

Christine defended me, "Hank would never."

Chester pointed out, "Right now."

Christine stated, "I gotta make us seem like friends for Hank. Is that all I can do? I will take the spot of Hank."

Sherry remarked, "You ain't Chester. I did it."

Christine admitted, "All we did for him."

Chester asked, "What's up with Hank?"

Christine answered, "Make a fist."

Chester added, "Then you turn it."

Christine asked, "What's it like to be thirsty?"

Mikey asked, "Are you thirty nine?"

Sherry stated, "At least we got him."

Chester guessed, "Maybe that's what Hank was doing here."

Christine suggested, "He should ask for a favor."

Mikey announced, "I think Hank is here," as I picked up the recorder.

I turned the recorder off and went with the tour across the bridge. While Gary had the tour group on the bridge I ran down to the lion spot with the recorder.

Very quietly Chester spoke, "I told you Hank would be here."

I asked, "Is anyone here?"

Christine even more quietly admitted, "I think he can hear us."

Sherry asked, "What is he doing?"

Chester asked, "Have you heard of him? Have you heard everything? That he ditched me here."

Sherry voiced her authority, "Let me hear of it."

Chester confirmed, "I swear that he did it."

Micah brought me my drink but as he went to put it down I said, "Not there."

Sherry stated, "I couldn't hear him."

Chester asked, "Can you hear it?"

Christine asked, "Was he talking to me?"

I said, "Feel free to talk while I'm away." I placed the recorder on the ledge.

Sherry asked, "Is that all he's doing here?"

Christine replied, "That's not what he usually does."

Sherry remarked, "I didn't think he was really over here. Is there any chance you can go get him?"

Christine answered, "I can see if I can do it."

Chester ordered, "You don't need to go get Hank."

Christine disagreed loudly, "Yes."

Chester asked, "What is Hank doing?"

Sherry suggested, "Let's go if we're finished."

Chester stated, "That is all we can do."

Christine announced, "I see Hank has got a hamburger."

Sherry asked, "Is that just all he brings?"

Christine replied, "That's just all he really needs. Hank won't be good. You'll see a different Hank."

Chester added, "Which. He might go back home. Or he may stay at home."

Mikey asked, "Can he go with me?"

Chester insisted, "Get outta here."

Christine remarked, "Playing closer."

Chester said, "If Hank won't answer. That's him right here."

Christine asked, "How do you feel?" She spoke, "I wish Hank was here."

Chester replied, "Crazy. Is Hank not moving?"

Christine plotted, "We are going to get back at Hank."

Chester remarked, "Hopefully he left here."

Christine asked, "What is he doing?"

Sherry asked, "Do you expect him?"

Christine answered, "Just like you said."

A new male spirit asked, "What are you doing here?" Then really quickly he said, "I better leave."

Chester stated, "Anyway."

Christine suggested, "I'll talk to Hank first."

Sherry replied, "But he's been here."

Chester commented, "I'll be here. It's confusing."

Christine added, "Making his order."

Chester told them, "We are going to the other lien. I see what he's doing."

Christine started to ask, "Can I..."

Chester finished, "Take him home. And see the left hand."

Christine replied, "And he heard a bird."

Chester stated, "Advance learning for Hank."

Sherry asked, "He did?"

Christine answered, "Take it easy."

Chester added, "And we knew all about it."

Christine told her, "It's one of those things about Hank."

Chester explained, "He wants to be perfect. But he can't so bucket. What's he up to? I don't believe in him. Did you bucket?"

Christine stated, "Now he's leaving."

Chester started, "What needs to be."

Christine asked, "Did you come for me? Hank wants to mate with me. There's nothing with Hank. Can you see anything?"

Chester suggested, "I should get to you."

Christine asked, "Are you too close to me?"

Chester started, "And one more thing."

Christine finished, "We speak Chinese. I can see bad things."

Chester added, "We different."

Christine announced, "I know where he is dammit."

Chester ordered, "That's everything. He should be healed. Get ready Christine."

Christine asked like it was scripted out, "Did you go through this here?"

Chester answered, "Let's see who's ready."

Sherry replied, "We live here."

Christine confirmed, "Yes we're ready."

Sherry remarked, "I do believe it."

Chester told her, "You should believe."

Sherry commented, "I miss going everywhere."

Chester stated, "A chance to give me something. I can see him when he's been here. If you need me."

Christine came back with, "Hank will be leaving."

Chester asked, "Did you help me?"

Christine answered, "Get here."

Chester explained, "I'll be the second one. I believe they're going. I'll wait for him to come pick up this. What we need is a banquet. He's everywhere. I see who he's with. He's got a chance already. I see everything."

Another spirit asked, "What is he doing?"

Chester asked, "Are you at fifty percent? Let's see what we can do. Can you see him? Where's Hank? Hear the music."

Sherry replied, "It's music. Can you see him?"

Chester answered, "I think more than that."

Sherry remarked, "I can hear Poison. If you think you can."

Chester told her, "Face it Homer. Maybe he went downstairs for a minute."

Sherry confirmed, "Hank went to do something."

Chester replied, "Enemy of the dead."

Sherry suggested, "Take it easy. If we'll take him. We can fix it."

Chester admitted, "I'll take it through this year."

Sherry added, "It's nothing but crazy."

Chester remarked, "Since you live here. I could take him already. If he comes through here."

Sherry asked, "What will you do to him?"

Chester started, "I'll get up from here."

Sherry asked, "Did you see Hank?"

Chester answered, "I'm guilty. Angels can see right through you."

Sherry asked, "What'd you make that for?"

Chester replied, "I'm making it for the hammer. And you'll see what we can do. Then you'll see me bonk head. Did you see Hank? Hank won't do that again to us."

Sherry added, "And you'll love the spirit."

Chester disagreed, "Probably not me."

Sherry stated, "Hank is gonna get it."

Chester told her, "He screwed me. Hank is someone you can see through. Take a picture. They're taking a bunch of pictures. What are you getting here? Y'all get ready for me. Basically what we do here. What's with Hank?"

Sherry suggested, "I don't think Hank expects anything. If you wouldn't use it then you wouldn't abuse it."

Chester asked, "Guess who's been a crazy boy?"

Sherry confirmed, "I don't think Hank would quit. Okay with what you're doing."

Chester added, "From those who made the bridge."

Sherry said, "Sandy."

Chester accused me, "Left the door closed, hey Hank."

Sherry asked, "Do you know Hank?"

Chester answered, "If we don't get back. I'm here to help you Hank. If you go back there. What is the scene? The beautiful bridge they built. Hank will know what to do. Hank you've done everything. Wait for me Gopie."

Sherry told him, "Say it."

Chester told me, "Hank can do like you do. Hank you cooperate. Hank make progress. There's no reason for what you're doing. Did you give up that easy? If you could write this in a book Hank. Then you'd be famous forever. Hank we're right here. Trust in me."

Sherry apologized, "Hank I'm sorry. You will break here. Are your feet getting tired?"

Chester stated, "Hank brought us here."

Another male spirit commented, "He married a native."

A second male spirit replied, "Paul was a native here."

Sherry told them, "Excuse me."

One of the male spirits replied, "Not worth it."

Chester remarked, "That was an idiot there. It might be like that last year. Hank was fifty years old."

Sherry asked, "Is he in here?"

Chester answered, "You'll see what it's about. It's just the problem. Are you going to be there for me? I won't stand for Hank."

Sherry replied, "That's very nice of you."

Chester advised, "Don't feed what the man gave to him to walk it. It's the fourteenth man. Hank's weird. Some people got to get their story straight."

Mikey suggested, "Wait till you hit him."

Chester asked, "Didn't you hear? I can feel what Hank's saying. Hank's here anyway."

Sherry commented, "Make your own little set of your chair."

Chester asked, "Hank what's over there? I'm here. What are you doing?"

Mikey asked, "Can you hear what he's saying?"

Chester confessed, "I need to think a little bit."

Sherry announced, "Hank is coming. Can you hear him say anything?"

Chester replied, "He talks dirty to me."

Someone laughed.

Sherry admitted, "I can hear."

Chester asked, "You want to put the table here? The best way to do it."

Sherry answered, "In a mystic clearing."

The tour came back into range of the recorder. Gary was talking to the magazine guys.

At a break in their conversation Chester asked, "Can you see what Hank is doing? Is he over the top?"

Sherry asked, "Hank what are you doing?"

One of the guys from the magazine said, "That's all you can hear."

Chester remarked, "I think someone dropped him on his head once."

Gary laughed and talked.

At a pause Sherry said like a bird, "I'm too pretty." Then back to her normal voice, "For Hank."

Gary talked about the spot on the bridge and as they were taking pictures Chester asked, "Hank what are you doing here?"

The tour group talked about their pictures.

When they were done Chester warned, "Walk back through here. I know you can do it. That's what you said. You're in Chesterfield without me. If you get to say that to me. I told him Hank would."

Mikey commented, "Wish the donkey was here."

Chester explained, "Paul made nationals and he left the Mike. Try not to leave. All you stuck up there. He's not too happy with his clothes on. He does not believe in us. You put the handle up. I just recognized it. There's something else in here. He jacked me up. I'm not too happy."

Sherry stated, "I've got the book. Let's talk to him. Let him see the future. Is there a brake on here? They see what happened. And the Hank got sent back. He smiles about it."

Chester asked, "What are you talking about?"

Sherry answered, "Did they teach us to be like that in school?"

Chester replied, "He's old enough now to take him. Hank what do I do with it?"

Sherry asked, "You'll take Hank?" as Gary came back in.

Gary and the guys from LA1Day talked a few seconds. The sound after that was so disrupted Gary's voice all but disappeared.

Chester asked, "Did you get a tear from me? We could drop Hank up there."

Sherry came back with, "He likes that feeling."

Chester suggested, "Let's think about this. On the one hand we could get Jack out of here. What nephew did he try to get it from? But he still did it in his house."

Sherry replied, "They are the same monkey."

Chester added, "I can't believe it."

Sherry asked, "What are you doing?"

Chester explained, "I'm supposed to see. Hank get through this part. I was talking to him.While he had his pop. I don't believe this would help."

Mikey replied, "Yeah you could save that."

Chester confessed, "I should trust Hank."

Gary and the tour group talked as they were leaving and I started back for the recorder.

Chester remarked, "We all missed Hank. You're all supposed to be after your life," with Sherry's help.

Sherry asked, "Now what's he doing? He's coming. I saw with him."

Then I shut the recorder off.

CHAPTER EIGHT

THE WANNA BE TOUR

*I saw many death masks this day, this
one looking out the window*

Another group of paranormal investigators called and asked to
go on the tour. In talking to them they seemed to know what they
were doing, but anyone who watches the ghost shows could pull
that off. We gave them a shot at investigating while on the tour
and they proved they were amateurs. I call this one the Wanna
Be Tour.

I went home and returned to the Village early to ask questions.
More important at the time was to have a heart-to-heart talk with
Chester and Christine. I decided the best place to do this was at the

doors to the pub as it was a little way from the walkway. It always looked like I was recording myself. I'm not sure if the spirits understood how talking to them looked to the tourists at the bridge.

As soon as I turned the recorder on Chester asked, "Are you wasted Hank? I don't think that we can do this."

I said, "Already we're recording, now I'm glad feeling."

Chester asked, "Hank. Are you stupid? I didn't think you would do it."

I said, "I know I'm kinda early but it is our business and we need to do it daily just at the minute."

Chester replied, "And we have so much to say."

Christine added, "I've got so much to say to him."

Chester started, "If you can be straight by the tour."

Christine yelled, "And could you hear it!"

Chester remarked, "I can't believe Hank would do it."

Christine stated, "That's okay Hank if you want to kill yourself. If he has to quit. I could help him stop."

Chester suggested, "I can do that too. I don't believe him. Let's go leave that to her." I thought he wanted to give up and let Sherry take me.

Sherry asked, "What, can I say it? We don't love him. He doesn't love you. I got a feeling."

I said, "I know you can undo that."

Sherry asked, "Can he hear me?"

I said, "Okay maybe we can talk."

I should add that I heard a noise from people that I thought they could get rid of with the machine. With it quiet we could talk again. The noise didn't come through on the recording nor did they hear it.

Chester stated, "He thinks he scared us. I know that feeling. I can't see."

I said, "That's sincere. I haven't touched the pipe in two days. I can quit when I want to."

Chester replied, "Then do it."

I said, "And I have that kind of will."

Christine advised, "Take a minute to think."

Chester remarked, "I guess he's a faker."

I said, "I just think it would be nicer."

Chester admitted, "I knew you could do it."

I said, "I could quit when it's easy for me."

Chester demanded, "Hank just quit right now. What do you think you know me?"

Christine interjected, "He tried to know you. That must be part of the plan."

Chester asked, "What do you think he does here?"

Christine answered, "I suppose he can't help it."

I said, "You may not understand the economics of it all."

Chester replied, "I understand economics."

I said, "I only have four hundred dollars."

Chester stated, "I couldn't hear him."

I said, "I have to pay insurance on my truck."

Chester asked, "Why is he talking about his insurance plan? I can't understand."

I said, "That's seventy dollars a month; over seventy."

Chester asked, "Is that what he's spending now?"

Christine asked, "Is that your finance charges? That's not very hard for you to do."

Chester complained, "I can't just sit here and think about it."

I said, "That gives me a little over four months of insurance. I don't know when I'll be making money so I don't know when more will be coming in."

Chester asked, "Hank what are you doing here? I know this has happened. Is that the only thing? I can go back where I came from."

Christine insisted, "No you can't go."

Chester replied, "I got better things to do than play. I'll give Hank one more chance."

I said, "And then this, I gotta get food, to save my life."

Chester summed it up, "I know what we're asking tends to put you down. I know you can quit."

I said, "But this is really a stressful time for me right now. That's why I'm asking if I can quit when it's easier."

Chester advised, "You just have to do it."

I said, "Then I can go through the stress and everything will be miserable but I'm going for it."

Chester warned, "Your whole life is in your hands right here. I'll cheer you up."

I can still remember the sensation after that. At the time I thought it was because I had poured all my worries out to them, but all the stress was suddenly gone and the weight bearing down on me wasn't there.

I said, "If that's what you want."

Christine replied, "I think we're getting through to Hank."

Chester announced, "I am the master of what Hank will say. If ever we were going to push Hank. You can do it."

I said, "Another thing I'd like to discuss."

Chester acknowledged, "I'm here. Christine is here."

Christine stated, "I believe in Hank."

I said, "There was a comment about the devil."

Chester replied, "That's the other spirits."

I said, "In Wicca, which I am a Wiccan witch, and I have reclaimed some of my powers"

Chester asked, "Is that the way you found it? It's just the magick. It's in there."

I said, "We do not believe in a devil."

Chester confessed, "I don't believe in a devil."

I said, "Nothing can be totally good and nothing can be totally bad."

Chester remarked, "I just know the fear. I know that Hank doesn't have the fear. But Hank can still be good. That's the way we think it should be."

I said, "We all have parts of the negative in us."

Chester agreed, "Yes we do Hank."

I said, "I even see negative in you guys."

Chester admitted, "I understand you doing that."

Christine admitted, "Yes Hank we can't help it. I think that will go as the answer."

I said, "I do not appreciate these comments about a devil okay."

Christine explained, "We couldn't stop it if we wanted to."

I said, "There's people coming tonight that are accusing you guys of being evil."

Chester suggested, "That's just their fear talking."

I said, "I don't think of any of you as demons."

Christine asked, "Is that a demon?"

I said, "Even the most negative is not a demon. It's just a negative spirit."

Chester told me, "That's the difference between the way you look at things."

Christine added, "And that's why we had to choose you."

I said, "Speaking of other things I see."

Christine asked, "What's bothering you now?"

Chester encouraged, "Let's give it, go with it. Give him some time."

I said, "I don't believe you guys steal."

Christine asked, "Is that what they are saying?"

I said, "I think what you do."

Christine asked, "Is that what you asked?"

I continued, "That is use the energy that is available."

Christine asked, "Does he know I'm faking?"

I said, "I have done this in this world."

Chester stated, "That is the answer."

I asked, "Can you tell me if I am correct?"

Christine answered, "Yes we can. Yes you are. That's just the way we do it."

Chester commented, "And you wanted to try to scare him."

Christine replied, "I just can't believe I fooled Hank."

Chester asked, "Is that serious the way you feel? I know you can taste it. I know what he's doing here. He's just asking everything he can think of. I told you Hank shouldn't be here. I told you we didn't have to be here."

Christine remarked, "I thought you'd go back there. He sure looked stoned right back there."

Chester replied, "But I didn't."

Christine asked, "Is Hank going on the tour?"

Chester answered, "Yes he is."

Christine stated, "That's the way we always do it."

I said, "I understand you can't tell me everything."

Christine admitted, "I try to tell you everything."

I said, "You almost have me afraid to ask any questions."

Chester told me, "You can ask anything."

I said, "I ask the wrong one and you didn't."

Chester finished, "I didn't tell you."

I said, "I got all."

Chester asked, "What'd he say?"

I said, "The sensation."

Chester confessed, "It's not your fault we couldn't tell you."

Christine added, "We could be here. And actually we wanted to."

I said, "Every question should be okay before you can answer them."

Christine guessed, "I think he thinks of us a lot. How can I say this to him?"

Chester asked, "Why don't you say it?"

Christine started to say, "Hank we never..."

I cut her off with, "The last thing I want to do is make you guys mad."

Christine started to say, "Guess you got a late..."

Again she was cut off. This time by someone yelling.

Chester suggested, "We gotta get away from here."

Christine asked, "Can we have this trouble here?"

I asked, "It would be nice if some people were going, right?"

The people arriving for the tour were noisy for about fifteen seconds then Chester announced, "It's getting Carol upset. I guess Hank was here before."

I said, "They feel like they know more than us; and we have been doing this so much longer than they have."

Chester replied, "I'd say good for Hank. It's the fear thing they have. They think there is a battle here."

Christine asked, "Can we tell who lives here?"

I complained about the narrow mindedness of the people going on the tour while they made a bunch more noise.

When we stopped Chester stated, "I can tell Hank is in an angry mood."

I complained some more about the people going on the tour and how they would interpret the EVP's I usually got.

Chester explained, "Hank you will just have to trust what we say."

More noise came from the people and Christine announced, "I'll fix it."

Chester remarked, "They say Hank's been here before."

The spirits from the pub in unison said, "Thank you for who you are."

Chester pointed out, "That's what Hank can do."

Carol gave her opinion, "Awwww. Hank is good."

I said, "I just want everything to go as normal. Pictures of orbs, full figure spirits if you can. These guys will take the tour; then talk about the tour and everyone benefits."

Christine came back with, "These people are nice. I'm just laughing."

Chester asked, "Is Hank even there? I don't think he knows them. Anyway he missed it. I'm first to go with Hank. Hank will be there. Just like he did. Don't you remember?"

Christine answered, "Let's hear."

I said, "If you're going to help tonight I sure appreciate it."

Christine decided, "I think we'll go back up in here."

I said, "We're ready to come."

Someone there for the tour stated, "I can't see Gary."

Christine replied, "I can't see much better."

I said, "I'll be waiting for your answer before I touch the pipe."

Christine suggested, "Just quit Hank."

Chester commented, "I hope he does quit like that. I hope that's not a fib he's telling me. Whatever Hank does do."

Christine agreed, "Yes."

Chester told Christine, "I'll help him. If you will ask him that."

Christine agreed again, "I will."

I said, "Thank you for talking to me."

Christine asked, "Is Hank through?"

Chester answered, "I hope so."

I said, "We will be going on the tour in a little while. We have to wait for everybody to show up."

Chester remarked, "I think they got here."

I said, "You guys are more than welcome to join us just like always."

Chester announced, "Looks like a better time tonight. I like the tour."

I said, "Thank you for the progress we made tonight."

Chester replied, "I don't think we made any progress."

I thought we did.

A man with the tour asked, "Anyone here with me?" at the fountain by the phone booth.

Christine asked him, "You want an answer?"

Gary said, "Elvis answered 'cause you wonder why, okay."

I believe they were talking about investigating Graceland.

A male spirit commented, "Now here's another."

Gary started the tour with, "There's always been a bridge across the river Thames." He went on to tell about the founding of London by the Romans. We went to the gate and heard that story. Then we heard the story of the land markers. Gary also

136

told of the pub and the paranormal activity there. Gary told the story of the lamppost.

We got to the phone booth and Gary told everyone to feel the phone booth because it was solid iron.

While they were quiet Chester remarked, "That's what you think. It's not Hank."

Gary began talking about the paranormal activity, but at a pause a male spirit stated, "In Lake Havasu."

Gary went on but when he said, "We get ecto of birds." A male spirit replied, "I can see it."

Gary said, "Sitting on top of it."

Chester announced, "I see Hank."

Gary went on to tell the Golden Unicorn story. At the end he said, "On top of that, in golden ecto a perfect unicorn."

A male spirit admitted, "I can't see that."

Another male spirit told him, "It's me see."

Gary had to re-explain the Golden Unicorn story for those on the tour that didn't get it the first time. He was talking about the séance they did at the Golden Unicorn when he said, "We got orbs." He paused.

A male spirit remarked, "Everything I needed."

Gary continued at the phone booth with the Marsha and Cheryl story and at the end he said, "I think with all the new technology we are going to learn a lot."

A male spirit replied, "It doesn't matter what you say."

Chester stated, "Hank's confused."

Gary explained the decision to sell the bridge and who to sell the bridge to, while we walked down to the water. He named everything that came in the bridge deal.

A male spirit announced, "I can see them."

Gary said, "Everything in the pub is from London." He started naming items.

After Gary's list, Chester guessed, "I think they're going with Hank."

Gary told about the bridge being in the Guinness Book of World Records.

As we reached the water's edge Gary said, "This is our new walkway."

A male spirit ordered, "Get over here."

Gary said, "They are going to carry it down to a new fifty two million dollar bridge they're planning to build across the canal."

A male spirit replied, "Nonsense."

Gary said, "I'm going to start a petition because this would put foot traffic out."

A male spirit stated, "I've seen that on the bridge before. You can take that when we go back home. He lost the table."

Chester remarked, "That was very crying of that Brad."

Brad told Chester, "It sucks."

Chester decided, "I'll go with Hank."

Gary said, "I'd like to put a black box on top of the bridge."

Chester stated at a much lower volume, "I don't think you'd get anything with that."

The people on the tour said how awesome that would be. They must not have heard Chester.

Brad asked, "Page each have their own quatrain?" Like he was checking the script.

Gary told the story of the rust spots on the footings of the bridge. At the end there was a pause and a female spirit suggested, "You can take her."

Again Gary had to re-explain the story because they just couldn't get it.

We headed over to Dead Man's Hole and Gary started the story there.

At a pause in the story and the comments from the tour Brad announced, "He's right here."

Behind Gary, Christine commented, "And a black list. Hank has ideas."

Gary said half a line and Brad suggested, "Accuse him."

In the rest of Gary's line, Christine behind him spoke, "I would give more to Hank than that."

Brad blurted out, "Smoke banana."

Gary finished that story but at the end Brad asked, "What's that for?"

Gary went on to describe the scene at Dead Man's Hole but between his words Christine called me, "Hank."

Gary said, "We have a song. It's called Meet Me on the Bridge."

Brad boasted, "It's my bridge."

One of the men on the tour asked a question. As he paused, Christine directed, "It's your turn."

Gary started another story as we headed for the stairs. He told more of the story on the stairs.

Chester commented, "I'll be glad when Hank gets a name."

Gary finished the first story on the stairs and Chester suggested, "Let's sneak in here first."

Gary said, "There's a law on the books that you're not allowed to hit the London Bridge with a hammer."

Brad remarked, "I wanna see if he hits it."

Gary said, "These are not the original steps."

Christine came back with, "These are steps."

One of the men on the tour talked about the orbs he was getting pictures of. When he had Gary's attention he went into another story. I felt he had a need for attention as he was not prepared to tell the story. Near the end of his story Chester whispered, "Don't believe it."

Gary started the Museum Tape story and at a pause Chester confirmed, "It's all here."

At Gary's next pause a male spirit stated, "I'm always here."

Almost at the end of the story Gary paused for dramatic effect and Chester asked ever so faintly, "Can you hear me Hank?" It was as if he didn't want to be detected by the other investigators.

Gary said, "Alright."

Chester repeated, "Hank," again faintly.

Gary finished the Museum Tape story and we headed up the stairs to street level.

Christine announced, "We're walking with Hank."

Sherry started to ask, "Is that what your Hank..."

Chester warned, "Be careful now."

Sherry replied, "He's nasty."

Gary said, "We're going to walk right over here and say hello to Mr. McCullough and Mr. Wood." Gary then said, "If we're all here."

Sherry asked, "Is that a computer?"

When we reached the statues at street level we talked about pictures. I told them we didn't get ghosts at the statues. If you turned back towards the Village you were at the same level as the floating orbs.

Just before Gary started the story Christine asked, "You will take him?"

Gary told the story of Mr. McCullough and C.V. Wood and then went into the cost of "putting a bridge in a barren desert."

After the dollar amount, Gary paused and Brad stated, "I just want to help a man."

Gary told how the pieces of the bridge were brought to Lake Havasu. Christine told me, "I'm right here Hank," at a pause.

Gary gave the weight of the pieces.

Brad pointed out, "That's Hank."

Maybe it was a joke. Gary did say twenty two million tons. I was going back and forth eating a sandwich once a day or once every two days.

Gary went into how General Patton used the area. When he said, "That General Patton put out there." Chester added, "Is Hank."

Gary explained what Mr. McCullough paid for the land to build Lake Havasu City. Then he paused.

Chester asked, "What did you say to Hank?"

Gary said, "He turned around and sold."

Chester remarked, "Since you're eighty."

Once I turned forty I started saying, "But I feel eighty."

Gary finished that story and then Chester asked, "Do you think I'm scared?" He started to fade as he told them, "Hank can ask for more money."

Gary started the next story with, "They liked to drink."

Chester added, "They drank too much."

Gary said, "They particularly liked to drink Jack Daniels."

Brad replied, "That's okay."

Gary told how the police picked up Mr. McCullough.

Brad suggested, "You should give it to me."

Chester told him, "Hank invented this."

I was mechanically inclined my whole life. I disassembled everything when I was young and have always tried to invent new ways of doing things. I can honestly believe that I invented something before coming to this world.

Gary finished the stories by the statues and we started our way across the bridge. He gave the dimensions of the bridge. Then the traffic started. The passing cars all but drowned out Gary and since the spirits speak at a much lower volume, there were no EVP's until the traffic stopped. Gary told about the lamppost on the bridge and the tour group was taking pictures of them.

Chester suggested, "Take a picture of Hank."

Gary said, "Over one hundred thousand people jumped off this bridge in London."

Chester added, "Tune in tomorrow."

Gary told of the diseases they were suffering from to make them commit suicide off the bridge.

Chester advised, "Trust us."

Gary said, "In the old days when you went into battle with your enemy."

Chester finished, "I'll talk to you later."

Gary told his stories for the next three minutes with a steady stream of traffic drowning out most of it. I thought Chester knew that was going to happen.

Gary said, "This is Charles Dickens' bridge."

Christine added, "Thank you for calling."

During the Charles Dickens story Brad said, "And he spent," before Gary said, "And he spent."

More cars passed by. On and off when the cars were passing by there was a disrupted sound. The car noise was there and then it vanished. It came back all in a rhythmic pattern. The last time out of the disruption Christine pointed out, "That's where Hank is."

Then another car passed and out of that Brad commented, "I give myself a week."

Chester asked, "That short of a break?" Brad was saying, "That was a man," at the same time.

Christine remarked, "A break would take him."

Chester stated, "Hank wants a nap."

Gary went on with stories while cars passed with little or no disruption and no one else was talking.

Then in between cars I got Chester saying, "That's Hank." Gary spoke. Then Chester pointed out, "Gary."

Out of a small disruption Brad asked, "What are you thinkin'?"

A series of cars went by.

At another break in the cars Brad asked, "What'd Hank say?"

Gary stopped talking as the disruption started and Brad stated, "We did know phone numbers."

After a one minute stretch of cars passing, and some disrupted sound, Christine confessed, "I will do some pacing."

Chester asked, "Hank can you hear what I'm saying? Do you know what I'm saying?"

Gary and the cars started up as we approached the end of the bridge.

Gary paused and Christine stated, "They need to be gone."

Gary started again and a few more cars went by.

At a break in the cars Chester told me, "Hank you can't do that. I'm trying to get you to quit."

I must have lit a cigarette.

Christine replied, "There's help."

Chester followed immediately with, "You can get to."

Brad asked, "Did he take something with him?"

Chester announced, "Hank is over there."

Gary told another story with a couple of cars going by.

At the end of the story Brad asked, "What's up with Hank?"

Chester answered, "I spent too long."

Christine added, "I can hear him talk too slow."

Brad replied, "That's weird that he talks too slow."

We crossed the street.

Between Gary and the tour group talking Chester stated, "Hank's in errors."

Brad suggested, "Hank can just go there."

Gary told a story on the steps about some WWII graffiti on the bridge.

As the tour group looked at it, Christine asked, "Can I tell a story too? That's all."

Gary gave some more information about the WWII graffiti.

Christine announced, "We can cross the bridge if you want."

Brad remarked, "That won't mean anything to them."

We started walking down the steps.

Christine complained, "I'm so tired."

Sherry asked, "Is that the same room?"

Chester admitted, "I don't see a reason for that. We should be home pretty soon."

Sherry and Chester told Christine, "That your Hanky."

Someone in the tour said something then Christine sang, "I'm going to the restroom."

Sherry asked, "Hank won't mind if she goes to the bathroom would he?"

Chester answered, "He won't even know," while a girl on the tour was talking.

Gary said, "It does not say soup."

We were near the passage door where we asked questions. The first question we usually asked was, "Is anybody here?"

This time Sherry sang, "Anybody here?"

Christine came back with, "He'll probably talk to me."

Gary said, "It's five foot zero inches up."

Chester asked, "Where's Hank?"

Someone from the tour remarked about what Gary said.

Christine volunteered, "I'll answer."

In a perfect example of a spirit talking through a machine Christine spoke, "To me."

Gary said another line.

Sherry asked, "What's that mean?"

Christine replied, "It's worse than that."

Chester asked, "Do people really want us to come back?"

Brad commented, "I'd like to be the monster right there."

Gary started to talk about the fifty caliber bullet holes.

Chester recalled, "I think we've done this before. You will be able to talk to Hank."

Brad confessed, "I don't know what to say."

Chester suggested, "Tell him just to be good."

Christine remarked, "Honk honk and you'll be there."

Brad replied, "Let's pretend we're dead."

Chester directed him, "You're with Christine. Don't go to Saturday night."

Brad asked me, "Can you hear that's a spirit?"

Chester told him, "That's what they're supposed to say."

Gary said, "A German fighter plane actually crashed on this side right in front of the bridge."

Brad announced, "I can hear the noise."

Gary said a line.

Christine and Chester remarked, "That's all we need together."

Brad warned, "Now your teeth are going to react about this thing."

Chester commented, "I don't get this."

Brad explained, "Probably he ate all this."

Christine replied, "Yes, it's Hank."

Gary took the tour group down the steps and into the parking lot of the Heat nightclub. He told them a story about the bridge.

When Gary paused Christine announced, "I might be here."

Gary finished that story and added another from WWII.

At the end of the story Chester ordered, "The wing is all that matters."

Christine confirmed, "That's more human."

Gary went into another story and at a pause Brad commented, "All the friends he had."

It sounded like they were checking out the wing book.

Gary continued until the next pause and Christine stated, "Only if you got him."

Gary finished that story then started telling about what was in the bridge now, and what was in it before.

He said the difference now was that there was only one service door. He talked about me and Zach going to it and asking if anyone was there. He told them about a voice coming back and saying, "Me."

Christine announced, "I'm right here."

Gary told about some of the first EVP's I got that he heard and between his words Christine confessed, "I can remember."

Gary told the Jack the Ripper story.

At the end of the story you could hear a lady at the Heat then at a much lower volume Christine spoke, "I think we're gonna get drop off. I'll call Jack in."

There were more voices from the club and the tour. They were talking amongst themselves and then Chester asked, "Where's Hank? Hank would gather for me."

Sherry asked, "Should we take off here?"

The tour group was trying to get EVP's. I was picking up a lot of conversations from the Heat.

Chester instructed with the music, "Go to the bathroom."

Christine replied, "I would," of course.

Gary said, "Yeah, we have to do this all the time," when the tour noticed all the noise from the Heat. You would never see the investigators on TV trying to do EVP's in a crowded situation like we did.

Christine commented in her most ghostly voice, "They're just there for me."

Gary started talking at this point I felt because we knew the spirits were mainly talking to me. I didn't think he wanted them to get any EVP's. I figured they would say they wanted to talk to me.

At a pause in Gary's story Christine stated, "I think we're done," and Gary finished.

Gary started another story and during a pause Christine told them, "I won't go drop him." At the next pause she added, "He stood backward."

At another break in Gary's story Brad commented, "I could kill her."

Gary said, "That's actually."

Christine told me, "Hank do it."

The next pause was strange. It sounded like Brad was trying to sing, "I can't talk to your mother."

At the end of the story Brad suggested, "Let's see what Hank's doing."

Sherry replied, "That's him go right back, right back here."

Chester asked, "Should I come back in here?"

Brad asked, "Embarrassed about Hank?"

The tour came back in, but then Christine asked, "There's more from Hank?"

Brad answered, "You'll hate what he's doing. He's smoking."

We went back up the steps to street level again and Gary said, "This side of the bridge is definitely more haunted than the other side."

Christine asked, "What's he talking about?"

Gary said, "People."

Sherry remarked, "That can't be good."

Gary said, "They've seen bodies; even British policemen."

Brad confessed, "I had no idea how far they go."

As Gary told of the full body apparitions seen on the bridge the cars kept drowning everything out.

When we got a break in the cars and Gary's story, Brad announced, "This one will do."

Gary said, "Now we have seven."

Chester replied, "We're two on two."

Gary was telling of some events in London arranged around the bridge when Chester confirmed, "It's all true."

Gary listed some more things and Brad asked, "So what'd you get here?"

Gary finished and Chester commented, "If Hank gets here."

Christine admitted, "I can't keep talking here."

Sherry asked, "Can he fuck up?"

Chester answered, "It's not just magick."

Sherry remarked, "That's weird."

Gary started telling about the Black Plague. At a pause Chester agreed, "So true."

Gary then related the Black Plague to the Great Fire of London and Chester agreed again, "That's true too."

Gary talked about Executioners Gate. At the end Sherry comfirmed, "I know what he meant."

Gary told the punishments they had. Cars were passing by but at the end Christine asked, "What's he doing?"

A car went by so we couldn't hear the answer.

Gary finished that story and started telling about Redbeard the Pirate.

After Gary said, "Sail up on a ship at night," Chester replied, "As if we didn't know."

Gary said, "They attribute that ability."

Christine asked, "And would you?"

Gary went on to tell how Redbeard was considered to be a vampire. Cars passed by as he finished the story.

Gary started telling about Blackbeard the Pirate. Cars continued to pass.

At a break in it all Christine suggested, "Let's see if he can do that."

At another break in the Blackbeard story Chester asked, "What did he do?"

At the next pause Chester suggested, "Hank will do it."

At another pause Sherry confessed, "We knew Blackbeard."

Gary finished the pirate stories with all the heads that were put on London Bridge.

Gary started the Lady in Black story.

At a break Chester claimed, "The last chance."

At the next break from Gary and the cars Chester uttered, "Hank."

Gary said a few words and paused.

Chester asked, "Can you get Hank to do that?"

A car went by and Gary paused again.

Brad stated, "I told Hank."

At the next break Brad remarked, "He didn't do it."

The Lady in Black story was about people jumping off the bridge to their death. I wonder if that's what they were trying to get me to do.

Gary finished the story with a lot of cars going by.

He started the next story and then a car passed and he paused.

Sherry asked, "When will Hank return?"

Gary continued telling the story until the next pause.

Sherry stated, "I came with you."

Gary was talking about the living conditions in London on the street the bridge was on.

He asked the tour group, "Have you ever heard the term London Mud?"

Chester replied, "I could make it."

Gary continued the story quite a while before there was a dramatic break.

Chester commented, "I want to."

Gary went on with the story to the end, where he said, "That's when they started putting in toilets and sewers."

Chester confessed, "I remember sewers."

Next there was a clicking sound like an old style camera.

Chester asked, "How do you get that to do that? I'm not that good with Hank. What do you say is the answer? I took him here."

We walked to the steps to go back down to the Village as Gary told another story.

I stayed at the top of the stairs while the tour went down and I picked up Chester asking, "What's Hank been doing?"

Gary told the lion story.

At his first break Sherry replied, "I've seen it."

At the next pause Christine asked, "We will see that?"

Near the end of the story Brad remarked, "She's only a spirit," with a lady from the tour saying, "Oh my God," in the middle.

At the end Gary said, "We never get anything that looks like a lion."

Chester announced, "That's his clue."

On the way to the last spot Gary listed all the ghost animals he'd taken pictures of.

Sherry claimed, "We haven't."

Gary talked about a ghost bear he got.

Brad commented, "That's cool."

Sherry added, "If he did."

At the last spot the tour group was taking pictures of the wall and Chester remarked, "I haven't seen that."

Brad insisted, "Somebody did that."

Gary asked, "What do you see?"

Chester replied, "A picture."

I took a picture of the wall because the people on the tour missed the spot that Gary pointed out. Gary asked for my camera.

Chester commented, "That's a good Hank," like I was his pet human.

Gary showed the picture to the tour group and then explained it.

Christine admitted, "I didn't know that."

Gary told a little more and Chester stated, "I gotta get to Hank."

Gary started telling of other sites with strange things on the walls.

Brad remarked, "Like hell they do."

Gary then told of another picture taken of the water break as we went back to the walkway through the English Village.

Chester asked, "Have you seen it?"

Gary said, "Olaf the Viking," in Dead Man's Hole and I turned the recorder off.

CHAPTER NINE

THE CHAMBER OF COMMERCE TOUR

*Brad in front, Chester in the middle, Sherry in back,
Christine with me*

The tour was getting very popular. Gary was told by the Lake
Havasu City Chamber of Commerce that the London Bridge Ghost
Tour was the number one tourist attraction in the city. I thought they
were basing that on what they were seeing on the city's website.

With so much interest in the tour they wanted to go on it to
check it out. Gary said it would be a different type of tour, more
formal, but we could still bring the recorder. I didn't want the
Chamber of Commerce to see me standing off talking to myself,

so I didn't ask any questions on this tour. I called this one the Chamber of Commerce Tour so I could have a file that was the Chamber of EVP's.

I turned the recorder on and it had so much static it sounded like an airplane was flying over.

The first words out of the static were, "I can see you." I couldn't tell who said it.

Christine replied, "I don't know what to say."

Chester explained, "That's why Hank came in here. I'll say something good. I know what you're saying. When you think that I don't. I can even hear when. You can't see me. I can't stand right here. Can you make extra room? Hank can you move out? I can barely breathe."

Christine asked, "Hank can you move a little bit?"

Chester told her, "Tell him not to clear out."

There was some brushing against the recorder.

Chester instructed, "Go ahead and ask him."

A combination of spirit voices replied, "That's the hardest did we ask that we simply made."

Christine advised, "Then don't do that."

Gary said, "This is our fountain."

I placed the recorder on top of the phone box of the phone booth we were in and went to join the tour.

Chester announced, "Hank is calling. I guess that's what it's like on the bridge. I will put this here. Hank answer."

Gary said a little about the fountain.

Chester commented, "Hank showed me where."

Christine remarked, "I can't push Hank. I think Hank went in here."

Chester asked, "Is it possible here?"

Christine asked, "Can't you see?"

Gary started talking about the phone booth.

Chester stated, "I hear they're smoking back here."

Gary switched to reminiscing about the pub with the Chamber of Commerce.

Christine suggested, "Hank would like that."

Gary said that he did EMF readings in the pub.

Sherry commented, "I don't believe that happened. I can't believe I'm on this. Hank is helping."

Christine replied, "I can see Hank doing that."

Chester remarked, "I don't think you thought I could wield that."

Sherry disagreed, "That's not what he said."

Chester explained, "Hank is here. Hank already got that. So don't push on that. I wonder if it's okay to change that. Some people were busy with that yesterday. Hank talked to you. And there's something about that. Hank is about to do that. Down there you were saying. That Hank would do it. I've done that."

Christine said the first half Chester the second half of, "I can't take a puff off a cigarette."

Chester added, "I would if I could. I'd like to do that now. I know it seems to take that I hope. That he will behave."

Brad boasted, "I bet I could change that."

Chester replied, "It doesn't matter if you change that. Tried to tell her. That monkeys still have lots of money. There's been mornings we don't go through there."

Brad remarked, "I bet Hank won't go through that."

Chester told him, "Hope you bet a dollar."

Sherry stated, "I won't give you a champion."

Chester announced, "Those who doubt the way of life. They are doomed right now."

Brad admitted, "I can do that myself."

Chester suggested, "Everybody come help me with Elvis."

Elvis replied, "If you won't take me." No, it didn't sound like "the" Elvis.

Brad ordered, "Stop the meanness. And we will see. And still for Hank."

Sherry faintly uttered, "Anything we can do. Like we did right here. Anyway here."

Chester exclaimed, "Then you'll take him outta my hair!"

Christine commented, "You can't get Elvis in there."

Chester instructed, "You gotta push hard on him."

Brad replied, "I think you got his dick hard."

Christine came back with, "I'm sure he'd like it if I did that."

Sherry gossiped, "Lizzy got prone with him."

Christine replied, "She would have done what I've been doing. Get close to me."

Sherry told her, "He's where he's supposed to be."

Christine announced, "Hank can do this forever."

Chester agreed, "Then that's what I'll have him do. I told you Hank would like to be right here."

Christine asked, "Just when is Hank gonna be here? I don't think he's over. I'll be proud of you."

Chester answered, "Hank will get you started. If Hank was here."

Sherry admitted, "I can't see Elvis doing that."

Christine confirmed, "I know he would. I didn't ask him over."

Chester asked, "Then you'll ask for help? If you could get out an answer. Only if you should move back here."

Christine agreed, "I comply to do that."

Brad remarked, "I didn't think you would."

Christine warned, "You're not ready for me now. When should I be here?"

Sherry answered, "Whenever you're ready."

Brad added, "I'd be first on it."

Sherry replied, "He told you he won't be ready."

Brad confirmed, "I know you will. It has to be. He's a blockhead anyway. I'll be back with just a mirror."

Elvis announced, "I can't see the Romans."

Brad asked, "How'd you do that?"

Christine answered, "I was right here."

Chester explained, "There was nothing you could do. That's what we got for the weekend. You've had a few to know that.

154

And there's no place like the bridge. Cathy hit me with her cane."

Christine told Brad, "You can have the stink pot. And it's right in here. Hank told me I could get out of here."

Chester replied, "I didn't hear what he said. Don't make it out so bad like you can say."

Brad instructed, "Please step inside the wall so it smells better."

A male spirit asked, "What'd he say?"

Brad told me, "We'll also be on Sioux City Hank."

Chester admitted, "I can't see Hank doing that."

Sherry asked, "But didn't you want this?"

Christine answered, "I bet Hank could do that."

Chester confessed, "I think I love him."

Christine assured him, "You just like Hank better. Hank can get out of there. I know he has to. He has to be the best of Hank."

Brad added, "Hank you got the kind of spirit we want."

Chester stated, "They're in this spot we think. I really not figure this. What do you say now after you have both halves of your drawer?"

Brad suggested, "Maybe we could name it after Hank."

Chester defended me, "He tried to do it right here. I'm sure he won't leave us here."

Brad commented, "Those who dreamt can dream. It was legal with Hank there?"

Chester remarked, "After the picture he took."

Brad replied, "Sometimes you gotta be open."

Chester told him, "There's a TV answer. Right now I gotta get out of this sit. Jack told me everything that you need to number. And you got a new top station. Hank will be lonely up here."

Christine asked, "Hank can't be doing this can he? He's right there. I've seen people. It's like they knew about this."

Gary came in starting the phone booth story as usual.

As Gary paused Chester announced, "Hank is not here."

Everyone was feeling the phone booth and Chester asked, "You numbered right?"

Christine asked, "Do they know what they're doing?"

Brad answered, "He told them right here."

Gary continued.

In between phone booth stories Christine offered, "I can take this down for everybody."

Gary finished the phone booth stories.

Christine demanded, "You can't leave us here. And you will take us. I need to go to the bathroom. You have to get back over here."

Sherry announced, "I think Hank's coming."

Chester remarked, "I need a creeper."

Gary started talking again but as some Chamber members were taking pictures he stopped.

Brad suggested, "The second story."

Gary said, "The more pictures you take the better off you are."

Chester admitted, "I can make them bolt right outta here."

Brad replied, "I'd love to see that."

Gary promoted his website.

Brad asked, "Can I talk to Hank for a minute?"

Christine answered, "I guess you can."

Brad told me, "I got a piece of bacon."

Sherry added, "A piece here."

Gary began the story again that he started before the pictures, but I went in the phone booth and turned the recorder off. I must have moved off from the tour because when I turned the recorder back on it was strangely quiet.

Sherry volunteered, "I'll take Helen to the tour."

Christine offered, "I will come after."

Helen admitted, "I want to know you better."

Chester and Christine asked, "Is your book done? Guess you have to draw more."

A male spirit announced, "I'd like to be moved."

A female spirit remarked, "It's not now a bridge."

156

Christine told her, "You have to explain."

A couple of people talked and we missed the explanation.

Christine confessed, "I don't think on that. I don't know what to do."

Chester asked, "Is Hank even here? You don't have to be here. You still should be getting him today. Wait for me. That's when he got here."

Brad replied, "Then you're pos...positive."

The clock tower chimed, coming out of that Brad pointed out, "He had a good girlfriend."

Chester asked, "Did you say something? That's the tree bird right there. I'll never ask Hank."

A siren went by as the clock tower made its last chimes.

Brad admitted, "I'm saving myself."

Chester explained, "And we got to do that with Hank. I see you're here. That's everything Hank can have. Hank will do this...do with this. And he will be successful."

Christine replied, "I am. His youth is very awesome."

Chester told her, "We better get Hank over here. And I'm afraid he'll dump you. I get mad just thinking about it."

Christine disagreed, "Hank wouldn't."

Chester insisted, "He will."

Echoing like she was announcing at the airport Sherry said, "Let's go around with that."

Chester asked, "Can you feel it? It seems to grow. Lookin' now at that boob tube."

Christine admitted, "I know Hank does. And that's just like Hank."

Chester announced, "I can't hear," as Gary said, "If you look out on the water-break."

When Gary got near the end of the story, Christine suggested, "Let's stay with Hank."

The Chamber of Commerce members were talking amongst themselves after Gary's story. Christine joined in the conversation right over the top of them saying, "You can see through with Hank."

I walked over to the stairs and asked, "Is anyone here?" trying to get the Gopie to say more.

Chester pointed out, "I think he walked over there. Hank we'll be right there. I didn't think he'd query."

Christine half yelled, "Let's get with Hank. Wait for us Hank thanks."

I asked, "Can you tell me your name?"

Christine asked, "Hank what are you doing?"

Sherry replied, "I'm right there tomorrow."

A female spirit offered, "I'll play with you."

Sherry yelled, "Here she comes!"

Christine arrived and asked, "What are you doing? No, he's a friend of mine."

The Gopie stated, "He will make us true."

I asked, "Do you stay at the bridge or do you travel around?"

Christine answered me, "I stay with you. What else would you like to ask Hank?"

The Gopie asked, "What'd he just ask you?"

Christine answered him, "Oh it was nothing. Hank what are we doing here?"

I asked, "Are you a ghost?"

Christine admitted, "Hank we're true burglars. Hank we shouldn't be here."

Sherry complained, "I can't get through here."

Christine replied, "Thanks anyway. It's clear for Hank. I'm glad we're through here."

Sherry commented, "I beat the last one."

Brad explained, "The people were in a hurry."

Sherry asked, "But what does that matter? You got to move fire when you do this. Can you do a dance right here? I am so done right here."

Chester confirmed, "I told you it would be fifteen minutes with Hank."

Christine consoled her, "Anyway you got to help."

Chester suggested, "I think we're gonna have to move on Hank."

A female spirit from the bridge warned, "That would make Hank hurt us some."

Chester asked, "What are you doing here? You didn't hear that about Hank."

Christine pointed out, "If they face right here. If you place this towards that room."

Chester explained, "I can't take this back over the same place. If you make orders to put it there."

Christine asked, "Do you think it'll make him dead if he has a cigarette? It is only one cigarette. I just think, I think we're just over reacting."

Chester asked, "Then you think you were right? You're better than Hank. I think you have poor attitude." He then sang, "I think you have a bad attitude." And musically came, "I'd rather do it with Hank. Do this with Hank. Leave Hank your answer. I knew you would do that."

Sherry remarked, "Plain clothes now we do. We got a few hundred back here."

Christine confessed, "I'm longing for that to work. I could do that in Hank's bedroom."

Brad added, "Then we know who shoved him didn't we. Here to make music. Music on Tuesday too. He pulled a discount even further."

Chester replied, "You do that so beautiful."

Brad admitted, "We said that wrong. Tom I keep doing it."

Christine commented, "Hank can handle that. In a mausoleum you can see 'em. Break through right here."

Sherry confirmed, "One moment I can do this."

Christine stated, "In that first need it."

Sherry asked, "What can you do with a whole turkey?"

Christine replied, "Then let's run down and get one."

Sherry came back with, "I'm on my knees."

Christine suggested, "You put that close to you."

Sherry asked, "Do you got a hold of him?"

Christine answered, "In the living room. I'm going to see him right now."

Chester ordered, "You're not supposed to be here. Yesterday you would be."

Sherry defended Tom or the turkey, "It's done nothing."

Tom asked, "And do you think I can do this?"

Chester challenged him, "And get your Mustang too. I dare you to face that."

Sherry warned, "I bet you know we're here."

Christine announced, "I said he's doing it. I don't believe he's doing what you told him. How do you suppose he's going to make it?"

Chester answered, "With that vehicle he's supposed to. That vehicle is not going to make it. I think so think that you will be right here."

Sherry voiced her authority, "You see there's a meeting up here."

Brad added, "After you guys go through me."

Christine pointed out, "This is where Hank will make a story."

Brad asked, "Do you think Hank will hear us?"

Sherry asked, "Didn't you bring him in here? Would he go for this? Would he answer too far?"

Christine stated, "Now people do when you make them seem like your best friend. I think we land-marked with Hank."

Chester directed, "Let's go to the next stand."

There was a person going, "Woooo." Chester waited on them.

Christine asked, "Are we going with Hank somewhere?"

Brad announced, "Here comes your last meal break."

Sherry asked, "You want me to feed back here?"

Brad asked, "Can you?"

Chester suggested, "If that's what you want to do."

Brad stated, "I'm getting thirsty here."

Christine asked, "Is he walking there too?"

Chester remarked, "Guess he would if you treat him nice. I can see how you move that thing up."

Christine ordered, "Get that thing moving."

Sherry fed back, "Get your horny sister right here."

Chester confessed, "That's the work I'm making."

Brad told them, "I could get back in here before. I'm not too pleased with what you're doing. If you see it, pick up here."

Christine replied, "You know I didn't do this."

Brad insisted, "Anything you can see wrong."

Sherry asked, "Did you ever get your horny sister?"

Brad ordered, "I just want you to clean over here."

Christine agreed, "I'm going to."

Brad asked, "Have you done anything? You'll think like this. Take it through here. And you wish you could be with me."

Chester explained, "He told Sherry how to do this. Get your horny sister here. You never will be take her."

Christine remarked, "Hank nobody loves you."

Chester instructed, "You don't need to take 'em."

Sherry commented, "I just feel like doing it."

Brad nagged, "If you ever bothered an attitude."

Sherry replied, "I told you it's not a big deal."

Christine confirmed, "I don't see a big deal."

Chester asked, "What is that that people are saying? You've got a meeting with Hank after this?"

Brad stated, "The big deal is here where we see them."

Chester suggested, "I think you can do what Hank is gonna do. It will take him years to go through this."

Sherry commented, "I hear the moon set."

Chester remarked, "I don't hear anything."

Brad guessed, "It might be our engine."

Christine decided, "Hank can do this when he gets back."

Brad offered, "I'll do everything in here."

Sherry exclaimed, "You're busted. Can you explain what Christine won't? I can't see what he wants in here."

Chester answered, "I gave you the story of what the book said."

Brad started, "I feel good." Sherry finished, "That Danny's back."

Gary and the tour arrived with Gary asking them to come down the stairs.

Brad tried to help when he announced, "Underneath the bridge is a magick tour. Got the juice if you're starting. Now do you feel like you finished doing that? Now they won't let me sleep after we put it here. Do you think he'll go with a magickal pipe? I thought you were done with me."

Chester confessed, "I didn't think it would hurt you. Hank wouldn't do that to ya."

Sherry suggested, "Let's do this."

Chester replied, "You remind me of what you did today."

Brad asked, "Can we be friends again?"

The tour started down the stairs with some board members talking.

Christine asked them, "Can you get Hank over here? Can't you get Hank already? Make some room for Hank. Who's the man with Hank though?"

Gary laughed then Christine complained, "Hank won't come to me."

Gary pointed some things out around the stairs.

Christine announced, "Hank is tired."

Gary gave the tour group his opinion of the layout on that side of the bridge.

Christine suggested, "They should put Hank over here."

Brad asked, "Can't they all see? Hank should be here."

Chester stated, "Hank could get through this."

Someone from the tour group asked a question and Gary answered with, "I'll be telling you about that in five minutes."

Christine told the spirits, "Hank gave us an answer. Hank will be coming here."

At times I could feel their anticipation. I would slip off by myself and speak quietly about my plan. I guess Christine heard me.

Gary said they needed a beer cabaret at that end of the bridge.

Brad gave his opinion, "I think Hank would be better. Now you stay here. I don't believe Hank is on tour."

Gary talked about going inside the bridge.

Brad started, "I'm looking for."

Christine finished, "Hank."

Brad started, "I've got to get," and Sherry finished with, "your Hanky pooh."

Chester disagreed, "Hank won't give you an answer."

Christine replied, "And that makes me feel good."

Gary started the tour again with a story.

Sherry asked, "Does he know Hank?" at the same time.

Gary finished that story.

Christine directed, "Come on down this way. And can you bring Hank with ya."

Gary started telling about the bullet holes. He finished that then went into the Jack the Ripper story. During that story the sound diminished to almost nothing but Gary stayed in the same place the whole time.

From the diminished sound Chester asked, "So what, you'll give Hank a short answer?"

Brad asked, "Did you ever fold them down to dress and make them all individual?"

Chester pointed out, "It's not a maintenance thing we got."

Brad remarked, "It sounds like an idea to me."

Chester corrected him, "But that won't make a difference. If this was fucking London you'd be a death monkey. Exactly where are you taking me?"

He and Christine confirmed, "Brian won't go through that corner."

By himself Chester commented, "All bridges must be like this. At midnight. How did you get to serve too much of the same thing every day? Usually a death occurs in life. I can make this happen. Let's give Hank a birthday."

Christine yelled from a distance, "That's a bad answer."

Sherry changed the subject with, "That's a beautiful knick-knack."

Chester asked, "Did you stay close, did you say something? What's he got in here?"

Gary came back in but after a sentence Sherry asked, "He missed you didn't he?"

Someone from the tour group made a remark.

Sherry denied, "I didn't do anything."

Christine announced, "I can't find it."

Gary and the tour group talked a few seconds.

Sherry asked, "Isn't that their side?"

Christine answered, "There's this damn story."

Sherry replied, "You can't touch this."

Christine asked, "That's what you're saying?"

Gary said, "That's a beautiful bridge you got."

Chester agreed, "That's for sure. There's only one good answer for Hank. Hank better come back through here."

Christine confirmed, "Hank will be here."

Sherry asked, "Hank for sure is coming?"

Chester guessed, "I think there's a reason he came today. Hank got the news on that thing here. I know Hank will be here."

Gary started one of the stories about the building of the bridge on their way back up the stairs.

At a pause Sherry commented, "This one fears."

Gary said another line then Chester remarked, "They're liable to be here for a while."

Sherry asked, "Is there a man among you?"

Christine suggested, "Hank might have to go with them."
Sherry stated, "I'm complete he's coming."
Christine agreed, "I am so sure."
Chester announced, "Hank is over here."
Brad again ordered, "And I told you ma'am, pick it up."
One of the male spirits went, "Boohooo."
Christine replied, "Hank would say that."
Gary and the tour came back in even though they were in the same place. Gary even told a story but it didn't get on the recorder.
Brad asked, "Is that the most Hank can bear?"
Sherry answered, "There's enough for you to say."
Chester added, "Hank won't understand though. That you could make that saying."
Sherry asked, "Can you make a?" Then there was a sound like four metallic whistles.
Christine asked, "Can you guess what Hank will say? Hank wouldn't be able to take that."
Chester commented, "And now if Hank would get here."
Sherry asked, "Does Hank know that we're here?"
Chester said diplomatically, "There are different opinions of that."
Sherry asked, "Is this the way that you stand?"
Christine answered, "I never really think about it."
Chester suggested, "You might have to stick to the script."
Sherry announced, "I decided he will be in here."
Christine warned, "He will play a game on you."
Sherry confirmed, "I know you care to see him."
Christine replied, "He'll be a man to you."
Brad came back with, "She knows a man to her. And he'll make you feel good."
Chester asked, "What did I told you? And now you shouldn't talk to her."
Gary came in telling the tour group about the Tower Bridge. Then I shut the recorder off.

Turning it back on I said, "If anyone is here please talk so that we may hear you."

Chester was telling Christine, "In his bedroom by his heater. I swear that he looked at me or something. And I know that he saw me coming. Years it would take the lion's head. He got me going over here."

Christine asked, "Are we supposed to meet up here?"

Chester answered, "You can say bucket right here. Everything is squared by the door. I've got to train to do something. I think I should cut down the post that's down here. There's just a lot of water to pick up. You're just Zamboning. I won't put up with that. But Hank will stand by her. Cause you might see us over here."

Christine added, "You may not see us here though. Wherever we'll be."

Chester remarked, "That's hopeless that's for sure."

Christine replied, "And people will take hands full of stuff."

Chester stated, "That's what Hank is doing. If they go in peace to the other side. His freak acts of walking. Five hundred years he's done that. He's supposed to be a poem star. He tried doing that before. He was years ahead. He asked about sisterhood. Stand right here for me."

Brad volunteered, "I'll give to Hank something. Dad's not hear from you. Watch yourself on the steps. We have no use for other things like that. You're supposed to stay here."

Gary said, "Let's walk down along here."

Chester pointed out, "That's when he says he's here. See how peace loving he will approach. Can you recognize a lot of Hank? Hank can get through. He did drop on there."

Brad asked, "Do you feel like telling him what happened?"

Chester answered, "We really talked through the computer to Hank about that."

Christine announced, "Hank is here."

Chester guessed, "I think he'll want to stand by you. He cares about you. You will act responsibly I hope. And you can help with this I should hope. Other times you can deal with Hank. If you could do that."

Christine replied, "I can do that. I can do some more."

Sherry stated, "I can just sit here."

Christine commented, "I think we'll get some answers. I can hear him back there. I can still hear him."

Brad confirmed, "I can see Hank."

Chester remarked, "Everybody can't see. Hank can walk through he's skinny. He can moderate some too."

Christine started, "On one hand."

Chester finished, "He'll do good."

Christine again started, "On the other hand."

Chester again finished, "He'll do beautiful. These feet are just to depend on you. In all that he'll walk like Stephen. I can see where you could make the back room much better. That should get down to its normal is good. Be sure to tell Richard let Hank take his shirt off. I only got to fix in here. Maybe Hank would rather take a long ass schedule time. You can't talk to him anyway. Because he can't hear you too. Good we got safety."

Sherry replied, "Here's talking to you already."

Chester added, "Now he's got the Buford. This is where Hank would be."

Christine stated, "I miss mostly who's right here."

Chester told Brad, "You'll never get this square, I'll get with this all day."

Brad asked, "Is there a beat when he comes?"

Chester answered, "Now you do forget to clean. Hank will be right there. That was easy. Let's see what he says."

But it was Gary that came in talking from a distance.

Brad asked, "If we drop those people do you think they would do anything?"

Chester replied, "If we could do that we could sign up for anything."

Gary can be heard again then Brad announced, "I can hear that."

After more from Gary, Chester told the spirits, "They're coming here."

Brad added, "Maybe Hank will be here too."

Chester ordered, "You should not do anything. Let Hank do this."

Brad remarked, "I just can't believe in Hank."

Chester asked, "You do want him here?"

Brad answered, "I can take him in."

Christine insisted, "Now you should thank Hank for this. You can't agree about that. Shake the hand of a man."

Brad admitted, "I'll have to think about that for a minute."

Christine suggested, "I don't think he oughta come here."

Brad stated, "I know these people from Saturday night."

Chester warned Brad, "I think you better get off it. You forgot to say."

Sherry told Brad, "I think they're talking to you."

Chester added, "When we first got the answer. You said you're not chosen Hank. But then lots of people seem to be able..."

Brad interrupted with, "You want me to sit for you?"

Chester ordered, "Walk with me and leave Christine."

Brad complained, "We'll come back and you'll also be doing it."

Chester replied, "Unless we have perfect timing."

Christine asked, "Is this what matters most. I can get up to your feet."

Brad admitted, "I don't need a broken finger that is right."

Chester warned, "After that the monkey would get you."

Sherry asked Brad, "Is that you leaving?"

Christine asked, "Is the dog coming with you?"

Chester explained to Brad, "You've been talking a lot of dokey doke. And I wish you happy. But his mother died on a Tuesday. And he might actually. Go at the same time. I know he's nice. And he'd be good at that."

A motorcycle passed on the bridge drowning him out.

Brad replied, "I think Hank would do. He's got a long time for it."

Christine announced, "Hank's here."

Chester added, "But now Jeff is here."

Sherry suggested, "Let's hear for a major."

Jeff said, "Dropping off today's invoice."

Sherry asked, "Does this seem weird? Can you take him somewhere?"

Brad guessed, "I think he's here just to see Hank"

Sherry asked, "Did you see Elmo come through here?" She then sang, "You've just become a secret. Hank was there for a little bit."

Christine remarked, "I sure wish Hank would get here."

Brad reminded her, "You said this would be easy."

Chester admitted, "I guess he went in for it. You'll suffer with Hank."

Sherry added, "That's a bitter one too."

Chester said in a hollow metallic voice, "Aw come on now." Then in a clearer voice he said, "I heard you were getting some."

Brad replied, "You should have drawn everything."

Sherry started, "He had turkey." Brad finished, "On his turkey."

Chester asked, "Is that what the street stands for? We gotta face the truth. Hank could copy me."

Gary came in with the start of the lion story.

After the first line Chester suggested, "You should stand up here."

Gary said another line.

Brad stated, "I don't see him."

Gary talked about his girlfriend and Brad remarked, "That's the lady you wrote about. I'm not scared of what he says to me."

Gary continued the lion story.

At a pause near the end Brad admitted, "I see what they're coming to get."

After the lion story was finished Christine announced, "I know what they're doing."

Gary said a little more.

Christine remarked, "I told Hank not to think of us."

Gary told the last story.

At the end Sherry asked, "When are you going to deal with Hank?"

We got the tour moving again and I shut the recorder off.

CHAPTER TEN

THE FIRST CAMCORD TOUR

Something trying to materialize on the bridge

Gary got his camcorder out of pawn. He and the boys were very anxious to try it. We watched some ghost videos on the computer that day. They were sure they would be successful with all the ghost pictures we were getting. I knew it was up to Chester and Christine if we got anything. This was the First Camcord Tour.

I turned the recorder on and immediately got Christine as she announced, "I see him."

Chester stated, "I can get an answer from him. I know what he's thinkin'."

I started at the Pub doors and asked, "Is anyone here?"

Chester asked, "Do you respect yourself? You're fucking up. I can't say that you told me. How to best deal with this. These people will have to get some."

Brad clarified, "They will get more than Hank will get."

Christine told me, "I won't go easy on you Hank."

I asked, "Do you like to talk?"

Christine remarked, "I can't believe yourself. I just know that you are in between."

Chester replied, "I probably shouldn't beat it to death."

Christine asked, "Those will do right?"

I asked, "I'd like to know your story, can you tell me?"

Christine answered, "I can only tell you something about it. This is just for Hank."

Chester told her, "I don't think you should tell a secret. Let him bucket. I know Hank can hear this. If he was smoking dope. He would think of something."

Christine replied, "That's not bad to me."

Chester announced, "Hank is talking."

I said, "Please say if you would like to establish communication."

Christine asked, "What kind of question is that?"

Chester stated, "I saw a piece of wood in there."

Christine confessed, "I won't hit him."

Chester insisted, "I will get you some. You might have to hurt Hank."

I said, "Thank you for talking to me," and then moved over to the phone booth.

Christine asked, "Where you going?"

I asked, "Is anyone here?"

Christine called, "I'm over here. Here's your answer. I always liked cooking."

Chester admitted, "I used to clean."

I asked, "Can you tell me your name?"

Christine pointed out, "Now we restarted. Well maybe we should be there."

Chester complained, "Damn, I don't want to go over there."

Christine replied, "Besides the walking is good. Hank came over here for something. I'm not going to go Hank."

I asked, "Why are you here?"

Chester answered, "I thought we'd get a better answer."

Christine stated, "You won't get an answer. It would be if he was over here."

Chester asked, "Should we go backwards? I didn't think he'd be here."

I asked, "What type of being are you?"

Christine demanded, "I want a piece of paper."

Chester replied, "I've got some here in here."

Christine threatened, "I'll get off of this Hank."

Chester commented, "I don't believe you wear us off."

Christine continued, "I will get him."

I said, "Thank you for talking."

Chester stated, "There was no sense in talking."

The clock tower chimed.

Coming out of the chime Chester asked, "Can you hear what Hank just said? We ought to get home."

Christine admitted, "I wish Hank was there. I'll be glad when he's home."

Chester suggested, "Let's take Hank home. Gotta get out of here."

Christine replied, "I don't think we can get him."

Chester ordered, "Tell Hank to come over here."

Christine asked, "How can I get him over?"

Chester answered, "Just get him moving."

Christine commented, "He wants to get out of here. I don't hear what they're saying. I can see some more."

Chester stated, "I'll bring Hank over. I can see him moving. I can move Hank over here. I could move him over there if I wanted to. You are walking over my way. He started to do it. Down where he's supposed to be in the car."

Christine asked, "How will he get home?"

Chester remarked, "I could send him ye-ow-ing. I won't give Hank any permanent damage."

Christine asked, "What is he doing? Where is Hank now? What is Hank doing? I can't see anymore."

Chester asked, "Do you want to leave with me?"

Christine answered, "I think I'll just sit right here on this table." That would be a table in their world because there were none in front of the Village.

Chester admitted, "I'd like to leave you here. And see what Hank would do. I'll buy you something."

Christine replied, "I'll get Hank to do that."

Chester guessed, "You'll go make him live somewhere. Where I can't get to him."

Christine suggested, "Get yourself ready to go. I think that Hank is coming. It will be okay. Can you get when something is coming?"

Chester answered, "I'll go in a bit."

Christine told him, "Okay but leave me here. I don't know what I'm going to do."

Chester came back with, "You will do what Hank wants. I want to take your plans. If Hank leaves buzz me."

Christine confirmed, "I know you will call. Totally got him. Where will you go with him?"

Chester stated, "I won't say that right here. I'll say that when I have to go. I know Hank will do good. I know he's going somewhere. You'll stay with Hank if you have to. Let Hank take you on the tour."

Christine suggested, "Go take a points lay-off."

Chester remarked, "Hank was looking up here. But he can't go in that room."

Christine asked, "When will you stop going in it? Can I go with Hank when he gets here?"

Chester ordered, "If you go with Hank you better stick with him. Why are you looking over there?"

Christine answered, "I'm looking for Hank."

Chester replied, "I hope you're not joking. Tell me it's not a joke. I know you're going to tell me something good."

Christine confessed, "I can't hear."

Gary came in talking about the bridge being built.

Chester announced, "That was Hank that just went through here."

Christine added, "Let me dance through here."

Chester admitted, "I can't quickly go over there."

Christine recalled, "I think we've gone through here."

Chester stated, "I know this is the way you take."

Christine replied, "I'll go back here."

Chester guessed, "Hank might like it. And he'd probably go through his progress. More quickly. I can't get there. You can wait right here."

A man walked by saying, "They're closed every time we come through."

Chester remarked, "I know people will come through."

Christine asked, "Is Hank going over there?"

Chester answered, "I don't know."

Christine asked, "What'd you say?"

Chester replied, "You'll remember when I get there. He's bored with everything."

Christine offered, "I can help with that. I should go be with Hank now."

Chester agreed, "Yes you can go court with him. I know you've got that coming. I'll just go over right here. I wish Hank was here."

Christine stated, "I don't see Hank anymore. I think he's over there."

Chester told her, "I know Hank was here. You can go up there if you want."

Christine suggested, "I could get closer to Hank."

Chester confessed, "I think I'll go wish on it. It's hard to be a friend to him."

Christine replied, "I'm in love with him."

Chester explained, "That's why you take a prior statement. I know he's going in there. Take it from an asshole. He might be going in there. You asked."

Christine asked, "Can we go over there?"

Chester answered, "I think he's right. Go with new stuff. I think we could do better. You'll have to stop with Hanky-pooh. I know he's been good to you. I know that it's been fourteen minutes. Yeah that we've been right here. I know Hank should be here."

Christine came back with, "But we talked with him. Did he think we're going?"

After five seconds of traffic drowning them out Chester admitted, "I had this idea of forty five junk folders in there. As soon as Hank gets here."

Christine asked, "Can we shut this thing off? I know what he would answer."

Chester suggested, "If you got tools you can do it. This thing really sucks. I know Hank would not think so."

Christine admitted, "Too bad I can't touch it."

Chester joked, "If you want to kiss him. You should pick that up. He's not your family so I'll have to change that."

Christine replied, "You're so funny."

Chester continued, "Come to me. I've got Hank in here."

Christine disagreed, "You don't have Hank over there."

Chester asked, "Where's your Hank, where did he go?"

Christine stated, "I'm happy with him."

Chester remarked, "I know, I've got to go somewhere."

Christine asked, "Are you going with Hank?"

Chester asked, "Can you see over there? Over and October. I think I'm going where he's going. You won't see Hank for a while. That's the rock you bought, the rock you bought. I don't think he pulled a double switch on you. I don't think Hank would ever do that. I know you've got a plan. I think you have a sure talking."

Christine told him, "If you do then he won't answer."

Chester suggested, "If you want proof then come over here."

Christine demanded, "Stop right there."

Chester replied, "I've got to go the way you want. I know you want to get an answer. I can answer that. I will only answer if you let me. I know you can't go on without that."

Gary yelled, "Hey Hank!"

Chester asked, "Did you hear that Gary called him?"

Christine guessed, "Maybe now I'll get an answer," behind someone laughing.

Chester added, "That's what you've been waiting for. Do you want him here?"

Christine admitted, "I've got that."

Chester told her, "You'll like this. Don't forget to punish Hank. I can't go to my appointment. I just heard the story that Hank just told. The spirits in the Pub. They got them on that camera. On their own."

Christine replied, "That's where he went off to then."

Chester stated, "Along the side of the building. Hank would never dump you. Only a dumbass would dump you. I don't think you'll get to Hank until the people get here. You will just have to wait. There's nothing wrong with fucking the whole thing and piss him off. That's the way you can get off this."

Christine asked, "Who said that I would?"

Chester answered, "They're all saying that you should do it. You would act just fine if you do it. I could leave if Hank walks in. Everybody says you don't have to wait for Hank. What does Hank say? You go play in the pool. That's what Hank told me."

Christine disagreed, "No he didn't."

Chester continued, "If you ask he would. I want Hank to do better. I just want to get close to you. Don't you know about doing that? Sidewalk became the street. Was it right to do that? I wish you had a good idea. What do you think Hank's doing? If you showed that to Hank he would take a shower."

By this time we had closed the store and the boys were out of school so it was a rare opportunity to get in the bathroom.

Christine pointed out, "I don't believe you talk first."

Chester suggested, "I don't think he wants to talk."

The people for the tour arrived at the fountain and they talked.

After them Christine admitted, "I know he's begging for it."

Chester said, behind a bird, "I'd just like to see the work that Hank brought."

Christine told him, "You will like it up there."

Chester replied, "It's not so good and that's a fact."

Christine guessed, "I bet before long you're back here."

Chester confessed, "I just want to make a shift right now. I'm already halfway down there."

Christine commented, "I just thought he'd never go. And now he can get lost there."

Brad remarked, "That really could happen."

Christine stated, "I've got to get going."

Brad asked, "Can I go with you? I will be just a guy going. You can't go without Hank knowing. If you leave I'll answer."

Christine instructed, "I love cooking."

Brad replied, "I already knew that one. You love picking on him."

Christine confessed, "It's a hobby."

Brad announced, "I've got a napkin."

Christine asked, "What's that for?"

Brad answered, "If Hank is hungry. Now what are you doing? I'd like to take that home. Don't know what you're supposed to do with that thing. That's what Hank was looking for. That's what you got there. That is good. I'd like to do something with Hank. He wants to go hungry like that. I could boost what he's eating. Actually force him to get well. What's he supposed to be doing?"

Christine told him, "He's expected to go big."

Brad asked, "Would you like me to do that?"

Christine added, "There's a copy in there."

Brad suggested, "That would make a secret place that you know."

Christine tried to discourage him with, "I can take Hank where we're going. I'd just like to leave you there."

Brad asked, "Do you want me to go with you? I don't have to go with you."

Christine answered, "I think you know that."

Brad replied, "I'll just stay here. You're going to take a better costume?"

Christine answered, "I think this one is good."

Brad told her, "I'm supposed to give you this. Hank is just the kind of people we know. That will make a difference. In the way that the bridge works. Did I just talk to you? So you think I'm good? You don't answer very good."

Christine remarked, "I told you he's coming."

Brad asked, "I'm supposed to be on top of something?"

As I entered the phone booth to check the recorder he commented, "Hank your behavior is broken."

Christine joked, "You whipped that into Hank."

Brad asked, "How do you know when Hank hears you?"

Christine replied, "He answers you."

Brad guessed, "I don't think he heard me."

Christine stated, "I can prove what Hank told me."

Brad confessed, "I feel like he answered."

Christine corrected, "I never heard him do that."

Brad suggested, "You ought to be going where you said. I could float on their boat. Ways I'm out of here. If you want me clear. I'll jump back in the boat."

Christine told him, "You can do whatever. Hank could help you. With what you are doing. Can you take over here? I can't wait to get over there."

Brad bragged, "I cleaned up the water here."

Christine commented, "You did a fast work. I know you can do that good."

Brad admitted, "It might be exactly what I'll be doing."

Christine asked, "You'll give that to him?"

Brad agreed, "Yes I will give that to him. You had better get going."

Christine announced, "I can go to the see a bucket."

Brad asked, "Would you like Hank to go too?"

Christine answered, "He could go if he wanted to."

Brad stated, "It's not like Hank to go away. I will show you what Hank will do. Hank will come over here. That's about what Hank would do. It's dusty over here."

Christine replied, "I can put him on this. Has he got here? I must get going."

Brad assured her, "Why don't you go and don't worry about Hank. I love him terribly now go."

Christine worried, "Hank doesn't know what's going on."

Brad confirmed, "I can tell him for you."

Christine agreed, "Okay."

Brad stated, "I will wait for Hank and do that here. You better get going. I'm here so you don't have to be."

A male spirit commented, "I think I'm here as well."

Brad asked, "What are you doing here Roger?"

Roger answered, "I'm just sittin' here."

Brad asked, "Can't you go and I'll talk to you later?"

Roger asked, "But what else am I going to do?"

Brad told him, "I won't take that as an answer."

Roger asked, "You want an answer?"

Brad ordered, "I want you to get out of here."

Roger replied, "Fine, I'm going then."

Sherry asked, "Is that the answer you got? Oh now Hank is here."

Roger came back to say, "I'm supposed to take this paper."

Brad admitted, "That was almost his fatal mistake for years. I know what he's supposed to do. I took the paper back."

Sherry remarked, "I can't wait. I can't wait to get off of here."

Gary said, "There has always been a bridge over the river Thames."

Brad asked, "Are they starting the tour? I know that there is something there."

There was the sound of a hit to the recorder and he decided, "I will leave it alone. I will wait for Hank over here. I could come over there with you. I can't bring this over there. I'm gonna start to come over to you there. I hope Hank will give us an answer. I could get her joking good. Hank just might answer me. Hank should do what you think. I got an idea we can discuss with Hank. Both Ethel and Charmaine should come over here. Now if I could just get Hank over here. I'm glad that you ladies are here. What I've got is the real deal. I already told you a little. What I'm trying to do with Hank is get him to eat."

Ethel asked, "And what should we be doing with Hank?"

Brad replied, "That's the way I think I'm leaving. Hank can come to the bathroom with us."

Ethel asked, "What is Hank doing?"

Some people walked by talking but Brad came back in with, "You two take him over there. What does safety mean? You don't have to go around the ceiling part. All that he can see is me."

Right before Gary started talking Ethel announced, "I hear him."

After Gary, Charmaine suggested, "Better try again."

Brad instructed, "Check for an answer."

Ethel remarked, "Hank is here."

Brad added, "Bring on the stray cat."

People went by talking then he continued, "I don't see Hank anywhere. I just wish that Hank would wait for me there. If you see him talking to himself let me know. Do you believe in saving someone like Hank here? He didn't know what to say about that the last time. That building right over there. Is where we mostly talk."

Gary said, "I know I take it all the time."

Ethel pointed out, "You know it's him."

Brad commented, "She doesn't believe in Hank."

Gary started the tour with the land markers and Ethel asked, "Is that what Hank would say?"

Brad remarked, "That's about what I could do. Now what we're talking about. He's just here on his own."

Ethel stated, "Nothing's moved for Hank yet. I'm waiting for that story."

Brad complained, "Your breath smells like bucket fish."

Ethel asked, "What has Hank been doing for him to answer?"

Brad asked, "Did I tell you he wants to come over to us? They hunted six hundred and fifty of them. Before they found Hank."

Ethel replied, "That's a lot."

Brad added, "And Hank's what they got going. So we got to get him to answer. The bridge will still go on like it always did. Now do you really want to do like me? That's what Hank is doing up here."

Ethel remarked, "That's a good answer."

Brad explained, "So you got to make the Applegate in here. We're talking here about what Hank experienced. Wait till you hear about that in his book. You're not as bold as Hank is."

I didn't know if there was anything bold about it. It was a trip where everything that could go wrong did. I was married with two kids at the time. We went from Reno over Donner summit to San Mateo for a holiday. We started by just making it past the point where they closed the road behind us for the snow, we had no chains.

Everything was good in San Mateo but on the way home the alternator went out in downtown San Francisco. Two hundred dollars and two hours later we were back on the road.

When we got to the mountains I bought chains and put them on hoping they opened the road, but it was closed at Applegate. We had to go back to the previous town to get a hotel room for the four of us. That turned into a three day adventure of driving to Applegate everyday to find out nothing gets past the Applegate. Late the third day they opened the road and we headed home.

The part that stood out for me is when we reached Truckee. We stopped at a truck stop to go to the bathroom and I could take the chains off. As I got out of the car I stepped into knee-deep snow slush and was instantly frozen and wet. I took the chains off while the wife got the kids to the bathroom. I lifted them over the slush.

I got everyone back in the car and I went in to the truck stop all wet and cold. I went to the bathroom. On the way out I used our last ten dollars to buy the kids the first Batman movie that just came out on VHS. The wife wasn't happy I spent the last ten dollars, but I told her we had to have some fun after all this crap.

After we got home I found one the kids' gerbils had chewed his foot off and I had to put him down before the kids saw it.

We had a child gate to keep the kids out of the kitchen that would be known as the Applegate that nothing got past.

Gary said, "I don't mind if you take pictures."

Brad instructed, "You don't have to be mad at him. They take pictures when they go around here."

Charmaine replied, "I can see it."

As the tour group started talking Ethel announced, "I can hear."

Gary told the tour a little more.

Brad stated, "I always wanted to get the perfect answer."

Gary told the lamp post story and the clock tower chimed.

The tour came to the phone booth and Gary told half of that story before the clock tower finished chiming.

Gary said, "One of my girls from my investigating team was over here doing EVP's."

Brad explained, "That's what Hank is doing."

Gary finished the phone booth story.

Brad tried to get through to me, "Hank I think you're hungry. Won't you come here for bacon? I'm getting through to Hank. I think he can hear."

I went into the phone booth and picked up the recorder.

Brad asked, "Hank what are you doing? He's leaving out of here. That's what Hank does. On the mail that he got. Can you hear the beep Hank? I'm talking to you. It's foggy why he did that to me. I did that to him yesterday. Yes Hank."

Ethel asked, "What is he wearing?"

As we were walking Brad announced, "Hank is coming. You have to move with Hank. Hank was here."

Ethel asked, "What is Hank doing?"

Brad complained, "Hank won't even listen to me. Hank is supposed to hear and answer me. Hank I don't think this is very funny. I think he's trying to make fun of me. You need to focus Hank. He thought he got rid of me. I want to see if Hank can actually hear us speak to him. Do you know how to do that Hank? You must be able to understand us."

Ethel replied, "Hank would just rather not hear you."

Brad suggested, "Hank should be ready to hear us. Hank is going to be up here. I know he's got a lot of people in his hair. Now you can hear him. The bald man has to do some shopping."

I said, "I ain't hurtin' if you did that. I ain't hardly supposed to help. That hurt to get the light from that storm."

I went on to finish my conversation with Zach about filming me with the camcorder. Gary instructed him to do so as I was having so much interaction with Chester and Christine.

Brad asked, "Did you hear it all? We should give Hank a favor."

Ethel sang, "No he's just a man. I know he deserves it."

Brad explained, "Hank doesn't treat us like that. Hank does exactly the opposite."

Ethel remarked, "I can't believe in Hank."

We reached the water and Gary asked the tour group, "You see all the stains up there?"

Brad pointed out, "That's what I mean."

Charmaine asked, "Doesn't he answer?"

Brad answered, "That's what Hank does."

Gary talked about the hooks that used to be on the bridge.

At a pause in the story Ethel eerily commented, "It cut deep."

Gary went on.

When Gary paused again Ethel asked, "By chance did you see him?"

Gary continued.

At the next pause Brad admitted, "I'm thirsty."

Gary kept on telling the story.

At another pause Ethel asked, "Is Hank in there?"

Gary went on.

At the next pause Brad announced, "He is a Wiccan male."

Gary said another line.

Brad corrected, "That's accusing him."

Gary finished the story but we stayed by the water while they adjusted the camcorder.

Between us talking Brad told me, "Hank come here."

We started walking towards the stairs and Charmaine remarked, "Hank kept looking at us."

Brad confirmed, "I told you Hank was different."

Ethel asked, "Hank what are you doing?"

Brad continued, "Told you he sees us. Hank doesn't have a big tour part right here. I've got to get Hank to come with me. Hank's supposed to be right here. If you stop doing that he will come back here."

Charmaine asked, "Stop being me?"

Brad answered, "No you just have to stop doing that. What do you think that he has to think? We have to give Hank a year to think. They bought that. Isn't that what spirit is all about? At this time we will be open to policy. I won't even be here to miss him. I can't get. I can't get Hank to eat for me."

Gary talked to the tour group.

Brad stated, "Now the tour is going to start again. This is where he bugs the fucking tour."

Gary started a story but at the first pause Ethel asked, "What do you want me to say to him?"

Brad suggested, "Just ask Hank to go down the road a bit. But you're better off walking."

Gary continued the story.

At a pause Brad confirmed, "That would prove Hank can hear us."

Gary went on.

At the next pause Ethel commented, "I think he heard."

Gary continued his stories by Dead Man's Hole. The tour was still talking about it as we walked to the bottom of the stairs.

At a pause Brad ordered, "Tell Hank to come over here."

Gary said a line.

Brad tried, "Hank come here."

Gary said a few more lines.

Brad replied, "Bring that question over." After a few more lines from Gary he added, "We could be helpful."

Gary finished the stories at the bottom of the stairs and we walked up.

Brad told me, "Things could be different. If you come with me. Come on Hank."

Gary rested on the stairs for a moment. He and the tour group talked.

Then Chester got back and asked, "Did you get your answer from Hank?"

Gary said a line.

Chester asked, "Did Hank say anything? But did Hank approach you first?"

As we climbed again Brad remarked, "I don't think Hank should be here."

Chester asked, "You don't think he's good? April we'll bring him back. I could get that for you."

Brad again complained, "Hank wouldn't give me an answer."

Chester asked, "What do you mean he wouldn't give you an answer?"

Brad clarified, "He completely avoided answering."

Chester replied, "I'll go give Hank a good talking to. I could bring him back. I'm glad you're here. Where's he now?"

I turned the recorder off.

I turned it back on at street level and traffic was heavy. I hung out at the statues and when the traffic died down Brad commented, "I just work here."

Chester admitted, "I didn't know you did the bridge."

Brad confessed, "Not all the time."

Chester explained, "That's why you don't care if Hank's here. That's not fair to do that to me."

Brad replied, "Yes that isn't too right. It's not like you would know."

Chester remarked, "That doesn't help me with Hank."

I put the recorder in my pocket and headed across the bridge. I just forgot to turn it off. On this tour we had five minutes of traffic and my pants rubbing against the recorder as I walked.

I pulled the recorder out of my pocket at the passage door.

Brad admitted, "I didn't think Hank would ever get here."

Chester told him, "When we take Hank over there we can't always be here."

Brad came back with, "I think Hank ought to be able to answer."

Chester suggested, "Hank could if he wants to."

Christine got back and asked, "Are we going with Hank to get wasted?"

Chester replied, "You made one."

I asked, "Is anyone here?"

Chester continued, "But he only answers Christine. Get up here."

Brad tried to tell Chester, "But Hank told me not to believe him."

Chester corrected him, "I don't think Hank would say that."

Christine answered me, "I'm right here Hank."

Chester insisted, "Let's hear Hank."

I asked, "Do you know I've been here before?"

Christine asked, "Hank what are you doing?"

Chester asked, "Hank what are you doing in here?"

Christine ordered, "Give Hank a better brain."

Brad again tried to tell them, "Hank said that he told me something. Then he'd be mine."

Chester reminded him, "Hank's here."

I asked, "You have spoken good to us before, will you speak to us now?"

Chester answered, "Hank we're always here."

Christine asked, "What is he asking now?"

Chester replied, "It's nothing."

Christine suggested, "Let's see if Hank can hear. I think Hank is calling."

I said, "I'd like to know why you stay here."

Christine answered, "Because we have something we need from Hank. What are you doing in here? Did you tell Hank what he is supposed to be?"

Chester asked, "Do you think Hank can hear? Days he'll wake up I'll be in here. Hank's still full on dope."

Christine asked, "Isn't he quite clear?"

Chester told her, "Not if he's doing it."

I asked, "Can you tell me anymore about yourself?"

Chester confided, "Hank you could not bear to see mine. I am here but you can't see me. And I will not be where you are going."

Christine asked, "Can you see what has happened here?"

Chester stated, "I'm safe from Hank's memory of me. The evil's gotten Hank most of his life. He had the nerve that he overcome it."

Christine announced, "He was here."

I said, "I'm going to go now but if you want to talk while I'm away, I will put this here and you can speak into that."

During which Christine asked, "You're gonna leave us here?"

After I left she remarked, "I can't believe Hank did that to us."

Chester replied, "He didn't give us nothing."

Brad asked, "What do you think he did that for?"

Chester answered, "I know Hank wanted us to be at this place."

Brad uttered, "At least he wants me."

Christine commented, "I didn't think he would leave. Hank come here. What's he doing? I'm thirsty. I think Hank will be here."

Chester confirmed, "I saw Hank, he stopped right there. I should just go to where Hank may be."

Christine asked, "Can you see Hank is he up there?"

Brad asked, "Does Hank believe that he'll be working with me?"

Chester told them, "I think he thinks what he wanted to. Let's leave him alone. Let's see how he likes being alone."

Brad added, "He's also being neighborly. He wants a conference with me."

The sound started vibrating when Christine remarked, "If you think this is a bird. You're sadly mistaken," during which the vibration fades.

Brad announced, "I think Hank is coming," with what made the vibration having an effect on his words. He continued, "He is with the Gopie. Did you not say he's going to be here?"

Christine admitted, "We just can't stand anymore."

Brad replied, "I just like the way he bugs me."

Chester suggested, "If you're going to need a favor from Hank. It wouldn't be that good. Hank seems to know what he's doing."

Christine requested, "Please take the Gopie out of here Bradley. I don't think he'll want to see. If Lonnie could see what Hank should be."

Brad asked, "Is that how you are going to do it? You'll probably scare Hank if you come here with me."

Christine told him, "Hank doesn't easily scare."

Chester advised, "We needed it the same if you can hear it."

Christine almost sang, "I didn't say anything. Hank is here."

Brad remarked, "I know he's been here before. Is he supposed to get married?"

Christine demanded, "Hank get over here."

Chester confirmed, "He's gonna get married right here."

Brad asked, "Who is here?"

Chester asked, "Didn't we tell you who he's gonna be with?"

Brad asked, "Who'd you find for Hank?"

Chester answered, "Christine will be."

Brad suggested, "You're kidding me with that. It's impossible with Hank. Is Hank supposed to be here?"

Chester told him, "Yes Hank should be here."

Christine added, "But you'll see that Hank won't be long."

Brad ordered, "But you can't stay here."

Chester asked, "What do you want us to do until he comes?"

Brad instructed, "You can set your arms right over here. Wait for Hank over by the boat."

There was no boat near the passage door; that part of the channel has to be kept clear.

Chester asked, "Do you think that's normal for him? I don't think so. You don't think he's mad do you? It's a situation. I don't think he believes in what we're doing."

A male spirit ordered, "We need to get the coat tails ready."

Another male spirit asked, "You're on board with the same family?"

A female spirit replied, "This seat is taken."

Brad asked, "Does Hank go with me?"

Christine asked, "Is Hank here?"

Brad confirmed, "I'll tell you when Mike gets here. Is he supposed to be right here?"

Christine answered, "Hank was supposed to be here."

Brad remarked, "I don't think he's coming here."

Christine spoke, "Hank's supposed to be in bed." She sang, "Bed for almost three seconds."

Chester asked, "You're not going to help with him?"

Brad answered, "I just can't have you stay right here. The patients need room."

Chester asked, "You'll help with Hank?"

Brad agreed, "Yes I still will."

Christine told him, "Hank likes you."

Chester asked, "And this is how you help me out? Wait till Hank hears it."

Brad guessed, "Hank will think it's fine."

Chester disagreed, "Not when you think about Christine it's not going to be."

Christine stated, "I'll just stand here with Hank."

Chester asked him, "Are you mad at anything? We can't have a problem here. Do you want to tell me a story? You can say it from over there."

Brad replied, "Say you got this thing for Hank. And then I'll give you help with him."

Christine explained, "I do believe in Hank and I. I know he can get my love. I know what they will say now only Hank talks to me. And you'll go right here."

Chester added, "If Hank gets here I'll be here. So play some music for me."

Christine asked, "What are we doing here? I'll sing for him with an accent. Do you want me to shake my stomach?"

Chester answered, "You'll do fine with singing. Make up what is Hank."

Christine remarked, "I can't get Marquez to do it. I can build it for you, Hank can only answer."

Chester instructed, "And sing your ditty right here. Show him the right things in here."

Marquez suggested, "Make him the salty dog."

Christine decided, "You'll be the same as Hank when it's finished."

Chester replied, "I thought you were doing this thing for me."

Christine directed, "Okay bring it now. Yeah we're going to sing it here. Make sure I know. If Misty starts her singing.

I think we'll start the music. I think we know what we're doing."

Chester announced, "I don't see Hank. If you can't stretch anymore."

Christine agreed, "We'll have to keep clear. I know what you're saying."

Brad ordered, "Get them from down there too."

Christine yelled, "Hey Brad it's clear."

Brad asked, "Are you going to sing or what?"

Chester asked, "Will you get on with it? I like sitting here do you like it here? I can see his mule deer. He will be happy that you're safe."

Brad asked, "Is Hank going to tell, tell a story right here?"

Chester answered, "We'll see that when Hank gets here."

Christine asked, "Is Hank here?"

Chester asked, "You don't have a grocery list on you do you?"

Christine replied, "I think that I do."

Brad asked, "Is he outside so you can make him talk?"

Chester asked, "How does it feel to be stuck like this again? In the bedroom he just takes it out. And plugs it into a machine."

Brad asked, "Is that how he hears it?"

Chester explained, "And that's why he goes. If we do stuff with Hank. It is in his room."

Brad said with his voice altered, "Been a long time here."

Christine started singing, "I could be a magick. If you could find a mirror."

Chester directed, "I can't hear you. Go get through the teacher."

Brad announced, "Here's Hank right here."

Chester suggested, "Sing for Hank while he's here."

Christine sang, "I'm being..."

Gary came in explaining areas of the bridge and drowning Christine out.

Brad said, at a pause, "They've been here for a second time."

192

Gary said a line.

Christine sang, "Can you see where Hank is? This is where Hank is coming."

Brad stated, "This is his song right here."

Christine sang, "You think so. Don't forget your book. That's all the book is."

Chester spoke, "Hank means to you." He then sang, "Now she's safe it's over here."

Christine announced, "And now."

Chester finished, "Both hands on tour special. I dare you to make it fall on his t-shirt. And then you'll have him in the bathroom finally. It's the kind of thing that people do."

Christine sang, "Smoke tobacco we all quit."

Chester spoke, "And me that do weed now. Hey Hank." Then he sang, "There's a ring." Again he spoke, "A female dropped it you can have it."

Christine stated, "If you read the right portion about me. Is Hank might be staying here?He won't come after us." She sang, "And now comes the part."

Chester finished speaking, "Where Hank leaves me. But will Hank do the same if he comes here? I think we're close to done here. Hank come here."

Christine ordered, "We're gonna stay right here."

Chester remarked, "I think you hit the jackpot. You wanna see if Gary's next? He's got two screws at night."

Christine commented, "Hank will be in his room. He's always in his room. It will be hard to nap."

Chester told her, "That's when you grow nice to me."

Brad gave his opinion, "I guess Hank's two-timing."

Chester replied, "It's a wonder that he's here."

Christine remarked, "Now you think you know it all."

Chester stated, "Hank's got this weird idea. He wants to handle all he paid for. I don't think Hank is good."

Brad announced, "Steven's been here. I can't make the call you do."

Chester asked, "Who is Steven? Who is he up here?"

Brad answered, "He would still be with Hank."

Chester asked, "You got to be kidding for real? Is Steven actually clever? That would be a help to us right?"

Brad suggested, "Hank would have no idea. Let's go get this through Hank."

Christine asked, "Hank would you please come over here?"

Chester was saying, "Jack is here," at the same time.

She asked, "You want to speak to both of them?"

Brad commented, "Hank shouldn't be like this. And he's got a real tank full."

Christine asked, "Is that what you wanted? He's not supposed to be here."

Chester answered, "Yeah I do."

Christine added, "They say you don't get better than Hank."

Chester agreed, "They've seen Hank, they understand about him."

Christine started, "Plus you'll never..."

Chester interrupted, "Hank's as close to the bridge as you can find. He's a mushroom as you can see. A free-for-all is not your answer."

Brad repeated, "Hank's supposed to be here."

Chester asked, "So that's what you'll think?"

Christine told me, "Hank it's for you."

Chester asked, "Why'd you get those piss ants that you get?"

Brad answered, "It's his first gift to me now."

Chester continued, "There is something that you can do."

Christine sang, "Use the bridge he knew."

Chester instructed, "This would be through with Hank doing this. Get Jack where we're going."

Christine asked, "Are we going somewhere?"

Chester answered, "Going where Hank will miss it. Hank will figure out who's who. That's as close as he's ever going to get."

Brad remarked, "Your hand is beautiful. But you're not going to give it to me."

Christine replied, "You know better than I do."

Brad asked, "You think I could? I knew how good this could be."

Chester told him, "You can answer a question for Damon's list."

Brad asked, "What are you doing?"

Chester suggested, "Look who came back yesterday. He'd come through here to avoid that."

Brad guessed, "He would if he's not too busy. And he'd totally like it."

Chester remarked, "Hank wouldn't let this get like that."

Christine told Brad, "You can build it."

Chester added, "Hank would let you do what you have to do. They never take Paul down to the Brooklyn Bridge. If you fuck this up you'll fuck everything every day. Hank will always make you look good."

Christine commented, "And you can fix a lot."

Chester explained, "Definitely Hank's got the music on the table. You could be next if you want that fucking bridge thing. Give Hank the difference right here. What'd you get when you hung the bathroom light on the ceiling? You can depend on Hank."

A soldier walked by telling a friend about Iraq.

Brad remarked, "They leave and then they go home."

The soldier said something else and Christine asked, "You hear them talking?"

As the soldier and his friend left Chester said, "Let's see if they're around here. Then I'm going to the bathroom."

Christine replied, "I don't think it's the same since he dropped now."

Brad boasted, "I took care of all the magazines."

Chester told him, "It's not the people, people that go to the bathroom. That you built for me. I do like it there. Hold on, are

195

you true level? Did you think I would buy this? You do have something Hank can do. I know the trick is tricky. I do have something to remember. When I leave away from here. You want me to accept this? I accept Chelsea in the magic mushroom. That leaves me open. I used to fear, do you fear what you got?"

Brad answered with, "I don't think I like the light here. Do you think I should move it?"

Chester replied, "Welcome to game trap."

Christine asked, "You found a use for Hank?"

Chester added, "I hope that you have done that. Hank has always burned. Give me back my hand. Do what Hank would do. We might have to leave before the Hank does."

Christine volunteered, "I'll take Hank."

Chester through in, "To clean his butt."

Christine announced, "Somebody's here."

That person said something then Brad suggested, "He can help me get rid of everything that I got."

Gary started coming in with his story.

Brad asked, "Does it have to be that much stronger?"

Chester answered, "Eighteen hundred pounds."

Gary said a line.

Brad replied, "I think we can get along."

Gary said another line in his story.

Christine commented, "They run their mouths out. You're zero from that."

Gary continued his story.

At a break Brad asked, "What if you don't have a pulley?"

Chester came back with, "I could get out and pull ya."

Gary talked some more then Christine offered, "If you think it doesn't matter I'll stop the paper bill. I know you think I'm a TV hater. Hank is coming here."

The tour got back to the passage door so I retrieved the recorder and turned it off.

I turned the recorder back on at the other side of the bridge where Gary did the lion story.

Christine remarked, "I doubt this is trying. And now he is..."

I asked, "Is anyone here?"

Christine answered, "Yes Hank I'm here."

Chester instructed, "We're going to do this right here. Going to have to make something perfectly quiet."

Christine added, "If Hank could hear us."

I said, "I'm looking for the person who."

Chester asked, "Did he call you?"

I finished, "Would like to talk to me."

Chester explained, "You can do that right here. This is all you do when you come back here."

Christine commented, "It's nice you like people."

Chester agreed, "You gotta like people."

Brad suggested, "Say the mountains are calling."

Chester replied, "It's nine thirty."

I asked, "What is it you want to say?"

Chester answered, "We're talking so you can hear us talk. I didn't even think you were coming. We're not supposed to be saying what we're saying."

Brad again suggested, "Tell him you will have to stop trying."

In the background a female spirit said, "And that's where spirits come from."

Christine added, "Tell Hank we're busy."

I asked, "Is there a message you're trying to tell me?"

Chester explained, "Hank you're not doing enough to keep living. I will have to take you Hank. There's two things you have to remember. For Hank it's personal."

The tour group arrived talking.

I asked, "Is there anything else you wanted to say?"

Chester finished, "You're going to be here."

In between the people talking on the tour Chester ordered, "You stay here."

I said, "Feel free to talk while I'm away."

Gary came in with the lion story.

During a break in the story Chester told Brad, "Let's go back to Hank over there. If you're not with me. Then Hank won't talk to you."

Brad insisted, "First tell me where we're going."

Chester replied, "We will be right here. Gary's going to start again."

Gary did continue the story.

At a pause Brad asked, "You want me to do that?"

Gary finished the story.

Christine remarked, "Hank is supposed to be here."

Gary told a short story then Chester asked, "What is Hank doing?"

Gary said another line and Christine confessed, "I can't see where Hank is."

Brad asked, "Is Hank in the mood for this?"

Christine informed him, "That's Hank on top of your feet."

Brad replied, "I know you would laugh at me."

Chester suggested, "Let's clear out already."

Brad stated, "I'm going to spend the night with him."

Chester corrected him, "You can't get to where Hank lives."

Gary said another line.

Christine asked, "Bet you don't know where Hank is?"

Brad answered, "He's right here. What is Hank gonna do?"

Chester asked, "Don't you think Hank's going home?"

Brad remarked, "And that's what I think. I know he's tired. Don't you think I should be with him?"

Chester asked, "What did he say? If only Hank would get here."

Gary asked, "What'd he say?"

Chester answered, "Get Hank."

Brad echoed, "Come get Hank."

Chester remarked, "I don't believe this."

Gary started telling the last story.

Near the end of the story Gary paused and Chester announced, "I knew he'd be here."

Gary finished the story and I picked the recorder up.

Christine remarked, "I bet you stop doing that."

Chester asked, "What'd you do with Hank?"

Brad asked, "Will you truck down the street?"

Christine answered, "Yes I will."

Another female spirit came in and asked, "Is Hank here?"

We started walking to Dead Man's Hole and I shut the recorder off.

We did go home and get the camcorder tape transferred to the computer. Besides the shadow spirit we got going through the glass of the Pub before the tour, when I was asking questions in the lion spot, a small white orb came off my elbow and circled around me three times. I thought it was Christine.

CHAPTER ELEVEN

THE WITCH TOUR

The lady in the phone booth was saying,
"There is a spirit behind the phone booth."

The next tour was small; three ladies. They were close friends with each other so they were having a wonderful time together. They were really into the ghost hunting also. It was only after the tour they revealed they were witches too. This fun tour I called the Witch Tour.

I turned the recorder on and got Chester saying, "There you are Hank. Wait just a second."

Christine remarked, "I knew you were coming. Let's hear Hank."

Chester stated, "I think he's coming."

Christine admitted, "I just want him to get here."

Chester announced, "Here's Hank."

I asked, "Christine, are you here?"

Christine replied, "Now Hank can see."

Chester confirmed, "I know Hank can hear."

Christine stated, "Hank will be here."

Chester ordered, "Rachel you come back in here. I know that you're supposed to be here. I know you think Hank will be here."

I asked, "We got a tour tonight, wanna help?"

Christine answered, "I'll do the best that I can with it."

Rachel asked, "What is Hank doing?"

Christine told her, "Talking with me. He knows what you're doing."

Chester again ordered, "I told you Rachel you should get back in here. Now come back in here."

Christine repeated, "Hank knows what you're doing. Why don't you get with Chester in the phone booth? I know you want to do this."

Chester admitted, "I know that you want to help."

I said, "We will be back here tomorrow night."

Christine remarked, "We will be here Saturday. How are you doing?"

I said, "I would most like your help."

Christine offered, "I will do what I can."

I said, "It's going to be a big tour with a lot of friends."

Christine asked, "You won't mind then?"

I said, "It's supposed to be a special night by my celebration."

Christine asked, "Guess what we're doing? I think you won't like it."

Chester asked, "Do you respect us Hank? Do you know everything that I know? I'm right here with you. Hank. He knows what he's doing. I can see just what you're doing. I don't like what you've been doing to us. I know what Hank is doing. You are in trouble Hank," with some brushing against the recorder.

I said, "There that's all I'll bug you about right now."

Chester remarked, "I knew it."

I said, "I hope things are better." Then I turned the recorder off. I turned it back on when the tour started with Gary talking.

At a pause in Gary's talking Chester warned, "I got you Hank."

The tour went into full swing with Gary stating facts up to the front gates. He continued about the gates as several people are picked up by the recorder yelling as they enter the Village. He moved on to the land markers as the background noise diminished.

Christine announced, "I know where Hank went."

Chester boasted, "I moved Hank."

Christine spoke right into the recorder, "See me. Hank will do it," as Gary was talking.

Chester confirmed, "Hank can go with me," behind Gary. Then by himself he added, "I knew that."

Christine called, "Hank we're over here."

Chester suggested, "Put your face upon the dirt here."

Christine replied, "That's what I was saying. I guess Hank will make it rain. He's mine here. He'd like to be here. He likes it here."

Chester started, "Hank."

Christine finished, "Wants to be my man."

Chester agreed, "Hank should be."

Christine asked, "Does Hank visit here?"

Gary finished the land marker story.

Christine announced, "Hank will be here soon."

One of the ladies on the tour said, "Let go of yourself."

Christine confirmed, "That's how you do it."

Chester asked, "You'll do it?"

Christine answered, "I'm broke. Give me a kiss."

Chester reminded her, "Hank will be here soon," at the same time Christine stated, "I will be with him."

Christine asked, "Do you know where Hank is going? Is Hank with us?" while Gary spoke.

She said by herself, "Hank opened this. I don't know what he wants but I'm about to see him."

Chester told her, "It doesn't matter."

Christine asked, "What did he say when you asked him? It's like fucking you."

Chester answered, "Then we'll catch him. Drop down the human race."

Christine stated, "Hank will take the bridge."

Chester asked, "Now will you eat some food?"

Christine commented, "And that's what Hank was supposed to do."

Chester explained, "I turned this over so Hank can get out. It's really beautiful the way that they work together. Hank you have to move the pager. Looks like Hank can always be better."

Christine asked, "Did he invent everything? It must not have taken very long." A few seconds later she said, "I love you. That's what Hank told me. I don't think he's very old."

Gary said, "The lamp post hasn't been lit in forty years."

Chester asked, "How do you get that on? I think you got it Hank. I'm sorry you had to put me."

Christine announced, "Hank is ready."

Chester asked, "Do you ever feel like me?"

Christine replied, "I control you. I'll be glad when Hank gets here."

Rachel remarked, "There is no way he'll stop."

Christine asked, "You want to bet me?" in time with my camera beep.

Chester commented, "I think you got us in there Hank."

We went on to the phone booth and Gary told the first part of the story. The ladies on the tour took pictures. Then Gary finished the stories at the phone booth.

Gary began telling about the Pub. As he talked about pictures of spirits at the Pub I added that I had gotten a picture of a woman outside the second story window looking in. She had blond hair pulled back and was wearing a period dress.

Chester added, "That is her dress."

Gary told the ladies the more pictures they took the better off they are.

Chester stated, "Hank is faster."

We walked down to the water with Gary telling stories the whole time. A few times he pauses but only for a second. There were short EVP's there. Chester was saying, "Hank I know." Christine was saying, "I'm with him," but I didn't separate them.

When we reached the water Chester instructed, "Now you can bring Hank over here."

Gary told more about the bridge.

After a story Chester remarked, "I think it's in Reno," with Gary saying, "Test," in the middle of it.

Gary said a line.

Chester asked, "Do you think Hank would do that? You stay with Hank whatever."

Gary said a couple of more lines as he got into position at the water's edge.

Christine insisted, "I want Hank over here."

Chester replied, "I think I can get Hank over there. It's not what you would think. It's stranger than you can believe."

Christine started, "I'd rather stay with."

Chester finished, "All you got on you."

Gary said, "This is our new sidewalk."

Chester challenged, "Bet you won't tell him."

Christine stated, "I can't tell him if I'm not sure."

Gary started the stories at the water's edge.

At the first slight pause Chester asked, "Hank are you here?"

At the next pause Chester warned, "You better give that to Hank," but Gary was talking about being hung from the bridge by iron hooks. I don't know if that was what he wanted me to get.

At the end of the story Chester remarked, "It's lost for everything. Can we mark it like this? See what Hank is doing."

We moved on to Dead Man's Hole and Gary started another story.

At the first pause Christine asked, "Did you talk to Hank?"

Shortly after there was another pause where Chester confessed, "I did it here."

At the end of the story Chester replied, "As smart as Hank."

There was some talking amongst the tour when the girl that I was attracted to said, "No."

Chester directed, "You got to get after Hank." Strangely enough the girl came over and talked to me after that.

Gary started another story but near the end Chester guessed, "He must be doing it."

After the story Chester remarked, "He got witch sense."

Gary mentioned what part of the story was on the website.

Chester ordered, "Now you can get back in here."

Christine asked, "Are you talking to Hank over there?"

Gary said a few things and Christine asked, "What are you doing with Hank's truck?"

Chester answered, "I just made some paper woody on it."

There was some talking between the ladies on the tour as we walked to the stairs.

Gary started the first story on the stairs.

At the first pause Chester suggested, "Let's go get Hank."

Gary continued.

The next pause Chester stated, "I wouldn't be in Jack's room."

Gary went on to the next pause.

Chester admitted, "I played a joke around here. It might be in the men's room right here."

Gary said a line.

Chester asked, "Did you see that?"

As Gary finished the first story on the stairs Brad shows up and volunteered, "I'd travel with Hank if you let me."

Christine joked, "I know where Hanky went to. Somewhere."

After a short line from Gary Chester replied, "I think Hank is gone back."

Gary said a line in the next story.

Chester announced, "Hank will help her."

As the ladies started taking pictures Chester decided, "I should get over there. There's no chance that Hank would get off of it."

Gary talking about his camera said, "It was made in Switzerland."

Chester added, "From a drawing made in Bingham. Is that how you do it?"

Gary got into the second story with, "You see the corners nice and sharp."

Chester asked, "Hank do you want to see them?"

Gary finished that story. He started telling about a paranormal experience he had with some clairvoyants and psychics who got ill during the experience.

Chester remarked, "That's not Hank."

Gary got into the story about two vortexes. He went into the background of the location.

Chester stated, "Hank would hear."

Gary finished the story.

Chester commented, "It must have happened before Hank. I'll just go get Hank."

As the tour started to walk up the stairs Chester called, "Let's go Hank."

At a pause in the talking going up the stairs Chester announced, "There's too many people for Hank to see."

As we came to the place for the next story Gary said, "I smoke too much."

Chester replied, "Then you shouldn't be with Hank."

Gary started the story.

At the first pause Chester instructed, "I'll handle everything. If you can get Hank over here."

Gary continued the story.

206

At the next pause Chester asked, "Is Hank supposed to be here?"

Gary talking about the Museum Tape said, "And he doesn't see a bridge."

Chester asked, "Should we come there?"

Gary said, "There's no bridge."

Brad stated, "It's my bridge."

Gary said a long line.

Chester remarked, "I know what he's doing." My camera beep covered the word doing.

Gary got near the end of the story and paused.

Chester asked, "Hank are here?"

Gary finished the story.

Chester voiced his concern, "I care what you do."

Christine confessed, "Hank we can't. We can't do everything for you. Did you already know that? I can't get an answer from Hank."

Chester asked, "Are we unstable?"

I turned the recorder off. I turned it back on when we crossed the bridge to go to the passage door. There was music playing at the Heat and Gary was describing what was inside the bridge.

As the words came in the song that was playing, it was Christine singing, "We need Hank. So sad that I don't know. Don't know what I need. Don't know what Hank wants. Like a long lost doubt see. He will stay forever. On this old bridge we're on. Right here on this bridge. Right behind me. And he is going to be. The big old hero. Of his happy thing he put on me."

Rachel sang, "I know he will be wreath me. Leave him too. But Hank is always. Always on me. He is alright. If he cannot see her. I don't know about Christine. Are you wish?"

Christine sang, "If I can tell you. Of my death right here. I got my meals at. And there were always people on the street with me. They were always there. They stared at me. And they would always laugh."

Rachel came in singing, "They would always laugh at her because. She was a sheep. And got her own soup and went home."

Christine sang, "And they had me. Believe me. They all leave me."

Rachel sang, "They all leave her."

Christine sang, "They all leave me. Leave me inside of me. Leave me alone. Where are you?"

Rachel sang, "You belong to her."

Christine sang, "Hank you will be madder than you want. So go in peace without being good for the asshole."

Rachel sang, "Take her to him."

Christine sang, "Now you know." Then very softly asked, "Did you like that?"

During the song Gary told the Jack the Ripper story. After the song he told of the movies about the bridge and Jack the Ripper.

We headed upstairs with another story at the top of the stairs.

I shut the recorder off after we finished on the stairs. We crossed the bridge and I turned the recorder back on at the top of the other stairs.

We were all having a conversation when at a lull Christine called me, "Hank."

Still having the conversation, one of the ladies told me I was pretty open. Chester asked, "Is it possible?"

After more conversation Chester confessed, "I can't do it."

At the next pause Christine told him, "Yes you can."

Before Gary started the story Chester admitted, "I know what you're doing." At the same time Christine replied, "That's Hank."

During Gary's story Christine asked, "What are you doing?" At the next slight pause she exclaimed, "Hank you're here."

At another pause in the lion story Chester remarked, "Hank would block some."

The next pause had Christine singing, "That is it." Then while Gary was talking she sang, "You know I've got to be there with the Hank."

Gary got to the end of the lion story and Chester told me, "Hank they're awesome."

As we walked down the stairs Chester announced, "Calling Hank to me."

Christine asked, "Can you hear this?" while she made a strange noise.

At the bottom of the stairs when Gary asked the tour a question Chester stated, "Hank is here."

Gary asked, "Do you see anything on the bridge?"

Chester asked, "That's not all do you see us? They don't think I'm serious. I want to see Hank here."

Christine told him, "You got me here with you," and sang, "We're all on the street now. And we're watching. Hank we'll do whatever you tell us."

Chester commented, "Hank that's good."

Christine stated, "They're not with Hank," as some people passed.

Gary asked, "How you doin'?" of the people walking by.

In the discussion amongst the tour group there was a pause and Chester replied, "I knew the answer." They were discussing a symbol that was raised up from the stonework so slightly you could only see it by taking a picture.

At the next pause Chester suggested, "Take a pickaxe."

As Gary explained more he paused and Christine announced, "It's over."

At his next pause Christine remarked, "People are bad enough."

Gary's next pause was long and Christine explained, "I know what he's doing. I want to take a crack at this. This is how you do it."

The next time Gary paused Christine admitted, "I'm so tired."

Gary talked to the end of the tour and I shut the recorder off.

CHAPTER TWELVE

THE PARANORMAL FAMILY TOUR

Full body spirit, girl looking in the Pub window

Much like Gary's family, two families who did paranormal investigation before, contacted us to take the tour. One family took the tour already and stayed in touch with Gary. Naturally I called this one the Paranormal Family Tour.

As soon as I turned the recorder on Christine asked, "Hank are you with me?"

Sherry insisted, "You have to go stay with, stay with Hank."

Chester stated, "All that is good Hank." Someone started to sing and he asked, "Is that Hank calling me?"

Christine half sang, "I'll meet Hank here."

Chester announced, "If you go to Hank's room. You'll see a neighbor."

I asked, "Christine are you with me tonight?"

Christine answered, "Hank I'm here. Hank you can tell if we're here."

Chester asked, "What did Hank say? Are you ready for a bad time?"

I said, "I'm not sure if you follow me around."

Christine replied, "Hank you've got me now. But Hank would never go to miss me. Do you want me to take him over there to you?"

I asked, "Is there any reason why?"

Chester remarked, "Now I've got Hank to talk too."

Christine suggested, "Hank could always speak through, speak through that."

Chester explained, "Hank would always be right here. Now you're going to take a walk."

I said, "We're going to follow, let's go."

Christine stated, "I will just go with Hank already. Hank are you ready? I can't tell him everything. I can't tell him about. What I know I'm going to do with Hank."

Chester ordered, "And you can't tell Hank anything about what we do."

Christine requested, "I wish someone would help."

Chester instructed, "Play it good with Hank."

Christine remarked, "You're only this small when you're with Hank."

Chester replied, "I hate Hank. For what he's doing to us."

I said, "Hello."

Christine told him, "He heard you say that."

Chester uttered, "He deserves it."

I said, "Just to let you know I did."

Chester remarked, "Aw here it comes."

I finished, "Hear you and I wanted to answer that question."

Chester guessed, "And he'll probably give me the wrong answer. Hank you going to answer. He should answer. Which one of us care?"

I asked, "Can you tell me how many favors?"

Chester answered, "I think you'll get about four."

I finished, "That you would get."

Christine added, "If you're special you get more. I think he believes it."

Chester told her, "I think we're in danger. I know that Hank will get two more. Then let's go easy. He'll be here soon enough."

I said, "All this sounds so interesting."

Christine announced, "He heard us."

Chester echoed, "And now he hears us."

I said, "I'm beginning to learn about the other side, I would like to know."

Christine asked, "What Hank?"

I asked, "How is it in your world?"

Christine answered, "You will know that when you get here. You can take us."

After some people finished yelling in the distance Chester directed, "It's over now with Hank. You can take the machine over there."

I said, "Once again I'm going to put the microphone out here."

A long sound came that was probably a truck horn in the distance. Out of that sound Chester ordered, "If Hank can hear us. He will go to Bullhead."

I said, "And you can just talk and I'll hear you."

Some spirit asked, "What does he mean when he answers?"

Chester spoke right into the recorder, "Hank never answers. Where is Hank? Make Hank an asshole."

I set the recorder outside the phone booth.

Sherry instructed, "You can take her back home."

A female spirit replied, "I don't like this."

Sherry added, "And you got them all."

I repositioned the recorder to get the built in microphone up to pick up more.

Christine stated, "I didn't think Hank would be here. I don't think Hank would miss court."

Sherry pointed out, "You're right here with him."

Brad commented, "I won't be here."

Christine remarked, "I'll be in here."

Sherry volunteered, "I'll tell Peter."

The clock tower chimed.

Sherry told them, "Hank was staying busy right here. Do you think Hank will get it home?"

Chester answered, "I don't think Hank would forget it."

Brad asked, "What do you want me to say on it?"

Chester replied, "Tell Hank you're here. What did Hank say to you?"

Sherry lied, "Hank told me to get out of here."

Christine disagreed, "Hank never said anything like that before."

Chester asked, "Did you hear what Hank said?"

Christine asked, "Well did Hank hear?"

Peter remarked, "Don't forget me."

Sherry announced, "He's here."

Christine half sang, "Now that you're here call Hank to come."

Peter called out, "Hank come here." It was barely understandable as an EVP so I wouldn't hear it out in the Village.

Sherry commented, "He didn't come."

Christine replied, "Hank comes here every day."

Chester reminded him, "You said he would come to you."

Christine stated, "He only comes to me. He won't even come here for me."

Sherry asked, "Can you ask Hank where he's going?"

Chester suggested, "You can both look at that book."

Peter agreed, "Then we'll both look at the book."

Sherry asked, "What did Hank do? Is that Hank coming over?"

Christine remarked, "And you'll both get an answer."

Sherry announced, "Hank's here now."

Christine repeated, "Now you'll both get answers."

Chester added, "And you will get to play with Henry."

Sherry admitted, "I can't get out of here."

Christine advised, "And when Hank gets over. Take it easy."

Chester announced, "Here he comes right here."

Peter replied, "I know where you'll be."

Christine called, "Hank you should come."

Chester directed, "And now you can get out of here. Can you drop what you're saying? If Hank wants to tell us something."

Sherry asked, "Is Hank still here?"

Christine commented, "I want to stay, stay with Hank. I'm asking to go to Hank."

Sherry asked, "You'd stay with Hank all day then huh?"

Christine answered, "I just want to visit Hank."

Chester replied, "Hank is gone already."

Sherry instructed, "Go give that to Henry."

Christine told her, "I can't bring Hank anything."

Sherry remarked, "Aw you're pitiful. So is he."

Chester agreed, "You got that right."

Sherry ordered, "Don't get too close to me."

Chester guessed, "I don't think Hank heard anymore."

Christine stated, "I know where Hank will be."

Chester admitted, "I should go there and visit Hank," with a beep at the word there.

Christine replied, "You can if you care to."

Sherry spoke, "I know where Hank lives." She sang, "If this is the thirteenth."

Christine sang with her, "Then I'll visit Hank."

Sherry sang, "If he goes to pull you. Hank believes in you Christine. Hank believes in Christine."

Christine remarked, "Hank will see me."

Sherry stated, "Hank will be with, with her. Then they will do something special."

Chester corrected her, "I know that Hank will think they did."

Christine decided, "I'll wait for Hank to get here."

Peter asked, "You'll be waiting on Hank?"

Christine answered, "Hank will be over here anyway."

Chester replied, "I think we'll touch up Hank better. I wonder what Hank will do. Say."

Christine told him, "Talk like me."

Chester commented, "I hope that Hank likes," then there was a metallic clank sound. He added, "We won't seem big. He better go home. And screw down all these mirrors. Don't be like what'd they say."

Sherry remarked, "I wonder if Hank would get that."

Christine said, "Laugh," in her little girl voice. In her normal voice she added, "That's what Hank should do."

Sherry asked, "What are you saying?"

Mark stated, "Hank is an asshole."

Christine replied, "I hate what Mark just said. About Hank," with a little girl's voice saying, "It's on."

Chester asked, "What do you expect me to do? I'll do what you expect of me. Only Hank should do this to him. You want to get back at him."

Peter suggested, "You'll like this thing with Hank. What did Hank do to deserve this? I think Hank is here."

Mark confessed, "I would go on to David if Hank was here."

Chester stated, "I feel good with Hank staying here."

Sherry agreed, "Hank should be here."

Christine added, "I'm inclined to agree with her. Hank wouldn't say that to you."

Sherry admitted, "I wouldn't take that to Leopold."

Christine demanded, "I want to stay here and be with Hank right. Then get rid of this asshole."

Mark replied, "I've been good since I've been here before."

Chester pointed out, "Now Hank won't help you. And you know where Hank would go. Would you stick with everything right here?"

Christine answered, "Yes, I'll write it with the paper."

Mark yelled, "And you're not worth this much!"

Chester finished, "I think we're done here. I think Hank should be here."

Sherry agreed, "Okay."

Christine stated, "I will be here."

Chester told them, "I will stay with Hank over there."

Sherry asked, "Do you think Hank will be there?"

Christine replied, "It doesn't matter. I think Hank is about ready to go."

Sherry asked, "Who will make a tulip?"

Chester answered, "You don't need a favor."

The people arrived for the tour and talked a little before Chester announced, "There you are Hank."

Christine ordered, "Let me see that. You turn around and face the wall. That's you now with Hank. I won't go with you now."

Sherry suggested, "Make it part of him."

Christine explained, "And now you pick up that. I will still give you a good number."

Peter remarked, "Charles has to take him."

Sherry asked, "Have you ever done anything like this before?"

Christine answered, "Yes when I go to the bathroom. That's what I'm talking about here," in her little girl voice.

Chester stated, "Hank won't be able to touch that anymore."

Christine decided, "I will take Hank away from here. I accept this journey."

Chester asked, "When did they say they would talk to you?"

Christine replied, "It should go better."

Chester admitted, "No one could do it better than you could."

Christine suggested, "Maybe the man should come here."

Chester commented, "If you go that far we could lien to it. I think we're in trouble."

Christine instructed, "Call Hank." Then there was a whistle.

Sherry replied, "He never would come."

Christine asked, "What was that?"

A female spirit answered, "Asshole."

Christine and Chester stated, "I visit Hank." It was very clear.

The Gopie asked, "But what are you doing here?"

Chester decided, "I should go where Hank is."

The Gopie stated, "I can't be wrong if you talk to me."

Chester announced, "Alright I'm leaving here. I won't step in it if you try it."

Sherry told Christine, "The Gopie said he talked to you."

Christine replied, "He'll take the summer."

Sherry remarked, "Especially with Hank."

The Gopie told them, "I can reciprocate with Hank though. Especially with all the good that Hank has done. Where is Hank now? Can you get Hank to come in?"

Christine answered, "I can go look for him. He might be near the bus driver. They're both magick."

The Gopie agreed, "Yep. What's that note behind you?"

Christine lied, "Nothing."

The Gopie asked, "What's the note stand for then?"

Christine confessed, "I've got his wing book right here."

The Gopie asked, "Did he come from a bad egg?"

Christine admitted, "That's a matter of opinion. Hank would say whatever."

The Gopie requested, "I would like Hank over here."

Christine offered, "I will bring Hank to you."

The Gopie stated, "It will take a little bit longer with Hank. I would like Misty."

Misty told him, "You might think there's a matter to resolve."

The Gopie replied, "But Hank is not here."

Misty pointed out, "You have everything Hank has ever done."

The Gopie confirmed, "I know that."

Misty asked, "So why can't you do it here?"

The Gopie answered, "I'm not going anywhere."

Misty disagreed, "I think you'll go where Hank is."

The Gopie asked, "And you think Hank will win? Hank should be here. I think Hank will answer a question right here."

Misty started, "You will have to," and with a little girl voice, "Come out." Back to normal for, "You will ask Hank," then to the little girl voice for, "Then go back. I could eat a doughnut."

The Gopie remarked, "That's more trouble than you need."

Christine announced, "But now I can bring Hank over."

Misty suggested, "You'll be done when Hank gets here. Do your thing when Hank gets here."

Sherry commented, "Maybe it will be different when Hank gets home. Brian get over here."

Christine offered, "I'll tell Hank whatever."

Sherry stated, "That's who he is going to be. Can you walk over there?"

The Gopie answered, "I can't go where others go."

Misty told him, "They can bring Hank over."

Sherry admitted, "You won't be with Hank. That's how we get over there."

Chester came back and confessed, "I don't know what Hank is doing."

Sherry asked, "Hank is over there?"

A siren went by.

Christine asked, "You don't believe I'll do it?"

Chester replied, "I know what Hank's doing."

The Gopie asked, "Can you go get Hank for me please?"

Chester answered, "I could banter with Hank."

The Gopie decided, "We will have to wait for Hank here."

Christine announced, "Now I'm ready. Let's get going." After a second in her little girl voice she added, "Now go back. Who are we going to bring with us? I'd like Tia to come."

Tia remarked, "Hank would never behave."

Chester suggested, "Bring your Uncle Chester."

Christine replied, "I will think about it."

Sherry asked, "You think Hank will come?"

Chester asked, "But don't we have to wait for him?"

Christine complained, "But I am ready to go."

Chester guessed, "I think that is the answer."

Sherry added, "And some of the people do."

Chester instructed, "But Hank won't know where we go."

Christine stated, "I'm aware of that." Then it sounded like she used the machine to say, "Escape."

Chester finished, "From here. You won't help with Hank?"

Christine answered, "But Hank can take care of himself. I think we can go. I think we can take a lot of people."

Chester explained, "But every time we go through that. We have to take the really big car. Maybe Hank could help us do this. Can you go see what Hank is doing?"

Christine asked, "Do you think Hank will remember?"

Chester answered, "Hank doesn't realize any of it."

Sherry announced, "I know where he's going."

Christine asked, "Where do you think Hank goes?"

Sherry replied, "I think he's gone into the men's bathroom."

Chester asked, "Is that the place that you were?"

Sherry remarked, "He told me we'd get an answer. Hank remembered. Where do you think you're going?"

Christine answered, "I'm going to see if Hank is over there."

Sherry guessed, "I bet you remember all of it."

Christine confessed, "I don't think I can say this. I can remember that. Hank moved just to be here. I can't help it with Hank."

Misty asked, "Can you get out of here?"

Chester remarked, "It doesn't do any good to ask about Henry."

Christine began to sing, "All is beautiful." Then spoke, "That's how we get thirty moons." She sang, "On and on and on. I could know you better. Did you hope to get all and meet us here? If you seem alright."

Chester commented, "I can wait right here. It's too late but whatever. You won't see the last of him."

Misty offered, "I will move this foot. Then you can pass."

Christine stated, "That's as cool as air right to it. Maybe Bones can get to it. I think you should be involved with everything."

Misty remarked, "I thought Hank would be a bit better."

Christine replied, "I'm not sure what Hank would say."

Sherry asked, "Did you hear what Hank said?"

Christine interjected, "And you also know me."

Sherry admitted, "That's what he said."

She then sang, "Did you want what Hank said?"

Christine answered, "I know he would answer. I have a new place with Hank."

Chester suggested, "Well get some moves with Hank. I guess Hank is getting ready."

Sherry asked, "Are you ready to kill him?"

Misty asked, "So what'd he say? Give him something to play with."

Christine said in her little girl voice, "Shut up with that. With that you have to fuck all that."

Chester assured her, "He'll take you back home to meet with him."

Sherry commented, "She'll marry Long Dong Silver. It won't take long."

Christine confessed, "And that's where Hank went wrong. I'm going here," combined with music. She then spoke, "I believe Hank could talk like that." She sang, "Now he sings to me. He's so easy. Let's just go to right here. While you're on it that's right."

Misty asked, "Did Hank say anything?"

Christine told her, "But I'll be up here, you say something. I didn't hear what you said. I want to be in here."

Sherry asked, "Did you telephone Hank?"

Chester ordered, "I want you to do that today."

Christine explained, "Goth told me to stand here. And you won't see me. I'll be better. I could stay right here."

Sherry asked, "Is that what you told him?"

Chester remarked, "I can't get Tony to come here."

Christine asked, "Who do you know that sings like that?"

Sherry answered, "This old man."

Misty asked, "Did he sing something before?"

Christine replied, "I wish Dean was coming."

Chester asked, "He did say he'd help? He might get along with Hank. Or you can't say what will be. We need to leave here."

Misty confessed, "I need someone's help to get out of here."

Christine remarked, "I will be with Hank over there."

Chester replied, "If that's where Hank is. If you go with Hank it's impossible. For us to get Hank to do."

Christine interrupted, "Still I'll take him there."

Sherry told her, "That's all if you take him there."

Misty suggested, "Get a room like Stacy's room."

Christine agreed, "Oh yeah we'd fuck like that."

Miles commented, "Hank was here on Wednesday. Same thing that babies do."

Christine asked, "Okay what was Hank doing?"

Miles answered, "He was riding on a bicycle."

Chester informed him, "Hank doesn't even own a bicycle."

Christine told him, "You don't know what Hank's got."

Miles gave his opinion, "I think he paid her."

Chester snapped back, "I should get after you for Hank."

Christine asked, "What's your big problem?"

Miles admitted, "I just want to help you two. I want to take the process."

Chester explained, "But you don't have to talk bad about us. Yes Hank paid for us. But we're still obeying what we thought we should."

Miles replied, "I'm so relieved."

Christine stated, "I bet your wife is home. I won't send him back to a monster. You don't think Miles wants in?"

Sherry pointed out, "There's something wrong over here."

Christine asked, "Is the pulley there? Here let me get that for you."

Chester ordered, "Go and sit with Hank."

Sherry resounded, "Go and check on Hank already."

Christine remarked, "He hates when I don't talk to him."

Chester said, "I don't even know if Hank can think right."

Sherry asked, "Didn't you say Hank has a simple mind?"

Misty admitted, "I thought they'd go this far to talk."

A person walking by said, "I've been to South Hampton."

Sherry replied, "I've been here."

Chester asked, "Is Hank going to be here?"

Sherry answered, "Yeah as soon as possible."

Christine confessed, "I know I can't go over there."

Misty asked, "Did you go in his bedroom?"

Christine answered, "I've been with Hank everywhere. Everywhere he goes."

Misty remarked, "Now that's interesting. Who'd you take through here?"

Christine replied, "The things that Hank can do aren't fun. If you take Tuesday out of here."

Miles announced, "I'm out of here."

Christine spoke, "I don't care what you have to say." She half sang, "Why don't you just go away. You don't have to get out of your seat. Everything you say is not true. Tell me you're out of here."

Miles commented, "I miss my dear."

Christine told him, "Don't let that door hit you." She sang, "He's gone forever. Make way for him now."

Misty asked, "Are you referring to Hank?"

Christine asked, "Do you know about a better man?"

Sherry answered, "Like Hank never does. But you say he looks bad."

Christine admitted, "I knew Hank could be better later. If he ever wanted to."

Sherry remarked, "I know you miss Hank. He must have a leather program. What do I mean then?"

She almost sang, "To see if Hank could stand it. That's if you ask me Grandpa."

She then spoke, "I think Hank is going over his head."

Christine replied, "There's lots of people who have seen us. Hank can barely breathe."

Sherry commented, "I bet he goes pee to piss off."

Christine asked, "What do you mean by that?"

Sherry answered, "I believe what I said. That's what I mean when I said. Hank said go around. Hank's not mad at you or something. Hank is getting scared of what he hears."

Misty suggested, "Maybe he doesn't understand what he's hearing. You two should be separated. Are you going to see Hank in bed?"

Christine remarked, "Maybe later."

Misty advised, "Maybe you should not go through this."

Sherry put it a different way, "Maybe you should be poof-poof."

Christine confessed, "I think I've done that."

Misty added, "Hank could miss you."

Sherry asked, "Do you know if Hank is stopping?"

Christine answered, "I'm not allowed to but you'll get ready."

Sherry announced, "I do believe he's here."

Misty told her, "Do anything to protect me."

Sherry remarked, "Hank won't be able to hear us."

Christine replied, "You never know."

Misty confessed, "I would like to kiss him too. Right now he's all you got. Why is Hank over there?"

Christine commented, "He has to wait there too. For all his fans to get there. That's why we are waiting for him. He's a fair man. His name is Henry. And then it changed to Hank. Hank needs a ride down the road. He does like me and get off of everything. It makes him cough," with a coughing sound.

Misty admitted, "I can see him."

Sherry yelled at me, "Okay Hank nothing's there."

Christine stated, "Hank is a big smoker. I've seen him smoke just about anything. With no reason to quit."

Misty asked, "Does he have some memory loss?"

Christine answered, "He hates his memories."

Misty replied, "That's a vague answer."

Christine resounded, "It's a vague answer to him."

Sherry confessed, "I don't care for memories."

Christine added, "I don't think that's a problem. Hank has always been a smoker."

Sherry suggested, "Hank needs to piss off."

Christine admitted, "He is a drop-out."

Sherry remarked, "Jeez he is a bitter man."

Christine told them, "He is almost ready to die. If you ask me it's not fair. He's not finished yet."

Sherry asked, "You put up with this?" at the same time.

Then Sherry apologized, "Sorry about the mean thing."

Christine asked, "Is that where we're coming from? I might as well take Hank out of here."

Sherry guessed, "Hank might not think that."

Christine replied, "I can't go to him."

Sherry came back with, "Ain't that a shame."

Christine sang, "Hank won't be here that's a shame."

Sherry admitted, "Yes it is, I'm crying."

Misty asked, "What are we supposed to do with a bad egg?"

Christine sang, "He's not bad."

Misty remarked, "I already know."

Christine insisted, "Hungry and humpbacked is Hank, you got that."

A car horn honked in the parking lot and Sherry commented, "Honk if you're horny."

I would tell people I got that EVP and they wouldn't believe it until they heard it.

Misty stated, "I didn't hear what you said."

Sherry replied, "I was painting you I'm sorry."

Misty suggested, "Wait till we get home for that. Anyway is Hank coming?"

Sherry answered, "He's coming Tuesday now."

Christine corrected her, "You know that Hank is supposed to be here this evening."

Sherry commented, "He's supposed to be like that tomorrow."

Christine sang, "You better hope he is. All of his friends." Then she spoke, "All are supposed to come here."

Chester came back with, "Hank just told you what he thought."

Christine ordered, "Let go of me."

Chester replied, "You'll tell Hank everything."

Christine disagreed, "I wouldn't do that. Hank has to go through this."

Sherry directed, "Go to it."

Christine asked with music, "Does he have matches?" She then sang, "What does he sing? Tell me he won't do that anymore. Now Hank won't go, go to beat it."

Misty remarked, "That's long enough."

Christine half sang without music, "Okay I won't sing through that." She then sang, "I can't sing over. I'll be singing it to him. If he could just get rid of these people. I just don't think he will."

Chester sang, "Sing me a favorite song."

Sherry sang with music "But I miss that song too."

Christine sang, "One of these days well I won't sing. By myself. I have to go on a rocket ride. It's all gone to get me."

Chester sang, "But you know when he comes back."

Christine sang, "I believe in him. Everything's with me, got it too. You'll be on my life. Everything's go to. Give me your world.

I will be gone. We aren't long enough. We're just human. I can't tell her about anything. We burned it all anyhow. You'll be the last man to get me. He should not be rich. He should not be mad at all. Because it don't matter how he survives. Goth only knew that you'll be my faithful phoenix after all. But to be with me is not too real. He'll whine after he barely gets done. You got to when there's no hurry on the song. It's gonna be a long night. He just got to turn down his work. To turn his world a world. He just can't believe his children. Cannot believe that they won't believe him. How could they not believe in Hank? Come and take me away from this old bridge. I can see through the end. I guess Hank ain't too ready. He's been ready to have to move it. Sooner or later he'll have to move. But it will be much better that this. I don't know why Hank won't go find a better place. Maybe he's not yet. He knows something here now. Hank will do the best that he can."

Chester sang, "Make him strong as he can be."

Christine continued singing, "I'll be in the bathroom. But don't go out and find someone else. Y'all make me hug. Got this old feeling on top. In that old camera that's picking up us. But it will be over and I'll be gone. In California. We've got a numbered house. You must enter the world to me. Got to stop smoking outside. When you're standing with somebody. And get over her. And I'll be gone. He tried for a time to get help from no one. From what I've heard. I know you can't believe in." She then stated without singing, "That Hank can grow better than this. It's so safe around here. I can't see Hank anymore."

Sherry offered, "I can go see if Hank is over there."

Christine added, "I could go with her."

Sherry told them, "We'll be right back."

Christine asked, "That's okay if we come back with Hank?"

Misty answered, "Then you'll know that Hank's coming back here."

Christine replied, "But Hank would be better off going home."

Sherry suggested, "Let's go see if Hank is over there."

Christine continued, "But Hank will always return. I won't care if he comes here. As long as there is other people."

Sherry asked, "Are you over this thing with Hank?"

Christine remarked, "I'll just be glad when it's all over."

Sherry announced, "I think Hank is coming over here."

Christine explained, "I just want him to get over here. I could visit Hank if he lives here. Hank and I will be together very soon."

Sherry asked, "And then you'll live somewhere next to him?"

Christine admitted, "I would just come here to visit him. If he can get to a better Hank."

Sherry replied, "It's hard to imagine Hank better. Maybe it's safer if we save a room."

Christine told her, "I don't care how you do it."

Sherry half sang, "You will be through and you will be you. When you'll be you. Will you still want to stay here? When you come to see how hard he's working."

Chester remarked, "That would be interesting to go through with Hank."

Misty asked, "Is Hank ever coming back?"

Chester answered, "Yes Hank will come through when he's touring."

Christine commented, "But I've seen Hank when he's already naked. That's the way he likes to come to me."

Chester asked, "Don't you think Hank loves you?"

Christine confessed, "I think Hank is interested in me. I've barely been with him."

Sherry asked, "Then you'll be gone?"

Misty asked, "How did you make out with Hank when you went over there to him?"

Christine answered, "I can't help him serve what little he's serving. I know he'll always be there."

Misty asked, "Have you ever stayed with him when he is empty?"

A female spirit voice came in saying, "I think they're going now."

Sherry uttered, "We'll return."

Christine stated, "Hank is still coming home. There's nothing wrong. Don't you think he made it here? Then Hank can be where he used to go."

Misty replied, "Well then I'm glad I got him here."

Chester asked, "What do you think of Mister Hank? Did you think he'd stay here?"

Christine commented, "Same time he'll be here every day."

Misty asked, "You say Hank will come this way through here?"

Christine told her, "Hank is always been coming through here."

Misty explained, "We got to stop this if we are going to get out of here."

Chester asked, "Is that the pump house here? I would love to get out of here."

Misty asked, "Is that the better way that he's going? Did you like the serious talk we did right now?"

Christine answered, "It's so nice that you said so."

Chester replied, "Guess the proof is in there."

Christine remarked, "Now he has something to listen to. At his home."

Chester ordered, "The both of you have to go."

Christine asked, "Can't we just go back out there?"

Chester admitted, "I won't like it if you stay there."

Christine added, "Hank will be there."

Misty stated, "I don't know where Hank will be."

Sherry explained, "First they've got to go away from that spot there."

Christine told them, "It'll take about that long with Hank. Now Hank has always been good about doing what he says. I'm going to play a song. Hank just won't be going without me. You've got so many parts to play. Now look at what Hank is always smoking. I'd like to have him be a better Hank. Hank will be coming here. And very soon you'll see. Hank will be a better man than he is. Can you see me next to him? If you don't like cooking."

Sherry asked, "Will you take Hank to the bathroom with you?"

Christine answered, "Yes and back to his room."

Misty directed, "Leave some space in here."

Sherry asked, "Do you see Hank coming?"

Christine announced, "We better get ready."

Chester remarked, "Hank already said he's coming. What's the matter with that fucking thing?"

Sherry pointed out, "If you like a better Hank. Then would you like him better than Hank?"

Christine replied, "Hank is better than most I've met. Bastard... wait a minute. Hank tell us how to fix this thing."

Sherry asked, "Do you really think Hank would remember this?"

Christine told her, "I think Hank could tell me what to do." The sound cleared up. "He made his own invention."

Sherry commented, "You didn't have to tell me. I already knew about it."

Misty suggested, "Then let's get you out of here."

Sherry asked, "Are you going to let them do this?"

Christine stated, "Hank is really coming. Hank won't expect anything. And Hank won't give up anything."

Misty asked, "Does he have to give up everything he does?"

Christine answered, "Almost everything he does."

Chester remarked, "Everything he does is dirty. He doesn't heal himself at all."

Misty asked, "What's that like?"

Chester answered, "He doesn't care if he lives at all. All these people care about Hank. But he doesn't care about himself. Everything he does is wrong."

Misty replied, "I've never heard of this before."

Chester told her, "I think everything he does is wrong."

Misty confirmed, "And you want us to scare him."

Chester challenged her, "If you think you can."

Sherry commented, "It's impossible to care about an old man."

Misty asked, "When does Hank come?"

Chester asked, "Does it matter if Hank's coming?"

Misty answered, "It is about him coming."

Christine remarked, "There goes Santa Claus. But maybe I praise on that."

Misty guessed, "Maybe Hank will get over there."

Sherry pointed out, "There's Hank right over there. Do you see him? Hank come over here."

Misty ordered, "Hank come here."

Christine replied, "I will go play with Hank. I could just stay over there."

Chester commented, "I'll go wherever. I'm going over to Eddie's house."

Misty asked, "Is Hank welcome?"

I started picking up some people walking by.

Misty remarked, "I can't see through all these people."

Sherry asked, "Have you had it with all these people?"

Misty admitted, "I know there's not much we can do. If I don't I'll see later. I need Hank to come over here."

Sherry stated, "Hank will soon be coming, stay longing."

Misty explained, "It's impossible to be longing. Hank just has to go through this anyway. Hank's not doing what he's supposed to so he's going to. He has to go through this courtroom thing."

Sherry suggested, "You will like Hank better. Let's just get this going."

Misty asked, "Does he know what we're doing?"

Sherry answered, "No he doesn't know about that."

Christine said from a distance, "I am coming."

Sherry called over to her, "But now we're doing it."

Misty corrected her, "Damn we won't go till Hank can hear."

Sherry asked, "Do we have to have him here?"

Misty replied, "If you want to do something."

Christine announced, "Hank is coming now."

Sherry confessed, "I can't stand to wait for Hank. Hank has been here before. If you're doing anything. I'm out of everything."

Misty told her, "Sherry you wanted to. How are you going to deal with Hank?"

Sherry replied, "Easy I'll make friends."

The Gopie remarked, "I hope you'll be freedom."

Sherry insisted, "Not with this. What if you amuse Hank? I just don't agree with Hank."

Misty asked, "Is Hank supposed to go here next?"

Sherry asked, "Are you almost through with me?"

The Gopie commented, "It makes her feel good."

Sherry stated, "I told Mister Hank. Hank won't believe us. Hank won't get out, I told him that."

Misty replied, "That's a stupid answer. I can't believe you want to do like this. Wait for me here will you?"

Sherry sang, "That's where I want."

Misty asked, "Can you be quite?"

Christine offered, "I'll stay with you if Hank can go with me."

Sherry remarked, "I'd rather he did not."

Christine told her, "Hank needs some spirit from you. Can you make it for Hank?"

Sherry replied, "Hank used to party a lot."

Christine asked, "Is that your final answer? Can you see what I can see?"

Misty commented, "You're not as stupid as I thought."

Christine ordered, "Tell me that you like his store."

Sherry sang, "Think you better not push me." She spoke, "Hank won't be here."

Christine suggested, "I'll go find him."

Sherry added, "I'll be your sister."

Christine replied, "That's what Hank would want us to do."

Misty pointed out, "You're good friends with her."

Sherry stated, "If you'll come back here."

Christine asked, "Can I bring my boyfriend with me?"

Sherry answered, "It doesn't matter with him."

Misty remarked, "I love it when you feel happy."

Sherry admitted, "I know he will be here."

Misty guessed, "You like to do that to her."

Sherry replied, "That's nothing like I do."

Misty commented, "That's what you did right there. Lying through your teeth. Just what are you doing here? You want to be guilty I'm sure."

Sherry confessed, "Close to Hank's back okay. Close enough to feel good. We like the Hank."

Misty resounded, "You just told me you didn't like the Hank."

Sherry clarified, "I don't like it when he's been partying. He's been here before."

Misty instructed, "You will stay for Hank. If you really like Hank."

Sherry confirmed, "I will be there."

Misty ordered, "Then you want to come back here."

Sherry suggested, "Let me tell you something," with a truck going by. She stated, "I just thought about Hank on something."

Christine commented, "I can't believe Sherry would do this."

Sherry went on, "If Hank were to do anything. I believe he would work. In top brain."

Misty replied, "That's not going to make Hank mess up. He doesn't have to do the two for two. It seems like you're looking for a mistake. That has to do with Hank."

Sherry stated, "There is so much he will have to do."

Misty told her, "I think you're through."

Sherry confessed, "I just want to miss him."

232

Misty insisted, "No, meet him outside. I think Hank will work out. I hear the bell."

The clock tower chimed.

Coming out of the chiming Misty said, "I think Hank will work here."

Sherry commented, "I think it's pitiful here."

Misty warned, "I think you better watch what you are saying. I think that Hank is going to be here," with a person laughing near the phone booth. She then stated, "I think they're coming over here."

Christine guessed, "I think Hank went to the bathroom. I could tell Hank about who you are. Hey Hank come over here. I can't believe Hank would do like that."

The Gopie replied, "I can't wait for Hank, to see Hank come."

Misty asked, "Are we okay here?"

Mark interjected, "I never met an asshole. Tell Hank that I did whatever. As soon as he gets out of the bathroom."

Misty announced, "Two minutes for Hank."

Christine called me, "Hey Hank, right here."

Misty remarked, "You don't do the favorite thing that I do."

Christine asked, "What does Misses Cat do?"

Misty admitted, "I like to flick them on their ear. You haven't been with us very long."

Christine confessed, "I don't care what you do. I only care about what I have to do. I have to wait for Henry."

The Gopie stated, "Hank's with a lot of people. Maybe they would like measure right now over here." He was talking about EMF readings.

Misty guessed, "I think they would let us do whatever."

Mark replied, "I think we'll go around. Before we do this thing with Hank. Everything will look a little different. I'll take the part that Hank won't like. Hank is getting ready to come over."

Christine tried to excuse herself, "I have to go with Hank."

Misty asked, "How are you supposed to be with Hank?"

Christine answered, "You might think I'm with Hank. That's what I said yesterday."

Misty asked, "What is Hank here for?"

Christine replied, "That's what I need to find out. Everything we told Hank. He liked what we were saying. I can't quite say if he would come here. If I wasn't here."

Misty admitted, "I never wanted to get off till this thing goes on."

Mark remarked, "I like what you have to say about Hank though."

Christine told him, "I'll talk to you more about that later. I knew Hank would come here when the little birdie talked to him. And now the bastard won't go away." That last line was so faint I knew I wasn't supposed to hear it.

Misty commented, "That's not a very polite answer."

Christine asked, "Does that mean I'm wrong?"

Misty answered, "I know what we got, here we go."

Mark asked, "You guys are ready now?"

Misty directed, "I know it's not the best of both worlds. But let's try to hold this thing together. I think Hank is almost here."

Someone in the parking lot revved their engine and peeled out covering four seconds of EVP's.

Sherry stated, "I don't know where you put the book."

Christine replied, "I wanna move past Hank."

Misty asked, "What are you mad at him for?"

Christine answered, "He's making a bad choice."

Misty disagreed, "I think you made a bad call."

Christine snapped back, "In the bathroom he did. He put his pants on backwards."

Mark gave his opinion, "I think it's about all the plans you have to worry about too."

Christine remarked, "I have to go with Hank."

Misty asked, "Will you never be like me?"

Christine recalled, "Maybe you already told me that. I'm just with Hank."

Sherry complained, "Hank won't be going right here. He can't help himself get off the cigarettes."

Misty advised, "There's an answer to that question too. Make him can't stand to smoke."

Sherry told her, "I think they already did."

Christine said from a distance, "Hey Hank is coming."

Misty warned, "Hope you are all ready for this."

Christine confessed, "I'm scared now."

Misty assured her, "Christine don't be scared. You made this so good."

Sherry added, "We've been with you all along."

Christine replied, "I know but Hank is coming."

Sherry stated, "I think your Uncle Tom is going to be here."

Christine announced, "I think Hank is right over there."

Misty explained, "Let's get ready to do this. I will always take care of things. Things that you would never. Expect to happen."

Christine started, "Thanks for doing this everyone."

Misty directed, "Let's go to page one. All the people are here."

Mark asked, "Is that okay with Hank?"

Misty replied, "Happy birthday to you."

Christine remarked, "I want to take the day off. What am I supposed to do?. I'll spend the day with Hank."

Misty instructed, "Hey Mark it's your turn."

Mark asked, "What are you going to do with Hank? When will you do that? I don't see Hank coming."

Christine commented, "Hank is on a stick."

The Gopie came back with, "That's not very nice."

Christine replied, "I'm just horny that's all."

Misty asked, "How are you gonna get some of that?"

Christine answered, "I don't know if he will."

The Gopie suggested, "Give him time to do that."

Christine asked, "Does that mean I can go with Hank?"

We heard Gary say, "There has always been a bridge."

Mark testified, "That's what Hank called me."

Christine insisted, "That's what Hank wouldn't do."

The Gopie replied, "Most of that is care about the wedding."

Sherry uttered, "Guess who's coming right here."

The Gopie remarked, "The walk is not very clean."

Misty agreed, "Boy is that true."

Mark asked, "Who goes through that fucking way right now? You don't bother with that."

The Gopie admitted, "I don't care about little things like that. Go with Hank if you can find a small bridge."

Sherry exclaimed, "Get out of here! With Hank."

Christine submitted, "I will go where you tell me."

Misty confirmed, "I think you understand that."

Christine offered, "I'll try to get Hank smoking out of smoking that too."

Sherry stated, "Hank should be here."

Christine confessed, "Hank won't do anything I tell him."

Misty instructed, "Bring Hank back with you, back to the hospital. Doctor Billy wants to see him."

Christine agreed, "I can do that with Hank. I think mostly Hank could hear this."

Doctor Billy ordered, "Get the pulse anyway."

Christine replied, "I can try Doctor."

Doctor Billy told her, "I could heal Hank."

Christine admitted, "I don't know if Hank wants to go through that with me."

Doctor Billy warned, "I will ask you both if I have to do this. Hank has to stop what he's doing. And bring the fire out."

In my astrological make up there's a lot of the fire element.

Christine confirmed, "I will make him do that too."

Sherry directed, "Tell Hank you're right here now."

Christine remarked, "I know I have to do that. But I have to ask if I can go back there?"

Misty asked, "Do you know about the meeting?"

Christine asked, "What's the meeting all about?"

Misty suggested, "Maybe you should come, I'll take you there."

Christine commented, "I have to go with Hank somewhere."

Misty asked, "Is there somewhere else you can go to?"

Christine answered, "I have to do this with Hank first."

Misty asked, "Can you bring him over here?"

Christine declared, "He might be going into the hospital."

The Gopie asked, "What would Hank be arrested for?"

Christine insisted, "He did not do anything."

Misty mentioned, "I think Hank would sue me."

Christine replied, "I think Hank would go peacefully like that."

Misty asked, "What do you think Hank should be arrested for?"

Mark answered, "Hank should be arrested for his smoking."

Christine remarked, "He can't be arrested for smoking. Maybe some other stuff."

Misty asked, "Why don't you stay with him okay?"

Christine asked, "Are you still mad at Hank?"

Sherry stated, "I just have to say something right here. Soon you'll be with Hank when he's arrested. Then what will you go through to be with Hank?"

Christine asked, "What do you think I'm doing here?"

Sherry insisted, "The police won't miss him."

Christine admitted, "I know he hasn't been an angel."

Sherry boasted, "I think my arrest is good."

Christine said emphatically, "Hank will not be arrested!"

Misty asked, "Do you hear what you're saying?"

Christine confessed, "I can't stand to see Hank go through that."

The Gopie explained, "But I think that's the way it's supposed to be."

Sherry agreed, "I think Hank should be arrested."

Christine replied, "But Hank is supposed to come here."

Misty declared, "We're not going to take him anymore."

Christine reminded her, "I thought you agreed to take Hank."

Misty told her, "I think we changed our mind. It will be alright. I know you've been expecting us to help Hank."

Christine started, "It doesn't matter what I thi..."

The Gopie interrupted with, "No it doesn't matter what you demand."

Christine, in her little girl voice pointed out, "I need that bottle. To make you actually see. The walls need vacuuming."

Misty replied, "I think you missed what Hank did."

Christine stated, "He went into the bathroom with me. Right after that he went home and took a bath."

Misty confirmed, "I know Hank was doing that."

Christine related, "I know Hank didn't do anything. After that he just fucking laid down."

Misty remarked, "I knew what he was doing."

Sherry disagreed, "That's not true. That's not the way it's supposed to be."

The Gopie asked, "And what did Hank actually do?"

Christine sang with music, "I could tell you now."

Sherry asked, "What do you think Hank would say?"

Christine spoke with music, "Oh wow." She sang, "I don't believe this."

The Gopie ordered, "Tell her what Mikey's supposed to do."

Mark told her, "Cut down all the fucking trees around here."

Christine screamed, "Why don't you just fucking do that!"

Misty stated loudly, "Mark will go!"

Christine commented, "Hank could only think a monster would do something like that."

Sherry denied, "It's not me that wanted to do that."

Christine spoke, "I talked to Henry about something." She sang, "That he better quit smoking." Then she excused herself with, "I've got to go where Hank is right now."

Sherry admitted, "But I think Hank is still just an asshole."

The Gopie replied, "I don't think you can do the things that Hank can do."

Sherry remarked, "I'm just saying that."

Christine confirmed, "I know what you're saying. I can talk to Hank about this."

Misty suggested, "Then that's what you should do."

Sherry asked, "Do you think Hank's an asshole?"

Misty related, "Hank can only be true."

The Gopie asked, "Can you be serious about Hank? I can tell when you've been with Hank."

Mark commented, "I'll be glad when you go back there with him."

Sherry stated, "I know what he's doing."

Mark asked, "Why aren't you over there?"

Misty expressed, "We need Hank to come over."

Christine confessed, "I have no idea what else to do."

Sherry asked, "Will Hank move in?"

The Gopie answered, "It could be better than you think," with Sherry saying, "Louder," over "better."

Christine announced, "I think I'll have to move here too."

Misty started, "I think we'll have to go with."

Christine finished, "All the lights are clear."

Mark asked, "How am I supposed to get in there?" He half sang, "If I stand right here."

Sherry sang, "If you could fucking see what I see," with Mark saying, "I don't care."

The Gopie warned, "I told you not to do that."

Sherry replied, "I feel free to do that."

Christine remarked, "I can't believe you blew that part."

Sherry sang, "That's how we do it when we're screwed."

Misty sang, "But then we go when we're told."

Gary came in giving the location of the land markers.

Christine sang, "Here they come now." She said, "Keep the magick mirror."

Gary started telling about the lamppost.

After Gary's first line Sherry commented, "It's all been done before. They all could have pictures of the mirror. Including Hank."

Mark suggested, "We should've had a boat there. Don't you see that boat coming?"

Christine answered, "That's what you should go down and play."

Misty ordered, "Now somebody come over here."

Sherry announced, "They're almost to us."

Christine guessed, "It seems they're fucking broken."

Misty told her, "You shouldn't of said that."

Christine sang, "In a time I'll wish for you."

Mark asked, "Do we actually have to say he will?"

Misty replied, "I don't think you have to."

Sherry sang, "And if it's cloudy."

Christine sang, "Hank won't be cloudy." She stated, "I think they're coming."

Sherry half sang, "Did you hear all that?"

Misty sang, "That'll be something."

Christine remarked, "I say. You're not supposed to be. Going away mad."

Gary came in with, "This is an original phone booth."

Christine announced, "Hank is back."

Gary started the phone booth story. The tour felt the phone booth.

Christine directed, "Now give the play boy."

We then heard the people on the tour talking about the phone booth.

Sherry informed the spirits, "They're talking about all of this."

Misty suggested, "Let's get started."

Mark admitted, "I have to go to the bedroom."

Gary instructed Micah on taking some pictures.

Sherry pointed out, "There's the asshole."

Gary said, "People come over from London and take the tour tell me."

Sherry stated, "We're all gone," at the end of Gary talking.

Mark confessed, "I made down some."

Christine asked, "All of it?"

Misty asked, "What is this?"

Christine mentioned, "They've got that now."

Sherry gave a reading, "I think we're about thirty now."

Christine instructed, "Turn it down some," as the machine started to vibrate.

The Gopie ordered, "Stay by Hank to do that."

Sherry replied, "We're all done."

We heard Gary again as he said, "We were supposed to do a séance at a place called the Golden Unicorn."

Christine warned, "Hank will see."

Gary said, "Two days before we did the séance."

Mark declared, "Hank's over here. Time to get dirty."

Gary said, "We were on a tour like this," with two notes from a piano. He went on to describe a picture taken of the phone booth.

Near the end of the description Christine directed, "We need to get this done. We have to get to Hank quickly."

Mark admitted, "I should move over there."

The Gopie remarked, "Hank won't believe this is happening."

Gary came back with a line.

Mark decided, "I should move this over here."

The Gopie asked, "Is Hank really ready?"

Mark answered, "He's got to be pretty ready."

The Gopie admitted, "Twenty year old me go through what he has. Doubt he has but he's got to get a publisher."

Misty confessed, "I think we can."

The Gopie stated, "Me thinks the Melbourne thing."

Mark commented, "That and the money from Marsha feels good. How can we get money from Carol? If we don't lie and fibbing about everything he says. Now the people say. They will take the third line. We need warp speed to do this."

Sherry asked, "Don't you think we're out here goofin' off?"

The Gopie insisted, "All this masterpiece has to be in."

Mark announced, "He's coming here."

The Gopie asked, "I can't let them take me first, do you understand?"

Sherry remarked, "It seems to be popular."

Misty instructed, "I think you better go."

Sherry resounded, "I'm ready to go."

Gary gave his guarantee, "I don't guarantee you'll get ghost pictures but I do guarantee that if don't take pictures you won't."

Christine declared, "Hank is coming. I don't think Hank will come back here."

The Gopie asked, "Is that Hank's thing right here? It's right here."

The sound disappeared like the microphone was covered.

He asked into the recorder, "Do you think I'm just Brad that has come here?"

Christine asked, "Do you think he has come here having fun? That he had to be here. Are you surprised?"

Mark answered, "To find him here."

The Gopie stated with Christine's help, "I am not just gonna be sitting and leave you alone."

Christine started with a guitar, "I can make my bed if I."

Mark asked, "Why do you sing that? That's Betty's stuff."

Christine sang, "But now you got me. Deal with my shit," when Gary was talking. "Then you'll learn to back off." Gary was still talking. Even when only Gary talked the guitar was playing.

The Gopie directed, "Make the exposure complete."

Mark suggested, "Time to go with me."

The Gopie asked, "Is that the end of the story?"

Misty asked, "Christine, are you coming? Hank has some pictures."

Gary said, "Step right out here."

Christine guessed, "I think that Hank will go with me. I can't turn the bridge like that. I think Hank is coming after me."

The Gopie assured her, "We all get scared like that."

Mark admitted, "I'm scared of the night train." There are no train tracks in Lake Havasu City.

The Gopie instructed, "Easy there boy. Plug that in here for that. That would be the second driveway."

Gary said, "What it was, was a truck."

Misty replied, "I've seen it."

Gary said, "That would drive down towards that side of the bridge."

Christine asked, "Any ideas about Hank?"

The Gopie answered, "That could be."

Gary gave a couple of lines about deaths on the bridge in modern times.

Misty announced, "It's Tuesday."

The Gopie stated, "Hank won't get hooked on this. Donna told me that."

Misty directed, "Stay with us."

We made it down to the water and Gary pointed out where the hooks used to be. Gary said, "They could get as many as fifteen bodies per hook."

Christine remarked, "I wonder if he'd like that."

Gary gave another line about the hooks.

Christine instructed, "We can't get off without Misty. What kind of bottle is that?"

I walked over to the stairs and said, "I came here a few days ago and was wondering if you found anything. I haven't had a chance to look for it."

Christine started, "Just go around with me. Go around back."

I interrupted with, "Say anything you'd like to say, I'd love to hear it," with Christine saying, "I'd like to go back there Hank."

Sherry disagreed, "But he won't like this."

I said, "No matter what you want to say I will not take it the wrong way."

Sherry sang, "You already said I was done right here."

Christine replied, "He did not know you were here."

Sherry argued, "But Hank just asked me."

The Gopie stated, "It's not his jury right here."

Sherry snapped back, "I already know that Gary."

I said, "I asked about dark spirits."

Christine ordered, "Not right now."

I said, "It wasn't here but it appears to be active wherever we are," with an electronic static that only they could cause.

Together Christine and the Gopie remarked, "That's not cool."

I said, "I was wondering about that."

Misty asked, "What does he know?"

I asked, "Think of anymore?"

Misty declared, "People busy."

I said, "You answered for me before I'm sorry I haven't opened for it yet."

For the first time there was silence on this tour.

I said, "Then I'm going to gain."

The Gopie replied, "That is true."

I said, "I want to know."

The Gopie added, "But he can't remember."

I said, "I worry about this."

Christine guessed, "I think that he's done."

I asked, "Would you like me to pick up early since I get more?" with Christine saying, "That should be all for now Hank," behind me.

The Gopie explained, "That is what the spirits stand for. We believe he may have betrayed Jesus."

I said, "That's okay."

Misty stated, "But we believe in Hank."

Christine called to me, "Hey Hank we're over here."

The Gopie suggested, "Maybe he knows about this."

Misty remarked, "It can't be fine. That he should be here."

Gary came back in telling about the bridge.

Misty commented, "Hank just went off."

Gary said, "If you look up here."

244

Christine announced, "He's bringing it."

Gary started talking about the stones in the bridge.

Christine sang with music, "He can't be a fool. Why won't Hank go with me over there?"

Sherry sang, "Maybe he's just the one."

Christine sang, "This is my song. And so far told. And a bucket on you."

Mark asked with the music still playing, "Did you find a piece of pie there Hank?"

Christine explained, "He won't give a guy an answer," as the music stops.

Gary came in with, "It's better safe."

Christine ordered, "Let's go Hank. I can hear the tour. Do you know what you're doing? Do you think they're coming over here? I can't stand to wait around."

Mark insisted, "We're not bringing the machine over there."

Gary came in again with, "Mainly the bridge was black."

Christine demanded, "You stay away from her."

Gary and the tour came in clearer as they approached us.

Christine pointed out, "There's a place for Hank and me."

Misty suggested, "Stay with Gary and me."

Gary told about looking for stories about the bridge.

Christine agreed, "Hank you were right."

Gary said another line very near us.

Christine remarked, "Now there's room for me and Hank."

As Gary went into the Museum Tape story Mark announced, "Hank's here."

At a pause in the story Christine replied, "But Hank is hungry."

At the next pause Mark echoed, "Boy is Hank hungry."

When he paused next Christine directed, "Keep it coming."

The Gopie declared, "Not with Hank."

At another pause Christine told them, "Hank won't like it."

Gary got near the end of the story before he paused again and Christine suggested, "Maybe Hank should go home. It's not safe being here."

Misty came back with, "Maybe you should go back with Hank."

Sherry reminded them, "Maybe Hank's got to be here."

Christine stated, "I could take Hank back with me."

Misty replied, "That would be better."

Sherry added, "Now we can do this whole thing, yes."

Misty announced, "Steve's here. Make Hank turn around."

Sherry explained, "That's what we mean when we say. Hank should not live here."

Christine related, "That's why Sherry might be where you go."

Sherry ordered, "Now tell Hank to come."

Christine remarked, "I am too busy walking with Hank right now," as the traffic noise increased like we were approaching street level.

I turned the recorder off and stayed a few minutes at the statues with the tour group. I then went ahead of the tour across the bridge and got set up at the passage door.

Turning the recorder on I got another song, "Tell me you'll get over me."

Christine mentioned, "Now we can hold the court here better."

Misty admitted, "Dan said I talk better. Over here," with an extra voice over her.

Christine reminded her, "You know Hank's supposed to be with me."

Sherry replied, "And if it's now it never fails."

Misty asked, "You'll be here?"

Sherry added, "Back where we began."

Christine answered, "All that green will be here."

Sherry remarked, "But I can't stand the things she does."

246

Christine complained, "It never fails she ditched me. It never fails. Hank would like to be here if he can. Hank will be a better man."

Sherry explained, "I think he'd make a bad Erwin. Now let me explain. Mark has seen him. Make a sandwich. Make dessert. When he's done with that. He makes it again."

Christine pointed out, "That's what he's got to make it over here."

Misty suggested, "Maybe Hank should eat what he's got to make."

Christine asked, "How can you judge him like that? I'm sorry Hank can't talk."

I said, "Hello again."

Christine replied, "Hank is talking to me."

Mark commented, "You should find Hank's story."

Sherry added, "And destroy Hank with it."

Misty stated, "I believe I've seen it. I think we're about done with this."

Christine uttered, "I got a bad feeling."

I said, "I haven't been able to listen to everything you said last time."

Christine remarked, "I was afraid Hank would say something."

I said, "I would like to know if there is something you would like to say."

Christine announced, "Hank has complete trust in me."

Misty insisted, "But I don't think Hank should live here. Maybe there's another bridge."

Christine disagreed, "You have to let Hank stay."

Sherry reminded her, "That's what the girl decided."

Christine complained, "But now Hank has to meet the maker."

Misty informed her, "He told me peace goes in peace."

Christine declared, "That would be like Hank. That's why he should be here."

Misty admitted, "I've got to give a hand to him. He's a very nice spirit."

Christine replied, "You don't seem to show it."

I said, "There is an interesting picture I got last night."

Christine guessed, "Maybe he got a picture of you or something."

Misty asked, "Does he always take pictures?"

Christine answered, "Man does he ever take pictures."

Misty asked, "Has he got it?"

I asked, "Who was that?"

Christine remarked, "I think that was Misty. I think you're getting a job for Hank. It says right here you can do that."

Misty came back with, "A job is a sacred experience."

Sherry ordered, "David, get over here."

David stated, "I live right here. Hank was right here."

Misty asked, "Did something happen right here David?"

David testified, "Hank started to move in here. Hank really started moving in."

Christine argued, "That's not something Hank would do."

I said, "I was once told here, that it would be very easy to be in trouble."

Christine asked, "Does that sound like a criminal to you?"

With Mark's help Sherry guessed, "He's not amused."

I said, "Trouble in."

Mark asked, "What are you trying to do?"

I asked, "With orbs that we get pictures of?"

Sherry remarked, "I think Hank is a bastard."

Misty replied, "He's not very scared of us."

Sherry complained, "But Hank won't respect us."

David commented, "Cause I can't believe I'm doing this with you."

Mark instructed, "Yeah but you talk when you're spoken to."

David uttered, "I wonder why I said that."

Mark declared, "Time to take David back up there."

Misty stated, "I haven't seen Hank to prove your idea."

Mark told her, "He's not anything like what he's supposed to be. They're calling over to me."

The Gopie started, "Hank," and Misty finished, "We could guess about him."

I said, "People would get really interested and we want to survive."

Christine announced, "Here he goes again."

I said, "Pictures of full body spirits."

Misty proclaimed, "We do not believe you."

I said, "Like what I got here."

Misty confessed, "I have no idea what he's talking about."

I asked, "Is there a way we can continue to do this?"

Christine answered, "Yes I'm here."

I said, "So people will understand that they continue to live on."

Mark admitted, "I know he's got their best in mind. But he's done about now. Are his feelings strong? All about her. I know he comes to see Christine here."

Misty commented, "But Hank has not been coming here so long."

Sherry added, "But I saw him here last night. After this he will do it all the same."

Mark asked, "Got any idea where?"

I coughed.

Misty asked, "Is that him coughing again?"

I said, "I'm going to leave the recorder right here," Mark sang, "God is everywhere," as I said, "If there is anymore that you want to say. I got it right there."

Mark asked, "Do you think he'll like the song I sang?"

The Gopie remarked, "I wouldn't say that."

Christine answered, "It could make Hank really mad. But Hank could get over it."

Mark suggested, "I think he should be ready for it."

Sherry replied, "Hank would get mad about anything."

Christine explained, "He doesn't need to know God is everywhere. I should take Hank back over there with me."

Sherry repeated, "Maybe Hank should go to another bridge."

Misty told her, "Already said that."

Sherry commented, "I'll be happy after Hank's gone."

Christine disagreed, "I don't think he should be gone."

Misty asked, "Is Hank over there?"

Christine called me, "Hank get back over here."

Misty stated, "Hank can be wherever he wants to. I think Hank should go to another bridge."

Christine started, "Hank should be where everything..."

Misty quickly asked, "Is he a bad person?"

Christine answered, "He is not a bad person at all. He understands everything. That he's ever. Ever said before. If there is a bad person. It won't be Hank. You want another bridge to have..."

The Gopie cut her off with, "That's what we got right here."

Christine again started, "But that's when he wasn't..."

The Gopie interrupted, "We all can see everything here."

Sherry replied, "I see a boat."

The Gopie remarked, "We cannot see through Hank though. Especially when he's being Hank."

Mark asked, "Did you hear how he does every day?"

Christine stated, "That's the only thing wrong with him."

Misty commented, "If that's true what I say stops right now."

Mark asked, "You ever seen Hank high?"

Christine declared, "That's nothing to do with Hank's spirit."

Mark guessed, "Days can go by and he'll still be doing it."

Sherry added, "Hank will never change that. Hank will never be. Ever sober."

Misty asked, "Does Hank ever purchase that?"

Christine explained, "Hank never purchases that. Hank should not be judged like that. Can I tell y'all something? Hank never purchases that stuff."

Sherry uttered, "I still don't like Hank."

Misty mentioned, "Hank would do better to stay off that."

Mark replied, "I told you Hank was high."

The Gopie disagreed, "It's not like that at all. I've seen him lots of times up here." He sang, "Does anybody wanna hear? Hank likes to party that's how it started with you guys. Don't mean I started with all my friends. Yes you bring I started."

Mark sang, "And I wish you're right. You'll be my boss here anytime. Was Hank here anytime without it? How does he seem on the other side?"

The Gopie answered, "Hank is sunburned."

Mark confessed, "That would be breaking my heart. But I'll break his heart. I don't think he's got the spirit. Behind your back here. We all drop him. I wish I knew one. I think he won't be sorry about it. He won't have to worry about it. We've all become extremely happy. Can you talk to Hank about that?" with help from an ecstatic Sherry.

Misty asked, "Can you tell Hank about this? Let's hear about everything," with Sherry singing in the background.

The singing continued over Christine saying, "I had a dream about Hank last night."

The singing was also on top of Misty saying, "I can hear that song."

Christine yelled, "I know," over the top of the singing.

Sherry admitted, "It makes me happy. Hank won't work on the bridge now." She asked, "Should I tell Hank right here?"

Christine answered, "Hank can't hear clear. I will take him home. Remember Hank still comes here."

Sherry asked, "Everyday will he be here?"

Christine replied, "Yes Hank will be here most every day."

Sherry asked, "Will you ask him please not to come around me?"

Christine remarked, "Hank likes you."

Sherry asked, "Why am I supposed to do this? With that asshole."

Christine asked, "You've had fun here haven't you?"

Sherry uttered, "It doesn't make much difference."

Christine explained, "It makes Hank feel good. Wanna make Hank feel good? You're gonna still see Hank."

Sherry confessed, "I still feel that I hate him."

Christine asked, "Did he do something? Like he did to me?"

Sherry answered, "It's just everything."

Christine apologized, "I'm sorry, he hasn't been feeling too good."

Sherry argued, "He will be a perfect angel for you."

Misty suggested, "You better bring him back here."

Christine confirmed, "I will go and fetch him."

Misty instructed, "We won't have to put Hank over here."

Sherry asked, "Is that gonna bring me right here?"

Misty admitted, "I'll have to think on that."

Sherry mentioned, "If it's too fast we're going through everything."

Misty ordered, "That's for you to do all after. We can all come back. He's supposed to be coming right back."

Sherry started, "But I can already see something. I cannot wait to get started. If Hank was here you'd be like..."

Misty interrupted, "Never mind about it."

Christine came back and stated, "Hank was judged last night. And that's bad he's not going to be here. He could be a help here. That's a journey. Hank needs me. If he needs me to come back another day."

Misty asked, "Have been able to talk to Hank?"

Christine answered, "I just told him what happened like that."

Misty replied, "I'm glad he got the message all right. Sherry you got the pencil ready?"

Sherry confirmed, "I'm ready with the snakeskin too. I just need to write down what I did."

Christine told her, "Know that you did stuff here too. Hank too."

Sherry stated, "I'll stand for whatever."

Christine warned, "You'll fucking die when I get home. And you'll feel like I'm a fake when I'm with you. You'll be such a mess."

Sherry suggested, "Hank should come here or something."

Christine commented, "He will go back in there. And you're stupid about Hank. He has already been in here. He was fucking living here. Hank has been here before. When he invented the machine that we have. That's how he knows what we are. And he knows just about everything. About some people living forever. These are the things that Hank already knew. He makes a spirit feel like they have known him. Hank has always been around here. And you think poor of him. Let me stay in the women's bathroom. Until I can find a good place for Hank. Maybe you should think before you give up on him. Damn you made a thousand spirits angry. You made the spirits angry. Cause you won't accept Hank. Hank could do this. Hank really does have the spirit. Hank does everything. That you think that I do. Hank won't believe all of this. He will pass this over."

The Gopie remarked, "He should put this down on paper. And this would make a very good book."

Christine replied, "He has the talent."

Sherry asked, "Is that forever?" Then she sang, "Oh if he does then I'll beat myself to death."

Mark gave the reading from the machine, "Seven eighty."

Misty stated, "Hank has been guilty in here. I can't believe that you stayed in any kind of place."

Christine snapped back, "Yes, I do."

Sherry apologized, "I'm sorry that I started all of this. Feels like I'm retarded now."

Christine asked, "Do you realize you shouldn't have started? What you don't believe you saw in every single moment?"

Misty guessed, "I don't think it would make it different."

Mark claimed, "You still have the weekend. That you could still undo that."

Christine asked, "Can't you see that I'm with Hank? Maybe he ought to take a picture. He could put the pictures in the empty journal that he's making."

Misty asked, "Has he got pictures of you?"

Christine answered, "He's got pictures of all of us. I'm sure he's got pictures you too. Just ask him."

Misty asked, "Should I ask if he got pictures of you?"

Christine replied, "I don't think it really matters."

Sherry remarked, "If you got him to talk to you it would matter. He is strange like that. Have you ever met him? There is no one else like that."

Misty confessed, "I can't tell if I am with him."

Sherry instructed, "You have to be with him and tell him."

Christine added, "Then you have to tell him something."

Sherry finished, "And he might give you an answer."

Christine asked, "And would you please talk to Hank whatever you think? I think he will know what you're doing."

Misty asked, "Am I going to have to dance with him this year?"

Christine answered, "It could be if you really wanted to test him."

Misty directed, "Wait till he comes close to me then."

Christine commented, "Hank has to come back here for this thing."

Misty asked, "Whatever shall I do?"

Christine told her, "It's easy to answer all the questions that Hank has."

Misty asked, "You have any idea what to say?"

Christine replied, "Hank did you see what Sherry started?"

Sherry remarked, "We've been through that."

Christine argued, "I don't think it should have been started. What do you think I should do about Hank?"

Misty ordered, "You can always meet Hank over here. I can see clearly now."

Sherry suggested, "We've got to clear the air about this."

Christine asked, "What are you trying to say?"

Sherry answered, "I think you knew what I was saying. What are you going to do about Hank?"

Christine instructed, "You shouldn't speak after what you already started."

Sherry confessed, "I know I shouldn't have instigated what I started."

Christine explained, "But now it's up to you to pay for that."

Sherry replied, "I said that I was sorry for it."

Christine continued, "But Hank's at rest again. Every day I'll be saying I'll tell Hank what you did. He's been lied to once before. You would not believe what Hank thinks about people lying."

Sherry disagreed, "I didn't start all of this."

Christine remarked, "Hank will see that different."

Sherry admitted, "I know what you're gonna say to him."

Christine informed her, "I'll just tell him it's all off. He will hear that you started. Maybe you should feel bad about it."

The Gopie commented, "The experience should prove fatal. Why should we all be here?"

Christine told Sherry, "You planned to take him down."

Sherry confessed, "Yes I did plan this. To mess with Hank."

The Gopie sighed, "Oh Sherry."

Misty ordered, "Now you should make things all better for Hank."

Christine sang, "I'll tell Hank what you had to do."

Misty mentioned, "The mirror is too wide for us."

Sherry replied, "There's not anything I can do about it."

Misty asked, "And what are we going to do about Sherry? And what to do about Hank?"

Christine stated, "Hank is open to be a free man. He will die an open man. Hank should come over here. You have punished him forever. Did you think that through? It shouldn't be the future of such a good man."

Misty remarked, "But Hank is not a good spirit."

Christine explained, "That is true because now he's just a man."

Misty asked, "How can we depend on his spirit?"

Christine answered, "Maybe you should see that I have been sleeping. With a good man."

Misty related, "We understand how you feel about Hank. But we also have a feel about Hank."

Christine asked, "Did you hear that Hank?"

Sherry advised, "Be nice what you say to Hank. Cause he is such a bad boy."

Christine replied, "He is not the asshole you think."

Sherry announced, "I think Hank is going back."

Christine asked, "You said Hank's coming back?"

Sherry confirmed, "Yes, it does look like Hank's coming."

Christine guessed, "Maybe he will stand for that."

The Gopie remarked, "That's a good thing for Hank."

Christine then stated, "Hank won't be standing for this, Hank won't be staying."

Sherry asked, "You think that Hank will feel? What we did to him."

Christine answered, "Master of faster."

The Gopie asked, "Did he pass through the people? He'll do anything. He's always moving too quick."

Christine said, "I know Hank is the better man."

The Gopie asked, "Did you feel what I'm saying to you?"

Mark asked, "You didn't see him did you?"

The Gopie guessed, "Maybe because he's got all the people with him now."

Mark commented, "I can't believe what an asshole he is."

The Gopie pointed out, "That was awful short of you."

Mark replied, "But he won't be staying for it."

Christine argued, "But he will be staying for it. When he's not so busy. He's been made aware of his plight. You think that I wanted..."

The Gopie interrupted, "No, I got a story."

Christine related, "Hank will be mad is the story."

Mark suggested, "Maybe you should let him hear the song. Now you can start that."

Misty mentioned, "There's nothing like it when we can hear the song. And we are supposed to listen."

Christine asked, "Do we really have to?"

Misty plotted, "Now let's bonk her."

Christine warned, "You just better back off."

Misty reminded her, "You know what that's supposed to mean."

Christine dared, "You just try it."

A man passing by asked, "Is there a reason I have to park out there?"

The Gopie proclaimed, "That's right we did this."

Misty replied, "I can't believe there's trouble here."

Christine explained, "Because of what all the spirits did to me."

Mark commented, "Let's not give anymore answers to Hank okay. You gotta make up with Christine for me. Maybe we can go through the bottom."

The Gopie asked, "Do we have the schedule?"

Mark answered, "We may have to put it down. It goes right on my shoulder do you get me?"

The Gopie asked, "How do you like the day so far?"

Mark and Misty remarked, "We hoped the bridge would help her. We just need the power with Hank."

Mark added, "Definitely has the nature for it."

Again Mark and Misty said together, "We gave Hank all that we want to give. Told you that already."

Misty suggested, "Maybe we could help with you."

Mark related, "If our backs aren't getting dirty. Hank might need to have a rescue."

Misty mentioned, "Hank wouldn't be paying for it."

Mark stated, "Hank could have a bleeding heart. If you ask me in his book. There's two thousand pictures of him in there. There are no pictures of him now."

The Gopie asked, "And you'd like to smoke with him too right? Maybe you both should be right together. Maybe Hank will invite us up here."

Misty asked, "Please give Hank another chance with a ballsy mirror? Can we talk to Christine when she comes back here?" with music playing, "Has he gone?"

The Gopie informed them, "I'll see Hank up here tomorrow."

Misty guessed, "Hank could tell me something with him."

The Gopie muffled replied, "Now the time has come. For me to be with him. Great they take tour. But what if they don't. Hank would not be able to tour because of us."

Misty muffled remarked, "I could step on Sherry."

Christine commented, "I think the zombies might have gotten her. If you play with Hank. You better get busy."

The Gopie ordered, "Let's go upstairs."

Mark told him, "But Hank is supposed to come through here."

The Gopie guessed, "Maybe he went shopping. You'd think a country club would have a few spirits though."

Christine advised, "Don't say that too very loud. Hank will hear."

Gary and the tour group arrived at the top of the stairs and he told about the white crosses.

The Gopie asked, "Is Hank with Gary?"

Gary said a line.

Christine asked, "Gary is Hank over there?"

The Gopie told Misty, "Hank forgot he's supposed to dance with you."

Gary mentioned the tongue of the bridge.

Christine asked, "Don't we have to go through that?"

Misty commented, "That appears to be seen."

Christine asked, "Will you dance with me? I'll try to dance right here for you."

Misty answered, "I should have a prize for stopping that way."

The Gopie announced, "Yesterday this would be number one. One through ten. Girl look at me."

Christine asked, "Guess who I found at Mike's? Crying about the guy who sent me. It only matters he's not here you know."

Misty confessed, "I had no idea they asked you to come."

Christine remarked, "A mirror of salt would make Hank go back to bed."

Misty asked, "What did you think a mirror of salt would do?"

The Gopie answered, "It drugs him." At the same time Christine admitted, "I got his hand to go through."

Misty guessed, "Hank won't come back though. I think he wants to like it here. Maybe he will have to stop here first. Maybe we're a rock over here."

Christine assured her, "You'll know about Hank later."

Misty announced, "Now Brad is supposed to be here."

Christine replied, "Oh I can see it now boy."

Brad yelled over, "Christine are you talking about me now?"

Christine answered, "I just want some friendly help."

Misty told her, "Now I'm gonna get ready, here he is."

Christine asked, "Would you ask the Gopie to move?"

Misty remarked, "Now he's got Brad worried."

Christine advised, "You shouldn't pick on Hank."

Misty asked, "Had any luck with him?"

Christine confessed, "I'd say he'd jump for me."

Misty commented, "That is just vile Christine."

Brad related, "Both of you are kidding. Both of you are like humans."

Christine corrected him, "You shouldn't talk like that. I just tried to help you. You made something more beautiful."

Brad asked, "So what are you all up to? Feels like Sherry's all pissed off."

Christine answered, "Not if I got here before this."

Brad asked, "Have you been waiting for him a couple hours today?"

Misty admitted, "If that's true I'd walk back. It's not like Hank is right there for me."

Christine announced, "Now he's right there. If y'all come back here. Hank just told me he'd come back."

Misty asked, "What about Hank though?"

The Gopie remarked, "Hank tried to go through me."

Christine assured him, "I will kick Hank."

Paul commented, "It's like fourteen to twelve."

The Gopie replied, "It's not healthy or helping when you're lying."

Misty started, "Now I must say to you."

Paul asked, "Are you talking about me?"

Misty finished, "Yes we're talking about you Paul. Maybe now you will pay my check."

Mark ordered, "Get in."

Misty advised, "Mark it's not his fault."

The Gopie added, "I sure hope you can explain this."

Paul came back with, "I believe that's her father's favorite daughter. Would you like to do something?"

Misty asked, "Aren't you glad that Paul is here?"

Mark asked, "You got your toolbox?"

The machine started making noises as Mark spoke.

Paul remarked, "There are spirits who do things like that you know."

Christine replied, "We've got the best man here." She sang, "If you go through the top. I would get Hank to fix this. But he is not going to live with you. With all the experience he's got." She then asked, "You want me to fix what you got there? You move that thing but not the ceiling. I need to tell Hank what we got this time."

Misty asked, "Is that Hank there?"

We heard one line of Gary's story on the return trip up the stairs.

Misty asked, "Did they stay over here long? Is he going to stay cool?"

Mark asked, "Does this attach to another boat? You only have Hank if he lives right here."

Christine asked, "You want to see if Hank would like to?"

Misty commented, "We could sound ghastly with things like this."

Christine explained, "Almost they got it. I doubt if it's gonna stay up. There that should do it. You want it all clear. But Hank might stay at home."

Misty mentioned, "Hank would be able to fix our boat."

Mark informed her, "We brought it back in here."

A spirit in the background confessed, "We tried."

Christine admitted, "For me it's kind of bulky. Is there anyone else in here who could help me?"

Misty remarked, "You must be crazy."

Christine replied, "He's coming around."

Misty guessed, "Bet you wipe it out."

Christine instructed, "I got the sail."

Misty pointed out, "Ooh what a strong man."

Christine suggested, "Hank could really fix this."

Paul said, "Boat," when Christine said, "This."

Mark warned, "Now see remember Paul could. Jack with you," and Misty whispered, "Stay with me," at the same time.

Christine claimed, "Get more done here. I've got it. Hold it not too far. It's too far on top of me."

Mark advised, "It was supposed to stay on the ground."

Paul asked, "Can we have music?"

Misty answered, "Not till I get do you like that."

Paul remarked, "There is nothing like that."

Misty asked, "Aren't you guys finished yet?"

Christine commented, "Don't mind that."

Mark asked, "Do we have to be talking in here?" next to the recorder. "I began the court. When I was underage. Remind me nothing can take that." He sang, "Way down in the middle of it," and apologized, "Oops I'm sorry."

Christine asked, "Does anybody have a red," then sang, "Day they call me?"

Mark pointed out, "Like everybody else. You must be getting happy."

Christine replied, "Maybe we shot that."

Mark asked, "Are you happy now Christine? Even though Hank's guilty."

Misty asked, "Did you really have to do that?"

Gary could suddenly be heard saying one line at the top of the stairs.

Mark said quietly, "I had no idea." Loudly he said, "What is that ailing thing you're talking."

Misty directed, "Now we're through."

The Gopie requested, "Go upstairs with me."

Paul commented, "I could assault Jack. If your name is Jack. Look at me."

Mark informed him, "You'll have to make a reservation with him."

Gary came back in explaining some of the damage on the bridge.

At a pause Christine announced, "Hank we're through."

When Gary got to the end of his explanation Mark admitted, "I still don't think he'll understand."

Christine suggested, "I will go back with him. Get after him about smoking."

Mark asked, "Did you say he's a broken man?"

The tour group talked as they got ready to move on.

Christine confessed, "I don't know what he's saying."

Mark stated, "Maybe I'll guess for sure."

Christine confirmed, "Yeah you are. And now you'll hear is anyone there."

Mark replied, "I think we got it."

Christine asked, "Is there a record of fucking up?"

Once again the tour group came in with Gary keeping his patience about how long it was taking them to get going.

As they quieted down Christine pointed out, "Yesterday Hank was here. You know Hank's with me."

In the background was The Offspring's Come Out and Play and I was dancing.

Christine asked, "Can you dance with me?"

Gary started another story with The Offspring still playing and I would bet no one got a picture of me and Christine dancing in back of the tour.

With no music Mark told them, "He pokes around."

Gary gave another line in the story.

Mark volunteered, "I'll jump on some of this next year."

Christine stated, "I accepted my post."

Gary said another line.

Mark guessed, "I think he had a tough break." After another line from Gary he asked, "Do you think you could use Jack?"

Gary said a long line.

Mark commented, "Never mind."

Gary talked a few more seconds.

Mark mentioned, "They got mad about Hank."

Gary continued his story.

At a pause Christine admitted, "I'm free but my time is bad."

Gary went on.

At the next pause Christine asked, "Can you hear me?"

Gary talked straight through the next fifteen seconds with Offspring playing.

At a pause with Come Out and Play in the background Mark related, "You got a funky beat going."

Gary finished the story.

Christine ordered, "Tell Hank," and Mark followed with, "You call Hank."

Christine remarked, "He knew what to say in here. And you're going to miss him."

Mark agreed, "I know."

Christine confessed, "Nothing. And walk around with Hank."

Then as the radio at the Heat announced Glycerin, a lady on the tour talked and drowned out any spirit voices.

Christine yelled over the noise, "Hey Hank there you are!"

Mark advised, "Give it up Christine."

The noise drowned them out for the next twenty seconds. I went and got the recorder and turned it off.

I turned the recorder back on at the lion spot. I went ahead of the tour so I could ask some questions over there.

Christine faintly asked, "What are you doing back here? There is no one around here."

Mark requested, "I want to take off."

I said, "I'm back again."

Christine commented, "I can't believe Hank will ask anything."

I asked, "First I'd like to know if Christine is still with me?"

Christine answered, "Yes Hank I'm here. What are you doing? That's Jack's room. And that might be your room forever. Does he think I'm going? Hank you're the bomb."

I said, "We heard a lot about the lion that appears in this area."

Christine asked, "That's nice Hank, what do you want?"

I asked, "Does anyone know about that?"

Christine asked, "What happened here?"

I asked, "Can you tell me anything about it?"

Christine replied, "I hear the music Hank. There's nothing to see here. Let's go back there. You can go back and say I'm sorry. And you can have everything you want then."

Jack asked, "Am I invading your room? What are you saying?"

Christine remarked, "I'll bet it's Hank's room."

Jack requested, "Well then do me a favor. Take him over to where he can help himself."

Christine assured him, "I'll be out of here as quick as I can. Maybe you could help him some too. Is that the Queen of Hearts there?"

Jack answered, "Yes I found it."

I asked, "Are there any questions you have for me?"

Christine asked, "Yes Hank can we have a cigarette and leave? Maybe we should have a bedroom here. Hey Hank let's go see the tour."

Misty asked, "What are you talking about with him?"

Christine confessed, "We're just visiting Jack. I've never been to Jack's on the tour. Is there a reason you're here?"

Misty answered, "I came to see if Jack would come with me."

Jack confirmed, "I'll do whatever they want me to do."

Misty remarked, "He asked the Gopie whatever he wanted."

I started, "Can we make that..."

Misty started to ask, "What's that nerd..."

I finished, "Lion or lion's head appear again?"

Jack stated, "There's nothing there. I don't think Hank knows we're here."

Christine reminded them, "But you know Hank's supposed to be in here."

Misty replied, "Not all the spirits are here."

Jack suggested, "Maybe he should come with me."

Christine asked, "Can we give Hank to Jay?"

Jack corrected her, "My name is Jack."

Misty answered, "I think Hank is supposed to be out of here."

Christine started, "Hank's supposed to be here every day for the next few..."

I interrupted, "Feel free to talk into the recorder if you have anything else to say."

Misty said into the recorder, "Me I sorta feel it's okay."

Christine pointed out, "That's where he wants to live here."

Misty guessed, "Maybe he ought to be here. Jack will be opening a station somewhere."

Jack interjected, "That would be sixty stations."

Christine commented, "I don't think I hear you in this thing."

Jack replied, "We're not supposed to."

Misty advised, "Forget about him."

A male spirit announced, "We're all listening."

A female spirit confessed, "We were just passing through."

The male spirit remarked, "Both of us have serious business."

Misty ordered, "Maybe you should go back to be with Hank. Now Hank's going everywhere."

Christine explained, "He has to."

Misty suggested, "Talk to me when I have a favor."

Christine guessed, "Well maybe Hank had to go to the bathroom."

Jack sang, "He's got the whole trash can. In his fucking knee. I think we could all do this the same."

Christine admitted, "Maybe we're not even."

Misty pointed out, "Jack is supposed to be here."

Christine declared, "I believe this will be Hank's room. When Hank becomes the Erwin."

Misty replied, "We won't promise you anything."

Christine sang, "You're not supposed to be here Jack. If he goes and gets my favorite dung hole Chester. But will he ask a favor? But it don't matter to me."

Misty remarked, "We could really use it. Do you ever hear the news around here?"

Christine related, "Hank should be the news around here. Have you seen Hank's truck that he brought down here?"

Misty confessed, "That's not quite what we had in mind. When he drove down here that far. Where's he going after this?"

Christine answered, "I don't think he has any plans."

Misty sang, "He might be dead after all."

Christine agreed, "Yeah he just might be after a while."

Misty said, "I guess I'll talk to you later."

Christine replied, "I'll see you not far off."

Jack remarked, "Don't catch me later on. If you need help with Hank."

Christine promised, "I'll see you guys later."

Misty assured her, "It'll be better."

Christine stated, "I sure hope that Hank doesn't stay. You go back without me. Pay for miles after miles." Jack was asking, "What'd you pay for forty eight?"

Jack announced, "We're taking off Christine."

Misty added, "Make a baby."

Christine sang, "You know we miles after all Hank. Can you go back? It will take us longer. I'll be glad when today is over. I think Hank's going to be on the bridge. Did you hear me Hank? And you should see how he's working. I'm about talking. Maybe he should talk. That's all I'm sayin'."

Chester came back and guessed, "Maybe Hank will be here."

Christine asked, "Do you want to be here when Hank returns? Jack will be here. They'll be here most of the weekend."

Chester declared, "Hank wait for you, he'll wait for me. Later on will he be coming back?"

Christine answered, "Yes he will be here. Make the miles and miles."

Chester admitted, "In his truck. I'll be right there."

Christine started, "Now you remember."

A male spirit playing a guitar spoke, "There's about fifty five grass holes."

Christine asked, "I'm talking here do you mind?"

Chester remarked, "If he has his truck I'm in trouble."

Gary said from above on the bridge, "It was right here last Christmas Eve."

Chester related, "There was something here last Christmas."

Gary gave a line from The Lady in Black story.

Chester mentioned, "I never heard that one. Peter can get..."

Peter said quickly, "Maybe I can."

Christine sang, "Maybe they can walk through."

Peter confessed, "But me and Jack jack hammered for a long time."

Chester added, "After the game he played."

Peter guessed, "Maybe he jumps alright."

Christine sang, "That's when he was across the street."

Chester admitted, "He said we could not be covered."

Christine sang, "But you told me for Hank it's easy. But maybe I should sing this one more time."

Peter related, "This means I could be easy on the bridge before."

Chester stated, "That's all Jack said."

Christine remarked, "Jack told me it was easy for Hank."

Chester announced, "Jane is supposed to be here. It's amazing how Hank can feel. Cause he has so much heart. Under his tee shirt."

Christine pointed out, "And we don't think Hank is enough. To be really happy."

Chester started, "And all his dope behavior. That has made him closer."

Christine finished, "To the friends he has out here."

Chester confessed, "I never liked friends like that. Maybe you should call him sweetheart."

Christine replied, "I don't believe that's what you want me to call him. I don't know if I can say it. I test drove what changed his mind. I put God in the courtroom. Just so Hank would think that's the way it is."

Chester advised, "You shouldn't do that when Hank's got to be perfect. Maybe you should have mentioned. Goddess in there. Now that people get hurt over these things."

Christine volunteered, "If you have a pencil. I will fix it. Did all you people around here see?"

Peter started, "Totally. There's a crazy lady..."

Chester interjected, "That's enough out of you."

Christine commented, "I can't believe that came out of Peter."

Chester guessed, "Hank must be gone."

Christine suggested, "When he comes get his stuff we'll get out of here."

A female spirit requested, "Help me."

Christine stated, "What we got we gotta take some."

Peter confirmed, "We've got thirteen."

Chester pointed out, "That's a talking mic. Hank's been here before hasn't he?"

Christine answered, "Yes he has been here."

Chester replied, "That's real smart."

Christine told Chester, "That feels real good. Peter dropped it."

Peter remarked, "It made quite a difference."

Chester related, "Baseball can't turn him down. Nice catch, they could smell the fear."

Peter announced, "You'll be a sports caster before the day is done."

Chester asked, "Did it fall apart?"

Christine commented, "Come to Havasu it might be better."

Peter admitted, "That's what we get for talking to you."

Christine joked, "After everything's all clear. I believe we'll take you too."

Peter confessed, "That table is done. I didn't drop many things."

Chester declared, "Gwar is singing."

Peter asked, "Is that that little thing? And I'll take that to our table."

Chester corrected him, "Wrong you found it here. That's the bridge to Hank that we're talking through. The guy probably has the first engine that he killed. He has the gas we gave, wouldn't he take me?"

Christine answered, "Yes."

Chester guessed, "Bet he can't talk to me."

Peter replied, "He'd have gonads if he talked to you."

Christine remarked, "But then you'd have to feel things for him. He's always got to feel like it's nothing."

Chester asked, "Are we talking about the same one?"

Christine sighed, "It don't matter."

Chester suggested, "This time let's see if actually if Hank's going back."

Christine asked, "Are you ready to see? Those can't make us outrageous. What would Goth really think about this?"

Chester stated, "He is supposed to get the paper. What page are you working on?"

Christine replied, "Two hundred and eight. I can't go back. With all that Hank could do for us."

Chester guessed, "Maybe there's proof of what I'm talking about with him. I could take them back if they're all ready."

Christine commented, "You might want to see. What you got me doing."

Chester asked, "Got any propane for the gas to come on? That's how you do like that?"

Peter blurted out, "We could rape Christine like that."

Chester remarked, "That's not very nice Pete. Glad you brought Peter along?"

Christine admitted, "I take them as I see them. Peter looked nice."

Chester mentioned, "Probably he should go back to the classroom."

Christine related, "As if a lot of shit is going on. Does he want what Hank's got?"

Chester answered, "He would take it for the chance to go with you."

Peter predicted, "Hank's not going to be good. He won't give."

270

Christine told him, "You haven't seen what I have seen. But he'll never give me the same. As he would give me when we mate."

Sherry yelled, "Where's your fucking mind?" She then sang, "Talk about it, talk about it, talk about Hank. That's what you do."

Christine confessed, "I don't think Hank would like that."

Sherry commented, "All you ever do is talk about it, talk about it, talk about Hank."

Christine asked, "Sherry what are you doing?"

Gary started coming in as the tour approached.

Sherry sang, "Get outta the way."

Peter stated, "You started all this shit."

Christine asked, "Is he in the bathroom? I cannot see the people."

Chester replied, "It looks like Hank's up there. You'll set up the band over there. As you walk out you can see them. You can put it right here where you dropped it. That should be fine."

Christine asked, "Is Hank still in the bathroom?"

Chester turned away from the recorder to ask, "Weren't you listening to me?"

Sherry sang, "Funky Town."

Peter gave a reading, "Eight ninety four."

Christine asked, "Can't you play what Hank likes?"

Chester commented, "Safe if I want to do this."

Sherry directed, "Get back the tour is coming."

Peter instructed, "This is how you do it," with Sherry warming up singing, "Get down."

Chester agreed, "That's the way it's supposed to be done for me." He turned and said, "And you thought Hank was still in the bathroom."

Sherry mentioned with the horns warming up, "And now I hope they do this."

Chester remarked with the horns playing, "You know that I don't like this music." Without the horns playing he told her, "Play some of that music."

Sherry replied, "We really don't know how to do it."

Chester suggested, "Maybe you would like to try. I know you want me just to sing."

Sherry admitted, "I can't keep from playing nearly everything."

Chester sighed, "Nobody's that bad." Then he sang, " Die," like he was singing Metallica's Creeping Death.

Sherry sang, "Whenever I do."

Chester ordered, "Schedule me some time."

Christine guessed, "Maybe we could dance up here. Are you going to do this? Maybe you should wait for Hank. Hank will soon be here."

Sherry offered, "Then we could play Funky Town for Hank. As soon as he gets here. Here's all the people we know. But Peter better Funky Town."

Chester mentioned, "Guess how long I've had this chair done. You'll be glad when Hank gets back in here."

Christine stated, "He won't be back here soon. Hank is in the bathroom."

Chester corrected her, "Hank's right here."

Gary came in with a line.

Christine greeted me, "Hi sweetheart."

Chester remarked, "Tell me that the asshole didn't want to go."

As the tour group got into position for the next story, Christine told him, "We don't have to go with Hank."

Chester admitted, "A lot of this scares me, I hate that."

Christine replied, "He's not all that strong."

Gary started the lion story with, "Let me tell you about my wife."

Chester instructed, "Easy there."

Christine directed, "You gotta keep away."

Gary talked about pictures taken on the steps.

Sherry sang, "I will fix them. I see Frank around him."

Christine suggested, "I'll see if Hank can go around and sense me."

272

Sherry commented, "You got your favorite now."

Christine agreed, "That's a fact."

Gary said, "Hey Zach."

Christine asked, "What's the matter now?"

Sherry answered, "I don't see how that Hank is smoking."

Christine confessed, "I know that Hank should quit smoking everything. But that's okay."

Gary started the lion story and Sherry started singing Funky Town.

At a pause in the story Christine pointed out, "That's Hank over there, you see?"

Sherry stated, "The movie theater won't be hard to do." There is one not far from the bridge.

Christine remarked, "We've been here before."

Sherry claimed, "We've got the centerpiece somewhere."

Christine informed her, "They saw the movie."

Chester added, "So Leopold can't make a difference."

Christine announced, "Last dance," at the same time.

Gary said, "I always tell this story."

Christine replied, "There's a story right here now."

Chester declared, "That will be something. Ready?"

Gary told about the time his girlfriend took a picture in that spot and got a lion.

Christine exclaimed, "That's Hank's lion!"

Gary went into the next part of the lion story.

Sherry commented, "I cannot believe this. Is that me?"

Peter answered, "Yes it is."

Gary gave the location of part of the event.

Christine asked, "Did you have to?"

Gary told about a lady on the tour who got an orb with a lion's face in it.

Sherry admitted, "I think I did it last time."

Christine remarked, "That's you."

Gary then told that they never got another picture of a lion.

Sherry confessed, "I was a small child."

It was four years since the first lion. After a line from Gary she asked, "Have you seen the bad about Hank? It's true."

As the tour group talked among themselves Sherry yelled, "People don't get caught in this loose stuff!"

Chester asked, "What effects did they leave behind?"

A female spirit answered, "I found a doll."

Chester replied, "I did not see that."

Peter stated, "That big tool constantly stays at the bridge."

A female spirit pointed out, "There's a man on the bridge. He does not look the same as the crowd."

Peter announced, "That's the chance we all take."

Christine commented, "The movie is right here."

Sherry informed them, "It's right here if you need it. They haven't seen everything."

Chester admitted, "I can't be able to do it. But Hank becomes a necessary part of the bridge that you have. I think everybody should get along close to Hank. Everybody."

Sherry acknowledged, "See if I can."

There was a laugh.

Chester remarked, "That is because you wish to screw it up."

Peter added, "We're at fifty percent agreement."

Christine replied, "That's a stupid answer you told him."

Sherry diasagreed, "But now he's got it right."

Peter confessed, "I'll try not to get it better."

A female spirit stated, "We love Hank."

Gary and a man on the tour talked.

At a pause Sherry told them, "You'll forget about Hank."

Gary told the tour he needed to check if he held the record for walking the London Bridge backwards. He then asked them if they saw anything on the bridge.

As they were looking, Chester ordered, "Stop that music. We helped you with locating Hank."

Gary asked if anyone had a camera. One person came forward and Gary instructed them where to take the picture.

Sherry commented, "I don't see it but it pretty much doesn't matter though."

There was more talking from the tour group.

Christine remarked, "That's music."

A female spirit admitted, "That's the way we feel inside about Hank."

Christine requested, "Then do me a favor."

Gary asked, "Did you take a picture of it?"

Christine finished, "Give Hank a chance."

Chester related, "I don't think it's much different than last year."

Sherry instructed, "Bring him over."

Peter added, "We'll just have to believe Christine," just as the tour was seeing the picture and remarking, "Oh wow."

Chester suggested, "Let me talk a little to both sides."

Peter asked, "Do you want me to bring that stuff with you?"

Chester answered, "That's close to pickin' up."

A female spirit asked, "What is that thing over there?"

Chester started, "Actually."

Christine finished, "It's Hank's."

Gary said, "Exactly right here."

The female spirit replied, "Good enough."

Gary said, "It's on this block."

Christine confessed, "I don't know if he's pissed off."

Gary explained the picture.

The female spirit guessed, "Maybe he needs more magick."

Gary said a line.

Christine started, "We had to..."

Chester interjected, "I had to check."

Christine finished, "If he believes in something."

Gary said another line.

Chester stated, "In the future the present is larger. Therefore."

Gary told the last story of the tour. He paused more after the story to add a few related facts.

Chester commented, "I wish Hank would come back in here to me. Move that stuff there."

Christine insisted, "Stop doing things that I know."

Peter confirmed, "Second time it's all ready."

Gary said, "People."

Christine added, "Don't see it all. All of them would like to."

Peter remarked, "You'll see a lot more of this when you get here."

Christine complained, "They won't even take pictures Hank."

Chester admitted, "I don't think it's much different."

Christine directed, "Back to the boulevard. To get ready."

A digital camera went off with a little chime.

Christine announced, "They missed us."

Gary talked to the tour group.

Christine asked, "That's what you came here for right?"

Peter asked, "They're all with Hank right?"

Chester commented, "They're all beaten down. Easier than I thought."

Christine suggested, "Let's see who's the next candidate."

Peter asked, "Do you include Hank too?"

Christine remarked, "They're all over on the thirteenth of January."

Chester figured, "Then it must be an accident. It shouldn't be that bad."

Christine asked, "Where are they found?"

A female spirit answered, "Not far from where you are."

Christine asked, "Next to me?"

The female spirit read, "Vehicle they're already planning to go home in. In the evening that's a fact."

Christine stated, "That will be after I'm done with him."

Chester replied, "Getting hurt with Hank."

The female spirit continued, "They all come here, there's propane."

Chester asked, "What do we have here to fix them?"

Peter pointed out, "Not very many of those."

Chester assured them, "I'll be back again."

Peter declared, "I'll be back right here. Left my computer home."

Chester mentioned, "Maybe you should try to go back there. They'll all be killed by the fire. They've got to make a cure. Better start now. Tell fucking Sherry what I'm doing."

With music Sherry sang, "I heard that. And I still don't like Hank."

Christine sang, "Don't do that. To Hank. Here he comes."

I shut the recorder off and you can imagine what was said after that.

CHAPTER THIRTEEN

THE GRANDMA TOUR

*Sherry, Chester, Brad, Misty, the Gopie, and
Christine at the passage door*

On the next tour there were a couple of little old ladies. We
thought the tour would be long and slow but they did a good job
keeping up the pace. I knew about the court from the last tour,
so I was very leery about how far I could push the spirits on
this tour. I started early by going to the phone booth and asking
questions. I was feeling out if I was still welcome at the bridge.
This the Grandma Tour.

I turned the recorder on and Chester faintly asked, "Hank are
you going to answer us? I don't believe it."

I said, "Well I hope you're here with me tonight."

Christine admitted, "I wouldn't miss this one for the world Hank. What is Hank up to?"

A male spirit stated, "I just came along to go on the tour. Tell me when I get there."

Chester greeted him, "I'm so glad you showed up."

A female spirit asked, "When did he decide to show up?"

Christine answered, "When he talked to Gary I suppose."

The female spirit asked, "When you all going to leave here?"

Christine replied, "After we get done talking to Hank."

A male spirit asked, "How do you like Hank?"

Chester confessed, "I don't think he belongs. Up on the bridge where we decided."

The male spirit confirmed, "I thought we knew that. I just have to tell Sherry."

Christine asked, "That will make her happy, but what about me?"

Chester suggested, "Let's get on it."

Christine asked, "Are you going to ask Hank about this? All he's got is the funny paper."

Chester asked, "What do you want me to do with him?"

Christine remarked, "I thought you were going to put him here."

Chester admitted, "I think I'll put him in another bridge."

I started by talking about the weather, "I think we end the breeze tonight."

Christine asked, "Does he know what we're saying?"

I said, "We can't stay here."

Christine declared, "That proves it."

I said, "The only reason I went to other places."

Chester asked, "What'd he ask?"

I said, "I thought the other spirits might be talking."

Christine replied, "That's okay Henry."

Chester asked, "Does he think we're mad?"

Christine answered, "He thinks that we're mad at him."

I said, "And I don't mind talking to you guys."

Chester asked, "What are we going to do with Hank?"
Christine asked, "Do you think he heard me?"
Chester guessed, "He's apologizing to you."
Christine confessed, "I'm not mad anyway."
Chester commented, "I don't think he knows that."
Christine suggested, "Maybe he's going crazy."
Chester remarked, "I don't think we've done that."
Christine mentioned, "Maybe he'd like to hear that song."
The other female spirit admitted, "I don't even know that song."
Chester confirmed, "I think Hank already knows it."
The other female spirit recounted, "I don't think I can do that music."
I said, "I want to ask about orbs."
Chester asked, "Has he gotten pictures of orbs yet?"
Christine answered, "Yes he has."
Chester ordered, "Tell Hank what he wants to know."
Christine started, "I will say..."
I cut her off with, "I get different colors."
Christine pleaded, "Please Hank."
I asked, "Red and blue, do the different colors mean anything?"
Christine stated, "The beautiful colors don't mean anything."
Chester asked, "Do you think Hank already knows about it? We should take Hank right here and now. I could take him right here."
Christine remarked, "Hank is with me."
Chester suggested, "I could take him in the bathroom. Then you won't have to go on the tour. I think Hank knows what we're doing. I think Hank has outlived the tour."
Christine disagreed, "That's what you think. No you won't."
I said, "We have a plan to start a church."
Christine predicted, "That's a plan you won't see."
Chester commented, "He has plans. That won't be successful. You won't be breathing. You'll stay right here."

I said, "In our plan we want to help people with food."

Christine started, "I think you should..."

I added, "They have a hard time getting."

Christine replied, "That's true I've seen it."

Chester admitted, "I think he knows what he's doing."

I asked, "Do you think it's a good plan?"

Christine answered, "Yes I think it's a good plan. But you can't make it happen. That's what Hank wants."

I asked, "Do you think it will be successful?"

Christine remarked, "Not for you Hank. I think more of Hank. He should make it big."

Chester explained, "He has to go big. For Hank's own self."

Christine declared, "I know that."

Chester confirmed, "I know that you know. But I think Hank should be big. What do you think Hank should do?"

Christine related, "I think he could write a book. About this."

Chester started, "That's what I think he could..."

I interrupted with, "I heard when you."

Chester asked, "What Hank?"

I said, "Just say please."

Chester promised, "I will try to remember."

Christine asked, "Do you believe he can hear us?"

Chester guessed, "I think he knows what we're saying."

I said, "As the people are getting the tour."

Chester requested, "Yes Hank."

I said, "It's really been getting hot."

Chester advised, "That's right. Now then Hank. You should not be sweating. It makes you..."

I interrupted, "Anything you can do."

Chester asked, "About what?"

I said, "To help."

Chester asked, "What is it Hank?"

I said, "With the tour."

Chester asked, "What does Hank expect us to do?"

I said, "Whether it's grab a person."

Chester confirmed, "I hear you."

I said, "Whisper in their ear boo."

Chester replied, "You know I can't do that."

I said, "Jump in front of the camera."

Chester confessed, "I could do that."

I said, "Let them get a picture."

Chester told Christine, "Ask Hank if that's what I have to do."

I said, "You are being nice and letting me do this thing."

Chester agreed, "Yes we are Hank."

I said, "We are selling the tour so other people can experience what I am experiencing."

Chester disagreed, "No we can't."

I said, "They really want to."

Chester explained, "But it's not their turn. That's what I think is wrong with him. I could just take Hank right here. Hank do you know where you're going? It's nice over here."

I said, "Well I guess I'm right here so the whole world doesn't think I'm a looney sitting here talking to myself. I'm leaving some room and we can come do the tour tonight. Thank you for talking to me and if you want to come on the tour you are more than welcome to. And I don't mind if you guys are the only ones talking or if other spirits talk too. That's okay."

Christine asked, "Isn't Hank nice?"

Chester acknowledged, "Yes he talks very nice."

I said, "Thank you for what you did for me so far."

Christine replied, "That's okay."

I turned the recorder off and went back to the fountain to wait for the tour. When they arrived Gary started the tour by the fountain and I turned the recorder on. Gary gave the history of the bridges over the River Thames. We moved on to the front gates and Gary started his story there.

When in the story Gary said, "A final joke on the bridge. When they put these gates up behind the Oscars."

A female spirit pointed out, "That must be Hank."

Gary said, "The stuff that they're made of is solid iron."

Christine started, "I should lean on his..."

Chester finished, "Head."

Gary said, "They were hand made in eighteen fifty one"

Chester admitted, "I could just piss on Hank."

Gary gave another line about the gates.

Chester asked, "What is this?"

Gary said another line.

Chester explained, "That's what makes Hank hurt."

Gary said, "I'll take it," as he got his drink from his son.

Chester complained, "I'm so pissed at Hank."

Gary said, "We used to have a little store down there."

Christine uttered, "I know."

Gary said another line.

Christine mentioned, "See the beard."

Gary gave a long line in a story.

Christine announced, "Hank is here."

Gary finished the story.

Christine echoed, "Hank's here."

Gary remarked on the story.

Chester stated, "You're ready and Hank's ready."

Gary started telling about the fountain.

Chester added, "I'm ready."

We moved near the fountain again with Gary talking and the fountain running.

When Gary paused Chester confessed, "I couldn't hear him."

Gary said, "It's on the website."

Chester claimed, "I missed it."

Christine related, "Oh you missed it. There's a seance happening. That's where I would be."

The female spirit replied, "I would rather just hear him."

Gary started the land marker story as we moved away from the fountain.

At a pause in the story one of the elderly ladies said, "There's voices in here."

Chester declared, "We got her."

As I moved back towards the fountain the water got louder but you could still hear Gary's story.

Then Gary couldn't be heard as Chester commented, "Happy birthday to Hank. I deserve what I got for Hank."

A male spirit asked, "What did you say?"

Chester suggested, "It's a gift that he ought to take. He ought to jump on it. That's what Hank should do."

Gary came through with a line.

Christine interjected, "I should scare the shit out of Hank."

Chester advised, "I guess that would be good. Hank should leave here now."

The male spirit remarked, "That's what he gets for asking."

Gary said, "There's a gas light right here," to draw the tour over to the lamppost.

Christine commented, "That's the tour."

Gary told the lamppost story.

At the end of the story the male spirit guessed, "Maybe Hank has some answers."

Chester agreed, "There's a chance that maybe he does."

The clock tower chimed.

Christine admitted, "I gotta get to Hank."

The male spirit figured, "Maybe someone can get some of the answers from him."

Christine offered, "I should try to get the answers."

The tour moved on to the phone booth as Gary gave the first line of that story.

Christine stated, "That's the good thing about Hank."

Chester mentioned, "He'd be a lot happier if he could just sit or lay down."

The male spirit confirmed, "You said what Hank has, it ought to be good. That tour's leaving."

Chester informed them, "I'm sure they're coming back over here. They'll be bringing Hank."

Gary came in with a couple of lines.

The male spirit asked, "Can Duran take us?"

Chester suggested, "Maybe Hank should test drive."

The male spirit asked, "Gallery of death isn't that?"

Chester guessed, "That ought to scare him."

Gary told the Marsha and Cheryl story at the phone booth.

The male spirit replied, "He's really good."

The female spirit commented, "Maybe we could see a little better."

The male spirit asked, "What's next on the order? So I'll see you when you are dancing."

Chester exclaimed, "So let's go do this."

Gary told the tour group to take a lot of pictures.

Chester pointed out, "They're busy. I think I can do this."

The male spirit instructed, "Say lots of things. Goth said something, there's a bunch of drugs he takes. What are the drugs he takes?"

Chester answered, "About four rapid hits of pot."

The male spirit asked, "Is that all he has to smoke?"

Chester explained, "Part of it is in this city. He doesn't have any jobs in this town."

The male spirit added, "There's tons of absences I was told about that."

Chester admitted, "I'm not sure where he's going. He always walks right here. Smoking right here. It's like he's absent. And he knows about energy."

Gary said, "You ask anyone here."

Chester guessed, "Maybe he's lonely."

The male spirit agreed, "That's it."

Gary told about the bidding on the London Bridge.

As Gary paused Christine confirmed, "Hank does that too."

The male spirit recounted, "We don't need Hank anymore."

Gary said, "This is my old store right here."

Chester announced, "Hank used to work here. Only get there."

Gary made a remark.

Chester declared, "That's where Hank should live here."
The male spirit asked, "How could he stay here?"
Chester asked, "Don't you have an idea?"
Gary said, "The Goth design."
The male spirit mentioned, "That's included."
Gary gave the world records the bridge held.
Chester stated, "This is what you have."
The whole tour remarked including me, telling them the current resident in the store used my idea as the London Bridge Psychic.
Christine commented, "They say that about her what Hank's been saying."
A ghostly female voice offered, "I'll move her."
As the tour quieted down Christine tried to say audibly, "Hey Hank."
Chester interjected, "Fucking up high again."
Over Gary and the tour chatting Christine asked, "Can Hank stay here?"
It was Gary that needed the first break and we stopped at the Jersey restaurant to sit at the table in front. Gary told the tour about his foot operation and why he still did the tour.
At a pause in the talking Christine confessed, "I still wish Hank was here."
The male spirit admitted, "We're no longer his friends."
Chester remarked, "That's a dirty blog," at the same time Christine started, "You know what I think."
Christine finished, "Hank screwed up."
The female spirit pointed out, "Both of you screwed up."
Christine asked, "What did you just say?"
The female spirit sang, "You know that we hate both of you."
Christine blurted out, "You bastard," over Gary talking. In a high pitched voice she complained, "You turned on us."
Chester replied, "Usually we don't worry about Hank that much." Christine in her little girl voice asked, "Want to see me bust eleven?"

286

Chester ordered, "Try to bring Hank over here," while Christine asked, "What's the pick up?"

Chester repeated, "Get Hank here."

Over Gary in her little girl voice Christine directed, "You stay with Mike."

Gary told the tour about where we were going next.

Christine echoed, "You want to see me bust eleven?"

Chester insisted, "Why don't you bring Hank over here," while Christine asked again, "What is the pick up?"

Gary told what he would like to see in the Village.

Christine asked, "You boys want some love?"

Chester remarked, "Just go give Hank a hickie. I think they will be going down here."

The female spirit admitted, "We're still mad, mad at her. I see 'em."

Chester asked, "You want to take Hank?"

Gary talked to the tour.

Chester advised, "Wait till you see a book."

We got to the water's edge and Gary started telling the story about the footings of the bridge.

At a pause in the story Christine announced, "I'm here with Hank."

The female spirit stated, "I'm pissed at him."

Gary continued.

At the next pause the female spirit suggested, "You better not bring Hank over."

Chester explained, "She says she's still mad at you."

Christine commented, "I'm with Hank so that's okay."

Chester asked, "Are you going to tell Hank about this?"

We moved on to Dead Man's Hole.

Christine figured, "There doesn't seem to be a place for Hank," while Chester informed her, "I pulled that already."

Chester declared, "We all wish some money for Hank," while Christine related, "Put your money on the front line."

Christine remarked, "I've never seen them like this."

The female spirit yelled, "Christine!"

Gary started the story at Dead Man's Hole.

At the first pause Chester announced, "Hank's here."

Gary continued but Christine behind him started, "All that Hank can really have..."

The female spirit interjected, "That's an extra space."

Mike joined the tour with, "Once we added this we're fucking dumping the tour guide."

Christine asked, "Don't like this? Are you still on the right train, I'm here. I got this on Hank's head," all behind Gary's story. She then sang, "I won't find it," like the song Heat Wave that kept coming in and out.

She spoke, "I remember when I got here. There was no one back. You see all that in Hank. And all of it. All the man I need is Hank."

She and some other female spirits continued to sing Heat Wave behind Gary's story. With Gary still talking she mentioned, "I keep calling Hank now but Hank called someone. On the telephone." In the little girl voice she claimed, "It's obviously."

The other female spirit sang, "Heat wave. Never mind about that. Man I'm over. Don't be on the side of him. Play hard on Donny. This ain't on you," as Gary started to come back in.

Christine disagreed, "Yeah it is," with Chester saying, "Quit talking."

The other female spirit complained, "I brought all of this. I'm going home. We were supposed to be talking and something."

A male spirit sang, "Does somebody need a hug?"

Christine in the little girl voice asked, "Is that a fool?" At the same time the male spirit sang, "Is that a fool going down the road." She replied, "I'm thinking Maz, I'm thinking," while the male spirit sang, "I'm thinking Mazatlan."

Chester advised, "People can hear that."

Christine asked, "Yeah what's her name Mike?" with the male spirit singing the same thing.

The male spirit sang, "It'll be me and Christine. Leave Amadeus, Amadeus. And freeze all of this."

Mike informed me, "That's King Edward."

Gary said, "They were very, very poor in White Chapel okay."

Christine suggested, "Maybe Hank could use this space," while Mike was saying, "Maybe I could space it."

Mike commented, "They're awful fucking rude. That's a cold move."

The male spirit asked, "What did you make of me on that?"

Gary said, "Wood was very expensive so guess what, coal won out."

Mike asked, "Was that in here?"

Gary said, "There was a hundred and forty years of coal dust."

The male spirit asked, "Do you even want me here?"

Christine asked, "Do you see what I'm marking?"

Gary said, "And these are a pretty good example of how dark it was when it got here." He was talking about the blocks at the bottom of the stairs. Gary finished that story with no extra voices.

Christine in her little girl voice related, "It's different down here."

In her normal voice she guessed, "Maybe they'll fuck me now."

In her little girl voice she exclaimed, "What a fuck."

Mike interjected, "Start my date with you."

Christine confessed, "I'm with Hank."

Mike replied, "Hank's a lucky man."

Gary started the next story about the blocks.

Christine commented, "I wish Hank was never here," at a pause.

Gary told the rest of the story.

Chester remarked, "Welcome to Lake Havasu."

Christine asked, "Where's Hank?"

A female spirit answered, "He's not far away. What will you do when Hank gets here?"

Chester admitted, "We're protecting Hank."

We reached the half way point on the stairs where Gary took a break.

Christine announced, "They always stop right here."

Gary started another story.

At a break the female spirit asked, "What are they doing?"

At the next break Mike asked, "What are they doing now?"

Gary told the bullet hole story.

Chester insisted, "I'll break Hank."

Christine asked, "Will you save him for me?"

Chester remarked, "I'll think about it when Hank gets here. Maybe you should wait right here."

Christine agreed, "I'll wait till Hank comes along."

Chester related, "Hank will do his thing up there. His restroom."

Christine commented, "Hank won't be mad at you."

Chester declared, "That's too bad for Hank. Hank knows the place we're doing it. That's all I'm saying."

Christine stated, "I'm going."

Chester demonstrated his power with a loud bang and Mike exclaimed, "Holy fuck!"

Christine replied, "Now you're just bullying us."

Mike requested, "I need a picture of you doing that."

Chester asked, "You want me to break my hand?"

Christine joked, "Hank would like to see that."

Chester dared her, "Go get Hank then. What's the matter? There's Hank over there."

Mike offered, "I could be you're extra man."

Gary started another story.

At the first pause Chester mentioned, "The birds told me to do this."

Christine remarked, "I don't believe that."

Gary a few lines to the Museum Tape story.

The next pause Christine pointed out, "Now then Hank's here."

Gary gave a line.

Christine asked, "What are you going to do to Hank?"

Gary said, "So he pulls down here to the sand dunes and there's no bridge."

Mike corrected, "There's a bridge right here."

Gary said, "He keeps looking and there's no bridge."

Christine confessed, "That's what I thought."

Gary said, "He finally sees the flag pole sticking out of the fog."

Mike replied, "That's it."

Gary gave another line.

Mike confirmed, "So there is a bridge."

Gary said a line.

Mike started, "Seek immediately, you're not a row but..."

Chester interjected, "Only if Hank wants to go."

Gary gave another line.

Christine admitted, "I want to leave."

Gary finished the story.

Mike suggested, "Let's go then."

Christine guessed, "I don't think we're free to. Hank still touring. Let's don't go Mike."

Mike mentioned, "You made it strong for me. I don't see why we can't talk to Hank here."

Chester explained, "Because there's other people around."

Mike confessed, "I don't see why Hank tours," with Christine saying, "Like you," in her little girl voice.

Gary said, "I'm glad that's over."

Christine commented, "I'm just saying you asshole."

Chester remarked, "I think he's done."

Mike asked, "Can you speak to Hank about her?"

Gary said, "We're going to walk over here and say hello to Mr. Wood and Mr. McCullough."

Chester answered, "I don't think Hank really cares. I don't think it would bother Hank."

Christine admitted, "I don't think anything bothers Hank."

Mike suggested, "I will go give Hank a try."

Chester told him, "I hope you know what you're doing."

Christine recounted, "I think we best get going."

Mike asked, "Without Hank?"

Chester replied, "Hank will talk to you at the lien."

Mike asked, "Hank will talk to you guys?"

Chester confessed, "I don't know what he'll say," as we reached street level.

Gary started the stories about the founders of Lake Havasu City.

At the first lengthy pause Mike asked, "You stay with Hank the whole time?"

Gary said a line.

Chester answered, "Once in a while."

Gary said another line.

Chester asked, "Can you remember Hank?"

Gary gave a long line.

Christine stated, "Hank is different."

Gary said another line.

Mike asked, "That's what you want?"

Christine confirmed, "I do."

Gary gave a short line.

Chester asked, "Are you gonna panic?"

Gary said a line.

Mike answered, "If Hank will."

Gary said another line.

Christine complained, "Why don't you just fuck Hank up."

Gary gave a long line.

Chester admitted, "He won't forget what we have done."

Christine pointed out, "But now you'll make us look bad here."

Gary asked the tour group, "Have you been out in the city at all?"

Christine declared, "I vote for Hank."

Chester commented, "Mike a good number of the streets are haunted."

Gary told the story of how the streets were laid out.

At one break when Gary was talking about Mr. McCullough, Mike stated, "He stays true."

At the next break Chester suggested, "Hank shouldn't be here."

Gary continued the story.

Near the end of the story at a pause Chester instructed, "Watch this."

Gary said another line but faded out before finishing.

Chester ordered, "Name this space after him."

Gary finished the story.

Christine asked, "Do you know where you're going?"

Gary told about Mr. Wood then everyone moved towards the bridge to walk across.

Before the first car passed us on the bridge Christine confessed, "Nobody can separate me and Hank." After a car passed she finished, "Hank and I will be together. I will make it here. That's how I'm going to make that happen here."

In her little girl voice she complained, "Now Chester gonna make me do that." Back to her normal voice after a car passed she stated, "I speak for me and Hank. I know that we can make it."

Mike mentioned, "I know you've been over here. Do you think I'm looking like you might be with me?"

Chester guessed, "Maybe you should visit with her. Maybe you could have her."

Gary came in giving the dimensions of the bridge.

When Gary paused with no cars passing Christine admitted, "I just want Hank to talk to us."

Chester confirmed, "Yes he will."

Christine blurted out, "I just want to say to him I love him."

Mike asked, "Are you divorced?"

Gary came in giving facts about the bridge.

At a pause Christine asked, "What's he got?"

Gary talked about Charles Dickens walking the bridge.

At a pause Mike announced, "I think he got his Jane in the picture."

Gary started the story about the lampposts on the bridge.

As a car passed Christine requested, "Give me a picture of Hank."

Mike replied, "I can do that. Don't you think Hank would want to know? Do you want me to tell Hank?"

Christine answered, "Yes."

Gary said a line in the bridge lamppost story.

Chester remarked, "I'm not sure about this."

Mike declared, "I got the camera all ready."

Christine asked, "Are you gonna take a picture?"

Chester figured, "They decided this on the tour. But who decides to do this?"

Mike answered, "Whoever we get when we take this."

Gary told more of the lamppost story.

Chester suggested, "Maybe you should check with Hank before you do this."

Christine guessed, "He looks like he won't mind if we take it."

Gary came back in with the story. He was able to finish the story with no spirits talking.

Not until we walked away from that spot did Mike say, "Maybe we should ask Hank about that."

Chester ordered, "You have to tell him about the picture."

Christine announced, "I got my picture taken with Hank."

Chester explained, "Hank would want us to do this. So I don't think you have to ask him."

Gary started telling about the suicides on the bridge.

Mike apologized, "Sorry I bumped into you."

Chester declared, "Maybe you ought to talk to Hank."

Christine echoed, "Maybe you should talk to Henry."

Chester added, "And tell him what you're doing. He can't live without this if you don't tell Henry."

294

Mike confessed, "I do believe it."

Chester replied, "That's what gave him lighter experimental girls."

Christine mentioned, "At first it was easy. He has me."

Chester insisted, "Not with the beard he needs to cut off."

Mike stated, "Hank's back here. I know Hank already."

Christine remarked, "That's what it should feel like with him."

Gary said, "A few years ago we had people that took the tour with us."

Mike commented, "We knew that."

Christine explained, "Hank won't take the tour. I know what's on the tour."

Mike directed, "Just a minute. I can take it from here."

Chester disagreed, "That's a bunch of bullshit."

Mike interjected, "They all close their mouths when they talk here. They have to stay in the parking lot. You got her?"

Gary started another story.

At a pause Chester reminded Mike, "Don't forget about Hank. He doesn't have any teeth."

Gary said a line.

Chester pointed out, "Look what you stepped in."

Gary said another line.

Christine replied, "I can't take you anywhere. I should just bring Hank over."

Mike remarked, "I know Hank would like that."

Christine added, "And you'd like that too."

Mike confessed, "I would like that for Hank."

Chester asked, "Can you bring Hank over to me?"

Mike called, "Come Hank."

Gary continued the story.

At the next pause Mike told Chester, "I can't bring Hank there."

Gary went on with the story.

At the end of the story Mike stated, "I know you were listening Hank. I know you."

Gary started another story.

Mike announced, "Hank isn't coming."

Gary continued the story.

At a big break Chester pointed out, "They're all with Hank. You're not up here."

Mike ordered, "Hank follow me."

Gary went on with the story.

At a pause Mike guessed, "I don't think he can see."

Gary continued to the next pause.

Mike offered, "I could get somewhere."

Gary went on with the story.

At the next pause Mike replied, "We're not gonna be able to get Hank to do this."

Gary continued.

The next time Gary paused Chester asked, "Are you through with Hank?"

Gary went to the next pause.

Mike asked, "We're going there?" He then stated, "That is with me."

Gary went on with the story.

At the next pause Chester confirmed, "I'll get you over there."

Gary continued the story.

At another pause Christine asked, "Will you bring Hank over there?"

Chester replied, "I won't answer that."

Gary continued.

At the next pause Christine announced, "He's here."

Gary went on to the next pause.

Chester admitted, "I know that."

Gary got a lot more of the story in before he paused again.

Chester ordered, "You bring Hank with you."

Mike disagreed, "I won't bring him."

Chester insisted, "Make sure that Hank comes. Make sure they all get across."

Christine requested, "I would like to stay here."

Chester instructed, "Christine go to where we go. Mike you know where we go."

Mike pointed out, "Look Hank. You're going with Christine. I don't think Hank can really hear us."

Chester remarked, "Hank won't always answer. Will you quit messin' with Hank?"

Mike replied, "I cannot let them go through there. I will not let them trip with that. They're across."

Gary started another story.

At the first pause Mike confessed, "I like her."

Gary kept telling the story until a car passed.

Mike announced, "I am on top of the bridge."

Gary continued until the next car.

Mike explained, "I've got to take Hank up here. There's a mass of people that are coming."

Chester asked, "Is Hank with them?"

Gary went on with the story ending with, "When they dug it up they found twenty five hundred skeletons."

Christine commented, "That's a boocu of us."

Gary gave a follow up to the story.

After that Mike confessed, "I don't like these people anymore. I just want to finish what we got."

Gary's next line has a pause in it where Mike guessed, "Maybe we could take her."

At Gary's next pause Mike admitted, "I'm really trying."

At the next pause Mike asked, "How many tattoos does he have? I don't know why he would want so many."

Chester remarked, "He paid for those."

Gary started talking again.

At a pause Mike replied, "I would change them." At the next pause he stated, "I would loosen them."

Gary continued.

As a car passed Mike announced, "I won't give him anymore. Hank will have to do."

Gary went on with the story to the end.

Mike interjected, "He doesn't look like Hank."

Chester suggested, "Maybe the two of you should look alike."

Mike confirmed, "I'll give them both."

Chester instructed, "Mind this. Give the best to Hank."

Christine in her little girl voice pointed out, "That is Hank." Back to normal with a lot of static she added, "I am with Hank."

Mike started, "What you got there is people. That can't smoke clear at..."

Christine jumped in with her little girl voice and demanded, "Just the bathroom asshole." Then normally she uttered, "Mike's an asshole."

Chester confessed, "I think it's all fair with Hank."

Mike offered, "I could make Hank, make him look like zero."

Chester advised, "I don't think you should do that."

Mike agreed, "I won't make Hank a zero. I should remember that."

Chester figured, "I think Hank could handle a fifty."

Mike replied, "I don't think he could handle a ten."

Chester guessed, "I don't know if Hank should really do this."

Christine commented, "Very good Mike." Chester said, "Mike," with her.

Mike requested, "Let me get through with this."

Chester suggested, "Let's go take Hank right now."

Mike admitted, "You can't say that I didn't do it."

Christine half sang, "Do you hear the music?"

Chester asked, "You didn't give much to Hank did you?"

Mike answered, "Just enough for him to work."

Gary talked to the tour group.

Mike informed them, "Yes the first thing Hank can do wrong. He'll get a big old breakfast on her." That did happen.

Chester asked, "What are you doing to him?"

Christine remarked, "I bet Hank won't feel it."

298

Mike mentioned, "There's something here that I do."

Chester joked, "Maybe you'd like to fuck Hank now."

Mike came back with, "I don't know if he can get naked here."

Chester guessed, "He only wants to live with her."

Christine confessed, "I'd like him to do better."

Mike stated, "But now that Hank will work better. Maybe you should just stay with Hank."

Chester announced, "Hank won't be coming."

Mike figured, "So I came to look, look at Hank."

Chester started, "Hank will probably listen..."

Mike interrupted, "Never mind. There she can take home to Jack."

Chester declared, "You'll be on the list already."

Mike replied, "It's all behind me if go technical. I can do her."

Christine disagreed, "I don't think so."

Gary came in during a story.

At a pause Chester asked, "He's an asshole isn't he?"

Gary continued.

At the next short pause Christine called me, "Hank."

Gary went to the end of the story.

Chester commented, "I wish Hank would come over here. Can you send him right here through the camera?"

Gary started to talk then paused.

Christine admitted, "I can't hear but I saw it."

Gary started telling the story.

As Gary paused to point something out on the bridge a passing spirit remarked, "The ring master has funny feet."

Christine snapped back, "I guess he has some you want some. Think bastard. Is it your family talking over here? I can't believe him anyway."

Gary said, "We have a picture on the website."

Christine asked, "Will you move Hank?" Would you help me? Would you put the mirror on your back? I think we'll go backwards over there."

Chester mentioned, "That's the most intelligent thing you thought. That's why most of them have long hair."

Christine replied, "I don't think Hank's hair is that long."

Chester stated, "I didn't say that it was. Mike is over there. I think it will be a while till we'll be over there. I think that he, yeah that's it. I think that you'll watch him. That you know we need him. Mike could fix Hank."

Christine remarked, "If he had me."

Chester asked, "You want me to do that?"

Gary said a line.

Christine admitted, "I really want Hank."

Gary said another line.

Chester started, "I know you..."

Gary interrupted with another line.

Christine half sang, "Should we draw a picture of what they wanted."

Chester commented, "I think I know what's the matter. I want Hank here."

Christine offered, "I'll make a sign I want Hank here."

Chester related, "That's a new one."

Christine assured him, "Don't worry Hank will be back here before long. Hank will miss me."

Chester asked, "Doesn't Hank seem old? Hank's always been a stoner. That's his whole attitude. But Hank as a stoner can't do no good, Now this won't hurt him after all."

Gary said a line.

Christine confessed, "There is something Mike could help with. I know he could."

Gary continued but between his words Christine called me, "Hank." Then, "Made you look at me," and, "Make him look like I did."

Gary went on.

At a pause Chester mentioned, "Hank would leave her tattooed."

Gary said a line.

Chester announced, "Jesus knows that Mike's gonna help us."

Gary went on to the next pause.

Chester demanded, "Give me those funny pictures. You can dance later."

Gary said a line.

Chester ordered, "Only your favorite dance."

Gary continued to the end.

Chester warned, "There's gonna be an accident when I call you Hank."

Christine advised, "You better do just what you started."

Mike commented, "And they really hate tattoos."

Christine asked, "Did you hear us last night?"

Mike answered, "That was quite a bad job."

Christine disagreed, "That was quite a festival. I think that I should have it. Quite often."

Gary said a line.

Christine again called me, "Hey Hank."

As Gary started the Jack the Ripper story she stated, "I want to feel something."

Gary said, "There's a million theories about Jack the Ripper."

Christine remarked, "He's got to be here."

Gary got a few lines into the story.

Chester declared, "I'm sure about Hank."

Gary said a line.

Christine admitted, "He may not be that cute."

Gary said, "And they were a bloody mess."

Christine finished, "And we're not into playing. Anymore. I wish Hank was here."

Gary said a few more lines.

Christine asked, "What do you think you would like from me?"

Gary gave a line.

Christine sang, "I'm just playing."

Gary went on telling the story.

As we headed back to the stairs and the passage door, Gary told the names they called Jack the Ripper. As he paused Christine announced, "I'm here."

Gary said a word.

Christine called me, "Hey Hank."

Gary said a line.

Christine warned, "You better get that mustache over here. Let's go with Hank."

Gary said a line.

Christine insisted, "Only Hank here."

Gary said, "Take you up there by that door."

Christine replied, "They're about to. That's what you like staying by here."

Chester asked, "Hank where you been?"

Gary said, "A voice said."

Christine bragged, "It was me."

Gary and the tour group talked.

Christine announced, "Hey Hank. Happy early birthday."

Gary and the tour talked some more. There always seemed to be a lot of discussion after the Jack the Ripper story. Gary then said, "Like I said," to get back to the tour.

Christine confessed, "I just want Hank over here."

Gary stated a fact about the bridge.

Christine remarked, "He's supposed to be right here."

We stopped just above the passage door while Gary went into another story.

At a pause in the story Christine explained, "And they'll do that."

Gary went on.

At the next pause Christine related, "It's not worth that. But the flatheads got it. In the second place."

Gary said a line.

Christine said, "I'll be here."

Gary pointed out markings on the bridges.

Christine asked, "Do you think he's awesome?"

Mike instructed, "I need him back over here," with Gary saying, "Bridge," in the middle of it.

Gary said a line.

Christine admitted, "I lost him."

Gary went more into his story.

At a pause Christine announced, "That's him."

Gary said a line.

Christine requested, "Send him back here."

Gary asked about one of the markings, "It looks like chalk doesn't it?"

A male spirit replied, "We're in here."

All of a sudden the recording had static on it so that only Gary could be heard.

After fifteen seconds of static Mike asked, "Is he coming over here?"

Christine answered, "Obviously he's mad."

Gary and the tour group talked.

Christine informed them, "Hank told me. That he wasn't mad at me. I bet we bug the crap out of him."

Mike guessed, "Maybe we shouldn't come back here again."

Christine suggested, "There is always the bathroom. I want to get out of here. Someone should go and measure that. I bet he won't even come down here. I tried to visit him last night. And he was reading his book. You don't think we lost him do you? I want Hank to be with me. I think he's waiting."

Mike asked, "Do you think he knows what he's doing?"

Christine stated, "Hank only talks to me. I'll get through to Henry."

Chester added, "And he'll go where he wants to go."

Mike asked, "Can you visit with Hank though?"

Christine remarked, "I can when he's at home."

Chester admitted, "I can visit Hank too."

Mike replied, "I would like to go visit him."

Chester commented, "I think we might be able to do that quick. Tell Hank to move down."

Christine pointed out, "Hey Hank is moving."

Gary came back with a line.

Christine explained, "I know what he's doing. Hank is only on the tour."

Mike asked, "Will you walk with Hank?"

Christine answered, "I think I might know where he'll go. Let's just do that."

Mike offered, "I'll pass that on to him today."

Gary came in with another story back on the bridge.

At a long pause Christine advised, "There is only one place for Hank. And Hank could be withdrawn. There are some banks over there."

Chester asked, "Whose the fucking boss at that bank?"

Christine stated, "Hank needs a job."

Gary warned the tour group about the cars as some people got off the sidewalk.

Christine remarked, "We're just going back with Hank."

Gary said a line.

Christine announced, "Somebody missed you with that. They could get as much as they want."

Gary said another line.

A song started playing. Christine sang the second line of the song, "Hank will you dance with me now."

The song dissipated and Gary came in talking.

At a pause Christine directed, "It's your turn Mike."

Mike instructed, "You turn it to thirty two to drop it. That's a bit more like it," with the sound vibrating. He then suggested, "Maybe you should try not to move it anyway."

Chester explained, "She has to unhook. I think she did it."

Mike confessed, "I feel like I'm at my bridge. Can you pick up on some other bridges here?"

Chester replied, "The other bridges wouldn't help."

Mike asked, "Does he know they got Captain here?"

Christine answered, "I think he does."

She ordered, "Worry 'bout this," as Gary started talking.

Gary gave his line.

Christine mentioned, "Hank knows about this."

Chester suggested, "Let's see if Hank knows alright. Bring him here."

Gary said a line.

Mike exclaimed, "They touched me."

Gary gave a short line.

Chester assured Mike, "It's gonna be okay."

Gary said another line.

Mike agreed, "I think it would."

Gary gave another line.

Christine called, "Hey Gary."

Gary continued the story to the next pause.

Chester admitted, "I can't hear Gary."

Gary said a line.

Christine called again, "Yo Gary."

Mike announced, "Hank is trying to get pictures."

Gary went on with the story.

At the next pause Christine commented, "Hank is really good."

Mike remarked, "Hank's never coming to us."

Chester replied, "I don't know about that."

Gary went to the end of the story.

Mike related, "That was the fire of London."

Christine claimed, "Hank. Everyone knows Hank here."

Mike explained, "That is the way they pick garbage pickers."

Chester confessed, "We got the birds to talk to him."

Mike told him, "Everybody does that."

Chester acknowledged, "That is good."

Then Christine did a bird whistle just like, "That is good." With Chester saying, "That is Christine." He then mentioned, "That is what we have to do."

Mike blurted out, "There's an idea. Let's get the birds to move him."

Chester interjected, "That is the opposite versus Hank."

Mike asked, "Think he'll hear?"

Gary went into the next story.

At a pause Mike asked, "What else do you think he has?"

Gary went on telling the story which could barely be heard because of all the cars passing by. He finished the story after the cars passed.

Mike stated, "I think you and Hank get together."

Chester remarked, "Definitely. I would just like you to help him."

Mike admitted, "I don't know if that's such a good idea."

Gary gave a line.

Chester guessed, "Maybe Hank is here."

Mike recounted, "I don't wanna have to go do this thing."

Gary started another story with no pauses until about half way through.

Then Chester ordered, "Go to the tea room."

Gary went on.

At the next pause Mike suggested, "You haven't seen me."

Gary said another line.

Christine interjected, "I don't think Hank was helping."

Chester replied, "Your man Hank."

Gary said a line.

Christine confessed, "I knew that."

Gary finished about Blackbeard the pirate.

Chester asked, "Is that your son?"

Gary told another pirate story with cars passing by most of the time.

At a pause Chester commented, "I don't see Hank anymore. There I found him."

Gary told of the heads that were put on the old London Bridge.

After the story Chester admitted, "I don't think we should have come."

A car passed drowning everything out.

Chester asked, "I'm tired of chatting about it when we're in his home? This is how David got it started. There's a job for Hank. There's some people over there. They're over their heads."

Christine came to my defense, "Hank wouldn't do that anyway."

Chester remarked, "I wouldn't want him to have to work here. Do you think Hank would like it? Do you think Hank would do that?"

Christine called to me, "Hey Hank you wanna work?"

Chester asked, "Now how am I going to do this?"

Christine repeated, "I don't know if that's such a good idea. That's what Mike said."

Chester acknowledged, "Yes I know."

Christine declared in her little girl voice, "I don't want you mad at me."

Gary said a line.

Chester replied, "I didn't know you had some."

Gary started another story. Several cars passed by as he told most of the story.

At a pause with no cars going by Chester confessed, "I'd like if you do this."

Gary said a line.

Christine guessed, "I think Hank would do this."

Gary gave a few more lines.

Chester commented, "I see zero for Hank."

Gary said another line.

Chester agreed, "I'd like to do that."

Gary started telling the Lady in Black story.

At a short pause Chester stated, "Got locks of hair."

Gary finished the story and a car passed by.

Chester announced, "They'll be coming through here. I suggest you all move."

Christine informed him, "I'm waiting for Hank to come."

Chester ordered, "We don't need you anymore. But Hank could use a number."

Gary started talking and a car went by.

As the car noise lessened Chester figured, "I could take Hank with me. And if I take Hank I could take Hank back with me. I could take Hank there. Don't you be testing me."

Gary started talking again.

At a pause Chester remarked, "Hank is still standing there. Maybe he could tell of it."

Gary gave a couple of lines.

Christine voiced her concern, "I don't think Hank should be standing here."

Gary continued to the end.

Chester confirmed, "Hank doesn't have to do this. There's no school that can teach any of this. Back to his plight. You can't take Hank with you."

Christine reminded him, "You said that you can."

Chester recounted, "But I'm not supposed to leave here till next week."

Christine replied, "Well then we could do this again."

Chester agreed, "Just till you have sex with Hank."

We started down the steps and Gary made a comment about how hard it was for him since he was four hundred years old.

Christine added, "That's not a fact."

Gary told a short story.

Christine admitted, "I think I can hear him."

Gary started the Lion story.

At a pause Christine told me, "Hank move over."

Gary said a line.

Christine remarked, "That's better."

At the next little pause Chester blurted out, "Hank heard."

Gary said a line.

Chester called, "Christine."

Gary said a couple of words.

Chester started, "Tell Hank this."

Gary finished that story.

Chester announced, "John is here."

Gary said a line.

Christine stated, "We come with Hank."

John asked, "Now should I say something?"

The tour group talked among themselves.

Christine directed, "You all will make me some. I'll tell this to Hank then."

Chester suggested, "Maybe he'd like to see."

A male spirit exclaimed, "This transport is see-through."

Chester explained, "But Hank is a spaceman."

That one surprised even me. I found it real hard to believe, but Chester felt very strongly about lying. I didn't think he would and in many ways it made sense.

A female spirit pointed out, "That's where we live in my room."

Christine comfirmed, "I've seen them."

John commented, "I got through the camera vision."

Chester guessed, "Maybe Hank will do better. Hank's a spaceman."

Gary asked the tour group a question.

Chester asked, "You are all docking here from the transporter? Ask Hank if he'll be safer. Tell Hank to get out here and take a picture of the bridge."

Christine related, "Here's Hank, he got the picture. Five fingers of what?"

Chester answered, "The screen Hank can use."

Gary asked a question of the tour.

Christine advised, "Maybe you should not fall back on that."

Gary said a line.

Chester asked, "Will you go get Mike?"

Gary went into a story. He told the whole story with no pauses. After the story he and the tour group talked.

Christine came back to say, "I went and got Mike. How has Hank been doing?"

Gary said a line.

Christine asked, "Hank didn't take a picture of you did he?"

Gary and the tour group talked again.

Chester admitted, "I think he's being safe."

Gary and the tour group talked more as we left the last spot on the tour.

Chester ordered, "Let's get back from here."

We got under the bridge and Gary said, "Olaf the Viking."

I shut the recorder off.

CHAPTER FOURTEEN

QUESTIONS AT THE BATHROOM TOUR

Other high ranked spirits show up at the beginning
of the tour at the land marker

Before the next tour I was still concerned about the court and even though I had talked to Chester and Christine before the previous tour, I knew I let them down. It was quiet at the Village and the bathrooms were locked so I decided to go over there to at least talk to Christine. Some of EVP's indicated that she wanted to talk to me at the bathrooms so I knew it would be okay. There was nothing special with the tour group so I called this one Questions at the Bathroom Tour.

I turned the recorder on and Christine exclaimed, "You came to me."

Chester admitted, "I can't believe Hank's here. I know that Hank knows we live in here. I didn't think Hank would be here."

I said, "Well."

Chester asked, "What do you think Hank is going to say?"

I said, "Maybe I should explain things. I think Christine you understand."

Christine replied, "I don't understand."

I said, "I don't know if who I think is Chester is here."

Chester guessed, "I think Hank is going to apologize."

Christine remarked, "Hank is coming to us now."

Micah came looking for me and I said, "We can wait for Micah to leave."

Chester declared, "That's okay Hank we're on it. We are doing it."

Loudly and clearly Christine asked, "Can you?"

Chester answered, "Yes I can. Hank can't hear you. He only thinks he can."

Christine confessed, "I'm not sure if he can or not."

A girl came up to me and asked, "Can you do me a favor? It's kinda weird of me asking people."

Chester commented, "Only Hank could help me."

I said, "Actually I was talking to my spirits. I'm sorry."

Chester stated, "Only Hank could have done that."

I said, "As I was saying."

Christine admitted, "I know what he's going through."

I said, "Explaining about myself."

Chester told her, "He thinks that I'm not here." He just barely got out the word here.

I said, "Marijuana."

Chester sighed, "Here we go again."

I said, "It makes me feel like the rest of the people. And you know I'm not like all these people."

Chester ackknowledged, "I know Mike."

I said, "I am totally different. Marijuana makes me feel like I'm part of society. It helps me keep my mouth shut and listen. It helps me when I'm waiting and don't have anything to do. And that's what we're doing right now is waiting."

Chester predicted, "Now here it comes."

I said, "So I hope you guys will be a little more understanding about that. Even though it's not so good for me. Once I get busy I can stop."

Chester remarked, "All the things he did."

I said, "It's not a problem right now when."

Chester related, "Just like always."

I said, "All this waiting. It helps me wait. It makes it okay to not do anything."

Mike admitted, "I know what he's doing."

I said, "So please be a little understanding about that."

Mike repeated, "I know what Hank is doing."

I said, "I've done it all my life."

Mike exclaimed, "I didn't know that."

I said, "And I'm gonna quit. I guess as soon as we get busy."

Mike asked, "Can he hear us?"

I said, "We're waiting right now on the government."

Chester stated, "I know Hank hates waiting for people."

I said, "You have to have a job."

Chester asked, "You're talking to me?"

I said, "In this world you have to do it really fast."

Chester replied, "I'm okay with that."

I said, "They rush you and rush you and you can't do a good job rushing."

Mike commented, "I know what Hank is meaning."

I said, "And the government takes it's time."

Mike sighed, "Don't remind me."

I said, "I could actually be collecting money now but."

Chester suggested, "You might be."

I said, "The government is taking a year and a half."

Chester remarked, "I didn't know."

I said, "It's not going to take us that long to get things running."

Mike comfirmed, "I think Hank knows what he's doing about this."

I said, "Asked last time about orbs, the fountain totally messed up what you guys said."

Mike stated, "I'd like to hear what Hank says."

I said, "It was too hard for me to get."

Mike asked, "Do you know me?"

I asked, "I understand the colors don't mean anything but was there anything else about orbs?"

Chester answered, "That is how we travel."

Christine added, "They have beautiful colors in them."

Mike admitted, "I don't think Hank knows very much about what we've been doing."

Chester confessed, "I don't think Hank believes he's a spaceman. I think Hank will disown me."

Christine uttered, "Whatever."

I said, "Then I asked about the church."

Chester commented, "I don't think that was such a good idea Hank. We don't like that idea. There are too many churches. You might as well be another offshoot. So don't do it."

I said, "Yeah but if it ever comes through it will be good."

Chester asked, "Are you listening? We don't want you to do that Henry. Are you there?"

I said, "I'd like to answer some of your questions."

Chester asked, "What questions were those?"

I said, "They were mostly Chester's, who I believe is Chester."

Christine related, "Hank is not sure about you."

I said, "I don't hate the tour. I don't hate the bridge."

Chester confessed, "I don't believe it."

I said, "I've just done it so many times, it gets a little boring. I care a lot about you guys."

Christine sighed, "I love him."

I said, "I nearly cried when."

Chester asked, "When Hank?"

I said, "When the one happened at the phone booth and Christine was told she couldn't be with me anymore."

Chester admitted, "I didn't know that happened."

I said, "It almost made me cry."

Chester claimed, "I don't think that happened."

I said, "I care a lot about you guys and care that you guys are with me."

Chester complained, "We care a lot about you. And that's a pity. You're not worth it. That's all I have to say. I don't think he can hear what I say. Now tell Hank what we're doing."

Christine declared, "Hank we're here for your death."

Chester added, "I don't think you're ready for it."

Christine remarked, "I'll be there."

I said, "You asked did we have a..."

Chester interjected, "I can't remember."

I finished,"More in sync conversation. Is there a way we can do that?"

Clear and slow Chester answered, "Only if Hank allows us."

Christine guessed, "Maybe he's not ready yet."

Chester asked, "Maybe you'd like to go with me?"

Mike explained, "We keep making Hank a spaceman. I don't think he can make it with her."

Christine disagreed, "I think he could make it with me."

Chester confirmed, "I think he will make it with Christine. I think he wants to be with her."

Mike insisted, "I don't know if he can have her," with some electronic interference.

Then the interference got real strong so that nothing else could be heard for two seconds.

Chester asked, "What was that?"

Christine replied, "That was the machine with Hank."

Mike guessed, "I don't think he even knew."

Chester commented, "I bet he doesn't care."

Christine directed, "I would like to have him push."

I said, "The tour is Gary's business."

Chester acknowledged, "I know."

I said, "Gary makes money off this tour."

Chester stated, "I know that."

I said, "I know the bridge seems out of control to Chester."

Chester recounted, "I don't know about that."

I said, "But this really helps with the tour. If people get pictures of these spirits."

Chester told me, "Yes Hank."

I said, "Running around as orbs."

Chester admitted, "I'm listening Hank."

I said, "Then they are really excited and they spread the word about it to other people. Then more people take the tour and Gary makes more money."

Chester asked, "What was that?"

I said, "I am living with Gary unable to pay him any money because I don't have much money and that gets into my ability not to eat."

Christine predicted, "But you'll die."

I said, "Gary has five children."

Chester again acknowleged, "I know."

I said, "I do not want to be taking food out of these children's mouths."

Chester suggested, "That's what you may have to do."

I said, "So I buy my own food."

Chester insisted, "You need to buy some."

Mike blurted out, "I got an answer."

I said, "Gary is always ready to give me food but everything in this world costs money."

Chester apologized, "I'm sorry."

I said, "We work to make money."

Chester repeated, "I am sorry."

I said, "And yet I cannot work in town. Christine you know that."

Christine remarked, "I know."

I said, "And it's from the prejudice of people because I have tattoos."

Christine sighed, "I'm sorry."

I said, "Maybe my hair too."

Christine related, "I'm sorry they can't look at your tattoos the right way."

I said, "Until these people lose their prejudice and know what a good person is."

Mike admitted, "That's true."

I said, "I'm not gonna be able to get a job. I'm not gonna make money."

Christine disagreed, "Hank we know better."

I said, "I can't afford to eat a lot."

Chester commented, "I can hear this later."

I said, "I can't afford to smoke a lot."

Mike pointed out, "That's good Hank."

I said, "I can't afford."

Mike directed, "Tell us something."

I said, "The machine."

Christine warned, "Careful now Hank."

I said, "I was asked about machines."

Mike asked, "What about machines?"

I said, "Machines actually tie us down."

Mike confessed, "I don't know about that."

I said, "This telephone I got."

Mike replied, "All the peeps do it."

I said, "As soon as it runs out of time, I've got to buy more time."

Mike told me, "I don't know about that Hank. Do you really need it?"

I said, "It will cost me money I can't afford to spend."

Mike apologized, "I'm sorry."

I said, "But I have to have the telephone because Gary's car is broken and he doesn't have enough money to get it fixed."

Mike asked, "What does that have to do with everything?"

I said, "If my car was broken I can't."

Mike exclaimed, "Oh my goodness."

I said, "Most of the money I have."

Chester yelled, "Hank gets money Tuesday," from a distance.

Mike admitted, "That will help."

I said, "On that car."

Chester announced, "They're about upstairs."

Mike asked, "Does he have to leave?"

Gary talked loudly to some people by the fountain.

Mike stated, "I know they're here."

Chester threatened, "Any longer and I might have to take Hank."

Mike confirmed, "I know that Hank is not being good."

I said, "I miss kind of the way this society is. They worship money more than their spirituality."

Mike asked, "Isn't that what you're doing?"

I said, "Which I would like to turn around very much."

Mike remarked, "I don't know if that's something Hank can do."

I said, "It's always see how much money you can get out of the other person. They don't care that the other person doesn't have enough money and needs a lower price."

Mike declared, "It sounds like he knows the problem."

I said, "They up the price and they're not selling a quality product."

Mike agreed, "That's true Hank."

I said, "Because of what I said before, they rush you and you can't make a quality product. They time and time and we needed to let time, it takes time to make a quality product."

Mike admitted, "I don't know what the answer would be."

I said, "I'm sure when you were alive."

Mike asked, "Who's that?"

I said, "That made in America meant something."

Mike confirmed, "That's right."

318

I said, "It no longer does."

Mike asked, "How can Hank say that?"

I said, "Cars don't last ten years."

Mike replied, "That's true Hank."

I said, "You're lucky to get your car three years."

Mike confessed, "I don't know what he's doing."

I said, "Mine is nine years old and it's been fixed three times."

Mike claimed, "It sounds like Hank knows what he's doing."

Chester pointed out, "But now you're leaning towards Hank."

I said, "I'm dissatisfied with the way this world is and I want to fix it."

Mike told me, "You can't fix everything Hank."

I said, "If I can't fix it I would be happy to come to your world."

In a hollow echoing voice Christine asked, "All of you hear Hank?"

A female spirit answered, "I think he said that he wants to come over here."

Mike remarked, "I can't believe he would do something like that here. Maybe he doesn't expect an answer to that."

Chester told him, "You don't know what he asked."

I said, "I'm waiting for Gary."

Chester guessed, "I think he's coming."

I said, "To get that business going and through that I may be able to help people understand what they're doing wrong and be able to change the whole world."

Mike asked, "Does Hank really think he can change the whole world?"

Chester explained, "I think that he thinks we can help him do that. I think that Hank thinks we can help him."

Mike commented, "I don't think he's ready."

I said, "I know I'm pouring my heart out to you guys."

Mike stated, "I didn't think we should do this."

I said, "And you're there for me. I appreciate that more than you can believe."

Chester recounted, "We don't mind doing it Hank."

I said, "I don't want to be a burden to you but I need your help." There was electronic interference on the recorder.

Mike guessed, "I don't think we can do this later either."

I said, "And if we're going to make the bridge a place that people come to we need the pictures of the spirits."

Mike related, "It looks like he's back on track."

I said, "Whether it's out of control or not."

Chester suggested, "Maybe he won't get so old."

I said, "People need to get these pictures, people need to hear voices, people need that assurance."

Christine replied, "I don't do that for everyone."

I said, "Religion in this world."

Chester tried to correct me, "Hank you have no idea."

I said, "Is based on."

Chester remarked, "Oh here we go now."

I said, "What happens after you die."

Chester asked, "Are you really going to pursue that?"

I said, "The evidence of you guys."

Chester repeated, "Here we go again."

I said, "It proves to them."

Chester asked, "Did you hear what I said?"

I said, "That there is."

Mike directed, "Listen to him."

I said, "Life after."

Christine confessed, "That's all I do."

I said, "So once again I ask anything you can do, please do."

Mike pointed out, "It wasn't really a question."

I said, "Thanks for talking to me."

Chester replied, "That's alright Henry."

I shut the recorder off. I went back to the fountain until we started the tour, then turned the recorder back on. The fountain was running so there was noise from that with Gary talking. We moved to the front gates and Gary told about those.

At a pause Mike admitted, "If it was you I'd feel bad."

Chester told him, "No you should be feeling better."

Gary said a line.

Chester remarked, "A big fat zero."

Gary said, "We're done here."

Chester stated, "He's gotta be bigger than his kids."

Gary brought everyone to the land markers.

Mike announced, "I don't think Hank is in there."

Gary started the land marker story.

At a pause Mike claimed, "We've been here before."

Chester instructed, "Mark don't step on that right now please."

Gary went on with the story.

At a pause Chester commented, "I saw what he was doing."

Gary got almost to the end of the story when Christine related, "I think he's done here."

Gary gave a couple of lines.

Mike insisted, "I don't think he could live right here."

Gary got to the end of the story.

Mike confessed, "I'm not scared of Hank."

Chester warned, "But you haven't seen what he can do. I have seen one spirit that Hank brought upstairs."

Mike replied, "I didn't see it."

Chester started, "Not the liquid..."

Gary interrupted with a line.

Chester finished, "He messed him up."

Gary said the first line in the lamppost story.

Mike started, "I didn't know he did..."

Gary interrupted with more of the story.

At a pause Chester admitted, "I knew he'd be in there."

Gary went on with the lamppost story.

At the next short pause Mike announced, "Hank is over here."

Gary gave the location of the other lampposts.

Christine gave her opinion, "I don't miss him."

Gary started the closing lines to the story.

Chester ordered, "To you he's a stranger."

Gary finished the story.

Chester explained, "That's what he gets when he won't help you."

We moved on to the phone booth and Gary started the story there.

Near the end of the phone booth story there was a long pause where Chester stated, "I don't think Hank is supposed to come over here."

Gary went on.

At the next pause Mike started, "I just want to see." After a line from Gary he finished, "I just want to see something."

Gary finished the phone booth story and went right into another story as the clock tower chimed.

At a pause in the story Mike admitted, "I think he knows what he's doing."

Gary went on with the story.

At a pause Mike told them, "Hank knows what he's doing."

After a few lines of the story Gary paused just long enough for Chester to ask, "Need a generator?"

At the next pause Christine confessed, "I can't hear it."

After a line from Gary Chester figured, "That's about it."

At a break Christine suggested, "Let's get out of here."

Then at the next break Mike remarked, "It's just my finger."

At another pause Chester confirmed, "I know he did that."

At the next pause Christine started, "Answer this."

Gary said just one line.

Mike agreed, "I said okay."

Gary said the next line with a pause where Mike asked, "What is he doing?"

Gary finished the story.

Mike stated, "I know that Hank is here."

Chester explained, "I just know where Hank is. I can't see Hank every day."

Gary and the tour talked a little on the walk to the water's edge.

At a quiet moment Chester commented, "They're better off with Hank here."

Gary and Micah talked a little.

Mike reported, "Hank is going about business."

Then we got a loud EVP among everything else that was soft. It was a passing spirit that said, "Witch. The dead they cannot hear you."

Chester mentioned, "There are some strange ones here."

Mike suggested, "That was part of his dreams."

Chester asked, "Why did you put him in here?"

Mike replied, "No answer."

Christine started, "Hank could be..."

Gary interrupted with a line.

Chester announced, "I'm ready for here."

We got to the water's edge where Gary and the tour group talked.

It quieted down and Mike pointed out, "Here is someone's case."

Micah talked to me.

Chester ordered, "Hank get over here."

Micah talked some more.

Chester confessed, "I miss talking to you."

Micah talked more.

Mike guessed, "I think Hank is a big brother."

Micah kept talking.

Christine instructed, "Those are Gary's."

Micah finished and Gary started a story but at a moment of silence Mike stated, "You get what you pay for. What is he doing here?"

Chester answered, "Taking pictures."

Gary talked to Micah.

Mike informed them, "Hank has a video camera."

Gary told Micah to take his video camera. He then told Micah, "I want you to video a lot of Hank."

Mike announced, "They're taking pictures of Hank. They know we're here."

Gary talked to the tour group while Micah stood next to me explaining how he operated the video camera. Micah finished talking and started filming. Gary got back to the stories of the tour.

At a pause Mike admitted, "I wasn't here."

Gary started the Dead Man's Hole story.

At a pause Mike exclaimed, "That's a win Hank."

Gary said a line.

Mike asked, "Can we fit through there?"

Gary said another line.

Chester replied, "We can slide through there. Now get back to the tour."

Gary continued the story.

At the next pause Christine remarked, "I can't hear him."

Gary said a line.

Mike asked, "Make a change wouldn't you?"

Gary told more of the story.

At a pause Mike suggested, "We could take Hank outta here."

Gary said a line.

Christine pointed out, "We got Hank right here."

Gary said another line.

Mike acknowledged, "Yes I'm right here."

Gary gave another line.

Christine declared, "Hank is backing down to the master."

We moved to the steps and Gary started the stories there.

At the first pause Christine encouraged, "We can do this."

Gary went on.

At the next pause Mike confessed, "We all tried this."

Gary said, "There is a law on the books that says you cannot beat on the London Bridge with a hammer."

Chester asked, "Can we beat on Hank with a hammer?"

Gary went on with more stories.

Micah talked a little as we climbed the stairs.

Mike guessed, "Maybe Hank's not watching us."

Gary went into the Bullet Holes stories.

At a pause Mike asked, "Did you ask your Hank?"

Gary said a line.

Christine answered, "Only if the yield's ready."

Mike offered, "We could get it ready for him."

Christine replied, "I hope you know what you're doing."

Mike admitted, "It's not that hard Christine."

Christine comfirmed, "I know you can."

Gary gave a lead into the Museum Tape story.

Mike announced, "Okay it's made to order."

Gary finished the lead-in.

Mike asked, "Can you take a picture of it?"

Gary started the Museum Tape story.

At a pause Mike mentioned, "I don't think Hank will feel it."

Gary went on.

At the next pause Mike asked, "Can you see that?"

At another pause Chester answered, "I can see that."

Gary got near the 'no bridge' part of the story and Mike sighed, "This again."

At the next pause Mike uttered, "I know there's a bridge."

Gary said the 'no bridge' line.

Mike declared, "Hank is here."

Gary said a short line.

Mike ordered, "Move it Hank," with my name fairly loud.

Gary said, "He looks up and he can see the flag poles sticking up out of the fog."

Mike remarked, "That's what Hank lives in."

Gary said the next line.

Chester admitted, "I knew he could do it."

Gary gave another line.

Chester claimed, "Hank's not even here."

Gary said, "Alright."

Chester recounted, "There he is."

Gary started winding up that story.

Mike suggested, "Let's do it."

Gary said the last line in the Museum Tape story.

Mike complained, "I don't think the yield will fit."

One of the people on the tour asked Gary if it was the Lake Havasu museum and he answered.

Chester asked, "Do you know what you're doing?"

Christine warned Mike, "Everybody's here."

We climbed the stairs with Gary talking.

At a pause Mike exclaimed, "Doggone it."

Gary said a line.

Chester started, "You originally."

Christine interrupted, "Catch Hank when he comes through."

Gary said a line as we went to the statues.

Christine guessed, "Maybe Hank will settle down."

Mike confirmed, "There will be a second chance to get Hank."

Chester instructed, "Don't worry about it neighbor. Never ask him to do that. I'll try it. If you could weigh it. I think you'll have to twist it."

Mike pointed out, "But Hank is here."

Chester confessed, "I just want to get this crap over."

Mike suggested, "Maybe you'd like Christine to do it to him."

Christine replied, "I saw Gary do it."

Mike offered, "Just let me do it."

Chester asked, "You won't bring Hank here?"

Mike asked, "What does Hank have? Could he die right here?"

Chester answered, "Hank has cancer."

Gary started the stories by the statues.

At the first pause Mike recounted, "Maybe you should do it."

Gary went on.

326

At the next pause Chester directed, "You'll bring Hank over here."

Gary said a line.

Mike ordered, "Hank come here."

Gary said another line.

Mike encouraged, "It's only a dream. Down here by Gary."

Gary went on with the story.

At a pause Christine told Mike, "You can do better."

Gary continued.

At the next pause Mike confessed, "Hank can hear us."

Gary said a line.

Chester asked, "Do you really think?"

Gary said another line.

Mike asked, "Got what you need?" It sounded robotic.

Gary gave a line.

Chester announced, "Hank is in here."

Gary said another line.

Chester remarked, "Let's see if that helps him."

Gary went on with the story.

At a pause Chester insisted, "Give Hank one of these."

Gary said a long line.

Mike asked, "Is Hank gonna be okay?"

Chester answered, "As okay as he ever is."

Gary gave another line.

Mike asked, "Is the Dungeon right here?"

Gary said a short line.

Chester replied, "No this isn't it."

Gary went on with the story.

At the next pause Mike apologized, "I'm sorry Hank."

Gary continued the story.

At a short pause Mike asked, "Did you hear?"

Gary went on.

At the next little pause Chester asked, "Did you?"

Gary said a long line.

Mike instructed, "Meet me here."

Gary went on with the story and a truck went by on the road.

The next pause had Christine singing, "I had fear."

Gary continued.

At the next pause Chester related, "It's not on you."

Gary told more of the story.

At another pause Mike asked, "Did you hear that?"

Gary went on with the story.

At the next pause Chester asked, "Is it Hank?"

Gary then asked the tour group a question.

While Gary waited for an answer Mike asked, "What would you like Hank to do next?"

Gary said a line.

Mike asked, "Can I help you with that?"

Gary continued the story.

At a pause Mike asked, "What's the matter?"

Gary said another line.

Chester remarked, "I shouldn't take you on the tour."

Gary went on.

At the next pause Chester admitted, "It's not you."

Gary finished the story.

Mike apologized, "I'm sorry. About me and Hank."

Gary added some facts after the story.

At a pause between the facts Chester guessed, "Hank won't do that."

Gary said, "General Patton used to hang out here a lot."

A deeper male voice replied, "I'm here."

Gary finished at the statues.

Christine announced, "Hank was here yesterday. But we helped him up here."

Chester commented, "Christine got him back for all of that. It's funny how we got here."

We started walking to cross the bridge.

Chester declared, "Next time we'll tell you about that."

Mike pointed out, "There is a box of what I've been cleaning for you."

Christine stated, "Hank would have asked me to do it. You don't think that Mike has some."

Gary and the tour group talked as we walked. Then cars started passing.

Gary began a story with the cars still passing by.

When no cars were passing, Gary paused and Chester asked, "Is that what he did?"

At the next pause Mike suggested, "Let's get out of here."

Gary went on with the story as more cars passed.

Sometime later everything paused and Mike asked, "Did you strike Hank?"

Gary continued the story and a few cars passed.

Everything got quiet again and Mike asked, "What are we gonna do?"

Gary said a line.

Chester answered, "Nothing."

Gary said another line.

Mike asked, "What'd ja mean?"

Gary told more of the story and a couple of cars passed by.

At a pause Chester warned, "He might hurt you."

Gary went on and a truck passed.

Chester mentioned, "He's done there," with the hum of the truck.

Gary said a few more lines.

Mike asked, "Did you see that?"

Gary went on with cars passing.

Between the cars Mike guessed, "He might be here."

At Gary's next pause Chester remarked, "I don't know if he'll do that." At the next pause Chester confirmed, "Hank is here."

Gary went on and several cars passed before it got quiet again.

Chester instructed, "That's what we'll put down later."

Gary said a few lines.

Mike confessed, "I don't know what to do."

Gary continued with cars passing.

At the next break Chester ordered, "Then we'll work on this tomorrow."

Mike disagreed, "I don't think we'll have to."

Chester guessed, "I don't think Hank will mind that."

Gary went on with the stories and Micah talked about going to a store there for dream catchers.

At a short pause Mike asked, "Did you hear that?"

At the next short pause Christine admitted, "I can't hear."

Gary and Micah continued with me acknowledging what Micah said.

At the next pause Chester claimed, "It's broken."

It must have been the machine that was broken because three seconds later everyone's talking breaks up for two seconds.

When they paused Christine announced, "I can hear him."

Gary and Micah talked some more.

At a pause Chester pointed out, "They must enjoy being together."

Gary and Micah continued.

At the next pause Chester stated, "Hank is back."

Only Gary talked this time.

When he paused Mike asked, "Who'd you have to kill?"

Gary said a line.

Chester answered, "Killed a man."

Gary went on.

At the next pause Christine asked, "Did you hear that?"

Gary continued with cars passing.

At a short pause Christine explained, "They're working."

Gary and the cars went on.

At the next pause Mike admitted, "I killed a man."

Gary continued with the cars.

It got quiet after a minute and Christine asked, "What is that guy doing?"

Mike remarked, "I think his dick is calling out for her."

Christine commented, "I don't know if I can deal with these two anymore."

Mike offered, "Maybe I should go trigger her memory."

Chester mentioned, "John said he wished on me."

Mike replied, "Enough about Chester."

Gary started another story and a car passed.

Mike confessed, "I know what you two are doing."

Gary continued the story.

At a pause Christine told Mike, "You're the asshole."

Gary went on.

At the next pause Chester confirmed, "There is no bigger asshole than Mike."

A car passed and then the tour group talked.

Micah and I went ahead of the tour.

Christine stated, "I think Hank will do it when he can."

Chester related, "Just like Bobby and Taylor did."

Christine added, "Only better."

A car went by.

Mike claimed, "Some people think that violence would not be hard."

Christine interjected, "I've been here before. I should see what Hank is thinking."

Mike asked, "Can't one or both of you do that?"

A car revved its engine going by.

Christine asked, "Don't you think Hank is special?"

Mike replied, "Maybe I should take a smoke here."

Chester agreed, "If that's what you have to do."

Mike remarked, "That's amazing that Hank's on the ground about that."

Gary came in talking again.

I told Micah the tour caught up to us.

Chester warned, "Careful Hank," as I was getting up.

Christine asked, "Do you need some help?"

Mike started, "Gary needs to."

Christine finished, "Sign up."

Mike claimed, "There's a kid bugging Hank."

Christine corrected him, "But Micah has a story."

Chester added, "But somehow he's into that."

Mike asked, "Yeah but can he do that?"

Chester answered, "Hank can do that."

Christine insisted, "Mike you're not supposed to be here."

Mike came back with, "I come here all the time."

Chester told him, "But you knew Hank was here."

Mike admitted, "I was sure that Hank would be here."

Chester explained, "Hank would be the part of why you shouldn't."

Mike asked, "Does he make a difference?"

Christine suggested, "Maybe you should let him try and do that."

Chester agreed, "Okay but don't arrest him."

Mike replied, "I wouldn't do that to Hank anyway."

Chester announced, "Tom's just saying they're ready. Regularly I would not let him do that."

Mike asked, "Hank will be here right?"

Micah started talking.

When Micah finished Chester confessed, "I'm trying to explain that to Mike."

Christine guessed, "Maybe you should try to rule."

After I acknowledged what Micah said Chester whispered, "Let's go in here."

Micah and I talked for a moment.

Mike informed them, "They're working already."

No spirits talked for about ten seconds.

Christine yelled, "Mike!"

Chester added, "Should not be in there."

Christine asked, "Should I help him out with that? Pick the key up!"

Chester advised, "Let him do that on his own. We're here if something happens."

Christine disagreed, "That's a bad idea. Maybe I could."

A girl yelled over at the Heat.

Christine finished, "Handle that. Hey Mike don't do that!" Maybe I should let him do that. Mike won't admit he doesn't know. Yo asshole! I don't believe this."

Chester commented, "Hank won't believe this."

A female spirit asked, "Can I see what's the matter?"

Christine repeated, "I don't believe this."

Chester figured, "Maybe you should let her watch this."

Christine remarked, "I don't care if she does."

Chester asked, "Did Mike do that?"

Christine ordered, "Let Mike do that."

The female spirit asked, "Is Mike an angel?"

Christine answered, "No he's not."

Chester stated, "I wish that he wouldn't be here. I think I should feel better. About Mike doing this."

Christine asked, "Did Mike hear what I said? I think Mike is finished. Make sure that Hank knows. How Mike shouldn't be here."

Sherry showed up and announced, "My hair is strong but it isn't long it isn't."

Chester mentioned, "Only you would say that here."

Christine asked, "Is that Sherry?"

Sherry pointed out, "Hank is over here."

Chester instructed, "Walk right up to her."

Sherry interjected, "And scare her."

Chester replied, "If that's how you do it. Guess Mike's over there too."

Sherry exclaimed, "Get out of here."

Chester explained, "Why don't you say whatever you might be towing the line. No Jewish community here. Yes you told me about that."

Sherry confessed, "But I didn't know this was about Hank."

Gary came in with, "Now this over here."

Sherry decided, "Better talk right here."

Gary went right into a story.

After the story Sherry started, "I don't think Hank..."

Chester interrupted, "He hangs over here."

Gary said a line.

Sherry corrected him, "That's where you got me wrong."

Christine greeted her, "Hi sweetheart."

I asked, "Would you like to talk over here?" Christine told Sherry, "I've got to talk to Hank," at the same time. She then admitted, "You got me right past Caesar."

Chester advised, "That doesn't even matter, you care about Hank."

Christine agreed, "Hank is still my favorite."

Chester stated, "You're just an asshole. Careful."

I said, "I'm not seeing a lot of you guys tonight."

Christine answered, "We're not gonna be here," as Gary talked the background.

Chester added, "We're the angel's maze."

Christine confirmed, "You got me."

I said, "I know you're here and maybe it's just one of those nights."

Chester related, "As you fear the night has come."

Mike told me, "That was Chester."

Christine yelled, "Mike you answered! Take Hank don't you ever ask me!"

Chester admitted, "I can't stand up to her this time. Guess she got on you. With a small chord from Amadeus. Now you know to stay in order. You're in cold blood here Mike."

Mike blurted out, "Hank's so busy."

I asked, "Can you impart any wisdom upon me?"

Chester answered, "We're both here."

Christine explained, "That is we're here. For you to live."

Chester mentioned, "But you have volunteered to come with me."

Christine confessed, "We can't always be here together."

I said, "Okay let's go back and get on the tour."

Chester remarked, "I don't know what you're talking about. I've seen it's on."

Sherry claimed, "But that sausage is in my hair."

Chester instructed, "But get it before it gets back to Hank. You two play over there where Hank is. I can't come over there."

Sherry suggested, "Maybe we're both satisfied."

Christine related, "Maybe we both dropped the ball then. All the time we spent together."

Chester commented, "It was a lot of time sweetheart."

Sherry acknowledged, "I'm aware of the time."

Christine declared, "All appears to be about Hank."

Gary came in with a line from the Jack the Ripper story.

Christine asked, "Did you hear that?"

Sherry answered, "It's all about Hank."

Christine insisted, "Say, do Hank is what we have. Hank is all there is," with my camera beeping.

Gary said another line.

Chester stated, "When we have to."

Sherry admitted, "I know."

Chester confessed, "We wanted fucking Hank to go through this anyway."

Christine corrected him, "That's no fair. You just say fucking too much."

Chester remarked, "I can't get any of the answers."

Christine related, "Everybody knows you don't need to."

Chester asked, "You know about that? Anybody down here believes."

Gary and the tour group came back in.

Between Gary's Jack the Ripper story and people at the Heat, Chester ordered, "See if Hank knew who he really was."

Gary started to talk but paused.

Christine commented, "I knew he'd know."

Gary went on with the story.

At a pause Chester mentioned, "Hank took a long time there."

Gary continued the story but even at the pauses it sounded like people at the Heat.

When the story ended Mike admitted, "I'm scared about you."

Christine told him, "You're not that good."

Sherry asked, "You got Jack here?" at the same time.

Mike confessed, "I love creepy Hank."

Chester replied, "Aw but is Hank done."

Christine demanded, "Go ahead I'm watching. Now did you hear that?"

Sherry questioned, "I don't know why you just can't stop it."

Christine reminded her, "It's all about Hank you know."

Sherry guessed, "Maybe I shouldn't have come here."

Christine directed, "But we already did that." Then using her little girl voice she yelled, "Catch him."

Sherry suggested, "Maybe you should bounce around there."

Mike asked, "Now does Hank feel it?"

Christine answered, "There is nothin'."

I may have bumped into someone when I said, "Oh I'm so sorry."

Christine ordered, "I think you're gone."

A few moments later she stated, "I know what Hank is doing."

Chester confirmed, "I called for you River."

Christine asked, "Why'd you do that?"

Gary said a line.

Chester descibed the bridge, "Two hundred and fifty two feet."

Christine added, "For Hank to love."

Chester asked, "Can you put it through there?"

Christine sang, "I hope you like it there."

Chester instructed, "That's not it, right through there. So did he have any idea?"

Christine replied, "He got her right."

I asked, "Christine are you here up there?"

Christine remarked, "Yes I'm always here."

After some yelling from the Heat she asked, "Where are you? I did that after the tour Hank." She was referring to the picture I got of her on top of the passage door.

Chester commented, "Female with the black heart of a female."

Christine claimed, "They lost their magick."

Chester stated, "I've been saving for Halloween already."

I climbed the stairs and rejoined the tour where Gary was telling a story near street level. When he paused the music from the Heat covered any EVP's.

Finally the music died down. Gary was talking about the blocks of the bridge being numbered.

Christine admitted, "I've seen that inside the bridge."

Gary said a long line.

A passing female spirit asked, "What are you?"

Christine half sang, "You know I'm a girl. See this male. He is from the Death Men. You best leave us alone."

The passing spirit asked, "Can I go right there around you?"

Christine replied, "I'm sure it's alright."

Sherry insisted, "I've just got to win."

Christine mentioned, "That's what you're always saying."

Sherry asked, "Did you talk to my sister? That's who just got it ready."

Christine ordered, "Help out."

Micah asked a question about recording the tour.

I answered his question.

Sherry joked, "Hank's so fat."

Chester asked, "What was she doing while you were over there? Smoking pot."

Christine remarked, "That's what I'm doing."

I said, "Don't say that unless you trust me first."

Christine exclaimed, "Hank just heard us."

Chester admitted, "That just proved I'm wrong. You should walk with Henry."

A car passed.

Chester commented, "Boy that just screwed us."

Christine related, "I think he was talking to you."

I said, "Saying anything is cool, but having questions to answer is the best part of what we're doing. Get it out there first."

Chester suggested, "First let's pull Hank."

Micah was saying how tired he was of doing the tour, so just to get him I asked Gary about the next tour and Gary answered.

Micah said, "Fuck you."

Christine replied, "Anywhere."

A car went by.

Mike announced, "I boosted Hank."

Me and Micah talked as another car passed.

After the next car passed Chester confessed, "I didn't hear what he said. There might be something."

Christine stated, "They're waxing."

Chester explained, "I tell him like it is."

Mike confirmed, "You're telling Hank."

Chester whispered, "That's not my answer."

He then spoke, "I've brought fourteen down here."

A car passed.

After that car passed Gary was telling a story.

Another car passed and Gary finished the story.

Mike asked, "What answer?"

There was talking amongst the tour group and Gary.

Christine pointed out, "See him over there."

Sherry remarked, "He does not care what you're doing."

Gary started another story.

Three cars passed before Gary paused and Christine asked, "Was he here?"

Chester mentioned, "I got a fear." There was a change in his tone when he decided, "I think it's not too difficult."

Gary continued.

At the next pause Chester declared, "I'm sure he can't see us."

A motorcycle and a car passed.

Chester asked, "Why are you trying to think with me?"

Gary went on to the next pause.

Christine convinced herself, "I can't be scared."

Gary went on with the story.

I fell behind the tour and said, "I wanna ask..."

Chester suggested, "You should ask us for some food."

Gary said a line.

Christine advised, "Easy."

Gary came back in and finished the story as three cars passed.

Chester asked, "Do you think Hank would kill for me?"

Mike asked, "Do you think Hank would miss. Your little troop?"

Gary started talking and several cars passed.

At a pause Christine asked, "Did you really talk to Hank?"

Gary said a line.

Chester asked, "Now that you did your thing. Whose got the screwdriver in their hand? Bobby knew that he had picked it up. I can't be happy with this shit we go through. All this time we've been with Hank."

Christine commented, "He has a brave heart."

Chester remarked, "He's just pissed off now."

Seven cars passed by before we heard Gary telling a story.

Two more cars passed as Gary started the Lady in Black story.

At a pause Chester admitted, "I would take her."

Mike confessed, "I would marry her."

Chester replied, "That's not good."

Two more cars passed by.

Mike asked, "Can you come up to my room?"

Chester answered, "I will be busy most of the evening. But tomorrow would be okay."

Mike pleaded, "You know that I'm trying to be a good guy."

Chester explained, "It seems like you're a poser. You are supposed to be an eternally helper. What have you helped us do? The next tour I'm trusting you."

Cars started driving past but there was just enough time between the second and third cars for Chester to say, "I know that Hank would like it."

As the fifth car passed there was singing behind it and as the singing stopped Mike called, "Christine."

Christine asked, "What do you want?"

A car drove by and Gary started a story.

At a pause Mike remarked, "I'll tell you later. That's alright."

Gary went on with the story and another car passed.

Mike boasted, "I'm a good guy."

Chester added, "We love you very much."

Mike suggested, "I got to get away from you guys."

Chester asked, "But where will you go?"

Two cars passed and Gary started talking again.

At a pause Mike commented, "It's not fair."

Gary said a line.

Chester demanded, "I want you to move Hank."

Gary said another line.

Chester started, "I think you should be."

Gary went on with a story.

At the first pause Mike agreed, "That's true."

Gary continued for a couple of minutes before the next pause.

Mike asked, "Where's Hank and them?"

Gary went on and another car went by before he paused.

Mike stated, "I'd like to take a whirly bird."

Chester predicted, "I don't think you will."

Gary continued.

At the next pause Chester related, "Hank's never been in a whirly bird," with Gary saying, "So," during it.

Gary went on telling about the suicides on the bridge. Gary then talked about the "Help me, my feet are broken," EVP story as an example of why they need a psychic. This time after the story Christine asked, "Did Hank even know her?"

We moved off the street level and Gary started telling the lion story.

At the first pause Christine exclaimed, "Hank answered."

Gary went on with the story.

At the end of the story I reminded Gary that I got a picture of a lion there.

Christine explained, "Hank got a picture of me and Chester."

They made a lion for me lying like the Sphinx.

The people on the tour started asking questions about the picture.

At a pause Christine told Chester, "That's what you did."

Chester replied, "Maybe Hank could do it."

I described the picture.

At the end Chester asked, "Does Hank know it was us?"

Gary asked the tour a question.

Christine admitted, "That was nice of you. Wasn't that nice Hank? Hank has duties."

Gary got the spotlight from Micah to highlight a spot on the bridge.

Christine remarked, "That's a good idea."

Chester asked, "Do you know what you're doing?"

I said softly, "Right now it's under the bridge."

Chester added, "It's coming through."

Christine asked, "Is that what you're doing? Colleen said something awful."

Chester advised, "That will make Hank all ready."

Christine confessed, "I knew Hank would do that. Let's not be together. I don't think." Softly she said, "Hank can do it." Louder she said, "Abuse..."

Someone from the tour talked cutting her off.

Gary laughed at what they said.

Christine called, "Hey Gary."

Gary talked about the object on the wall.

At a pause Christine judged, "Guilty."

At the next pause Chester asked, "Is Hank upset?"

Several seconds later there was a pause where Chester asked, "Does Hank know we're gonna do it?"

Gary finished the story and gave some facts after it.

Gary paused and a lady on the tour answered, "Yes," with Christine behind her saying, "He's talking."

Gary gave a line.

Christine admitted, "I knew it."

Chester remarked, "Not in his head."

The tour looked at the spot on the bridge again.

Chester ordered, "We gotta show Hank that picture."

Christine asked, "How can Hank see?"

Gary talked as we walked under the bridge where he said, "Olaf the Viking."

I shut the recorder off.

CHAPTER FIFTEEN

THE TV46 TOUR

Micah checking his camera for orbs while
they passed by him

A local TV station had a show about things to do in the area and since we had the number one attraction in Lake Havasu they were real anxious to get us on. We knew it wasn't anything big but you never know where these things will lead.

I got there about the same time as I always did but everyone else was running late. The fountain wasn't running and it was quiet in the Village so I went to the phone booth to talk to Chester and Christine. This is the TV46 tour.

I turned the recorder on and Chester announced, "Hank is here." As I got settled in the phone booth he asked, "What are you doing Hank?"

Mike stated, "I'm ready for him." He then asked, "Hank with me?"

Chester ordered, "Not on the tour. Get back over here."

Mike greeted me, "Hank."

I said, "I don't know what to."

Chester asked, "What is that?"

I said, "What to do was before."

Christine sighed, "My Hank."

I said, "I learned nothing from Christine."

Chester replied, "I know."

I explained, "My knowledge comes from this world."

Chester directed, "Maybe you should rehearse that."

I said, "As I say before."

Chester admitted, "I wouldn't be here. If I wasn't gonna be here for Hank."

I said, "There are things I do in this world."

Chester suggested, "Look around home."

I said, "I can only guess that you do the same thing in your world."

Chester started, "Careful what we."

Christine interjected, "Move Hank. Hank what are you doing here?"

Chester remarked, "Hank wants to come to our world. And be the Erwin."

Mike started, "I'll try to do whatever I can to make him..."

I cut him off with, "I was wondering."

Chester pointed out, "Hank enjoyed that. Here he comes with it."

I started, "Is Robert."

Chester commented, "I don't like waiting."

I said, "McCullough."

Chester related, "Not in your head."

I finished, "Here at the bridge?"

Mike confessed, "I couldn't hear what Hank just asked." We could hear a motorcycle out on the road.

He then added, "I'm not working with Hank anyway."

Chester explained, "But Hank, is here. I don't think he's clear. They don't have to know."

Christine announced, "Jack is tardy."

Chester stated, "Hank will disown me. Forever."

Mike asked, "What are you going to do?"

I said, "I wanted to let you know that uh."

Chester asked, "What'd he say?"

I said, "TV cameras are coming tonight."

Chester told Mike, "Hank knows her mentor."

I said, "Ah it's a local channel of TV."

Mike replied, "I don't think it really matters."

Chester advised, "I wouldn't tell Hank. Hank would turn on us. There is no room for error."

Mike asked, "Are you gonna live with Hank?"

I said, "So we're trying to look good."

Chester remarked, "You're failing Hank."

I said, "My battle with smoking is going pretty good."

Chester instructed, "I'll do the magick now. I'll do what Mike did before. I won't wait till everybody is all around. I've got some training for Mike. Start the balling right here."

I said, "Gary should be getting here real soon. It's kind of up in the air how late it's going to start and..."

Christine asked, "What Hank?"

I said, "How long it's going to take. Usually when the TV comes you have to do it again and again."

Mike agreed, "That's right."

Christine commented, "Hank that's awful," as I said, "So."

I finished, "We will see what happens."

Chester requested, "Give us a minute," very clearly.

I said, "In that respect."

Christine confirmed, "Now we got it."

I encouraged, "But like I say if anyone wants to join us it's fine with me."

Chester yelled, "Hey Mike, Hank's not angry with you."

Mike remarked, "That one went much better."

Chester stated, "Hank was good for us. Double winners."

I turned the recorder off.

Everyone showed up later. The TV people told us how they wanted to film the tour but the beginning would let them get the feel for how Gary did the tour. We started the tour normally with the history of the bridge by the fountain. I turned the recorder on.

Gary gave the first line of the story and paused.

Chester suggested, "Let's stay with Gary."

Gary said the next line.

Mike agreed, "I can do that."

Gary told more of the story.

At the next short pause Mike offered, "I will do it."

Gary related the Village to the bridge and told of the beginning of London.

At another pause Chester asked, "What will you do?"

Gary finished the story.

Chester commented, "Up at the bridge."

The people on the tour remarked on the story.

At a quiet moment Chester asked, "Did everybody hear that?"

Gary and the tour group talked.

At a pause Chester pointed out, "Look at this."

Gary and the tour group continued.

At the next pause Chester directed, "Not here."

Gary began the story of the front gates.

At the first pause Christine ordered, "Don't do that."

Gary went on with the story although a few people continued to talk.

A female spirit asked, "Is that Gary?" at a break.

Gary mentioned the land markers.

At a pause Chester uttered, "Whatever."

Gary carried on with the front gate story.

At the next pause Mike announced, "Hank was here."

Gary finished the front gate story.

Mike repeated, "I'm sure that Hank was here."

Gary headed over to the land markers and told that story with a lot of talking in the tour group.

At one pause Chester claimed, "Favorite." At the next he warned, "He ought to put it down."

You could only hear the tour talk after that.

As the tour quieted down Chester demanded, "Give it to me."

Gary squeezed in the lamppost story and told about the fountain but there was a point where the sound started vibrating. He went on to mention EMF readings while they were at the fountain and then he had to explain EMF readings.

As the explanation ended Christine called me, "Hank."

Gary started telling about the ghost box.

At a pause Mike acknowedged, "Here I come."

Gary finished telling about the ghost box.

Mike asked, "Up there now?"

Gary told about one of his EVP's from the Village. He then talked with the female host of the TV show about other paranormal research.

At a pause Chester ordered, "Do it now."

Gary and the host finished their conversation.

Christine mentioned, "I'm mad Hank."

Mike apologized, "I'm sorry."

Chester started, "But she," at the same time Christine sighed, "I don't mind."

Gary went back to the lamppost story.

At the first pause Chester exclaimed, "Live."

Gary went on with one of the TV people talking the whole time.

At a short pause Mike pointed out, "Right there."

Gary finished the lamppost story.

Christine directed, "Come back here."

The tour group (mostly TV people) talked among themselves.

We moved to the phone booth.

At a pause when the tour group was talking Mike admitted, "I don't need it."

Gary began the phone booth stories. After the first story Gary, the host, and the director all talked so when one paused two were still talking. When they got to the ghost topic they took turns talking.

The clock tower chimed.

Gary got back to the phone booth stories.

When Gary said, "My name is Marsha."

A female voice replied. "I'm here."

Then when Gary said, "Hello my name is Cheryl," a female spirit remarked, "My name is Cheryl," Gary said, "Okay," in the middle of it.

Gary explained EVP's a little more.

At a pause Christine asked, "Think he'll do it?"

Gary asked me what the name was of the girl that I kept getting EVP's of. Then Christine announced, "I'm here."

I said, "Christine."

Gary said, "He gets Christine almost every time we come down here."

Christine insisted, "I'm with Hank."

Gary began telling the Golden Unicorn story.

At a pause Mike claimed, "I'm in love."

At the next pause Chester remarked, "No you're not."

At another pause Mike argued, "I am." At the next pause he apologized, "I'm sorry."

Chester instructed, "Closer."

Gary continued, "In perfect golden ecto is a unicorn."

Mike asked, "In here?"

Gary finished the Golden Unicorn story.

Chester mentioned, "He likes you."

348

Gary started talking as we got moving.

At a pause Mike declared, "I've seen this before." With the rustle of us moving he claimed, "I could live with her."

Christine remarked, "I can't believe this."

Gary asked Micah to carry something.

Another male spirit complained, "I can't hear."

Gary started another story about the bridge.

After the first line there was a pause where Christine suggested, "I think he wants attention."

Gary went on with the story.

At a pause Christine figured, "I'll put Hank over there." At the next short pause she explained, "They're talking."

At another short pause Chester ordered, "Get it on."

The next pause was long and he stated, "That's what we have for Hank right here."

At the pause after that he announced, "Mike's over there. Where Hank is."

Gary began another story.

At a pause Chester directed, "Go put Hank there."

At the next long pause he asked, "Don't you hate doing this?"

Gary told more of the story.

At another pause Chester asked, "Where's Hank, what's he doing?"

I went with the cameraman ahead of the tour to set up at the next story spot by the water.

Chester admitted, "I don't know what a tripod is. Maybe it's an American ingrate. That would be something Hank would know."

Christine commented, "Hank is doing business."

Chester asked, "Is he here?"

Mike confessed, "I don't see him."

Chester stated, "It's not the cafeteria."

Gary and the tour came back in.

At a pause Mike claimed, "I would like to be with you."

Gary said a few words.

Mike asked, "Can I come with you?"

Chester asked, "They're going to film us right?"

Gary started another story.

At a pause Chester confirmed, "I think you got him."

Gary and the TV people got to where we were. They were having a conversation.

At a pause Mike announced, "Hank's here."

Gary and the TV people finished their conversation.

Chester remarked, "Betcha don't."

Gary said, "Okay."

Chester explained, "That sounds too much like you."

Gary started the next story with a question.

Christine declared, "I can see them."

The TV show host answered, "Yes."

Christine claimed, "They're awakening."

Gary got the story going.

At a long pause Christine admitted, "I heard her."

Chester ordered, "Go see Hank."

Gary went on with the story.

At the next pause Chester asked, "Are all the spirits together? That's okay if Mike stays."

Gary continued.

At the next pause Christine directed, "Look right here."

Gary went to the next pause.

Chester demanded, "Make it work. Who's here?"

Gary talked a little more.

Then Chester made an announcement. It was loud and clear unlike most EVP's when he told everyone, "Watch out for blue seals."

Gary added more description to the story at the water's edge.

The TV people talked about it.

At a pause Chester advised, "Understand the tour."

We moved to go to the stairs and Gary started the Dead Man's Hole story.

When Gary paused Mike asked, "Did you forget about food stamps?"

Gary continued the story.

At the next pause Mike asked, "Are we through?"

Gary went on.

At the next pause Chester insisted, "That's as good as you'll get Hank."

Gary talked to the next pause.

Chester ordered, "Georgia (my mother) can't see what we do to Hank."

Chester did get her for me. It took five seconds for him to leave, get my mother, and come back. It happened in my room.

Gary gave one long line.

Chester instructed, "Just wait and see."

Gary said a line.

Chester announced, "June is here."

Gary gave a short line.

Mike reminded them, "You're forgetting about Hank now."

Gary went on with a boat rumbling by.

When he paused there was still some boat noise as Chester demanded, "Just get over here. I'm so sick of Hank giving up. Mike do you know what you're doing?"

Mike answered, "Yes sir."

Gary continued to the next pause.

Chester suggested, "Let's go see how Mike is doing."

We got to the stairs and Gary began the stories there.

At a short pause Chester stated, "I can hear."

Gary gave a line.

Mike admitted, "I can hear him."

Gary carried on for a while before the next pause.

Mike claimed, "I can see."

Gary said another line.

Chester mentioned, "I'm doing it."

Gary gave a short line.

Mike insisted, "Don't serve it to Hank."

Gary continued.

At a pause Chester directed, "Get in the chair."

There are no chairs near the stairs.

Gary said a short line.

Mike confirmed, "I did."

Gary gave another short line.

Christine announced, "I still can't hear."

Gary finished the story and the tour group talked. We then climbed the stairs to the next spot with Gary talking.

At a pause a female spirit asked, "Isn't that him?"

Gary worked his way into the Bullet Hole story.

At a pause Mike started to say, "Later me and Hank..."

Gary came back in cutting him off.

At the next pause Chester requested, "Let me hear it."

Gary went on to the next pause.

Christine asked, "You got David?"

Gary continued with the tour group talking some.

At the next pause Chester asked, "What do you want with her?"

Gary finished the story.

Chester remarked, "I got too many spirits in here."

We started climbing the stairs again and Christine cried, "I just need to be with Hank."

Gary said a few words.

Christine stated, "Only Hank lives here."

Gary began talking but the sound was interrupted. The sound straightened out just before Gary paused.

Christine offered, "Here's some paper." The paper rustling could be heard.

Gary said a few words then started the next story.

At the first short pause Chester admitted, "I hear him."

Gary went on with the Museum Tape story.

At the next pause Chester asked, "What is Hank doing?"

Gary continued the story.

At another pause Mike announced, "I can do it."

Gary kept telling the story to the 'no bridge' pause.

Mike commented, "Wonder what Hank's doing."

Gary said, "He can't see anything."

Chester ordered, "Tell Gary we're here."

Gary said, "Keeps looking."

Christine asked, "The Gopie?"

Gary said, "He sees the flagpoles sticking out of the fog."

Chester stated, "His name is Hank."

Mike replied, "I love the Hank."

Gary finished the story.

Christine blurted out, "The video tape is on her."

Gary said a few words.

Chester requested, "Let's do that again a little bit. Yeah Mike would hate that."

Gary said a few more words.

Chester told Mike, "There's this thing we want to do to Henry."

Gary and the tour group started talking.

At a pause Chester complained, "He makes my stomach hurt."

Gary talked all the way up to the street level and the statues. He paused when we got there.

Chester remarked, "Hank's back is fucking short. And there's nothing we can do about that."

Gary began to talk about the statues but the passing cars covered up what he was saying.

After a car passed Gary wasn't talking and Chester advised, "Hank should have been here. Where would he might have gone?"

Mike wished, "I'd love to be up there."

Chester offered, "You could be here."

A truck passed.

Chester admitted, "I can't do most of everything."

Mike explained, "There is only Donny and I. Not that you care about that."

A car passed.

Chester mentioned, "Donny could not be here. Even the other spirits do that."

Mike confessed, "I thought Hank was supposed to be here."

Gary and the TV people talked.

A car went by and only Gary was talking.

Two cars passed.

Chester stated, "Hank is right there." My camera beeped.

Chester warned, "Now that Hank's on the move he'll be hard to get."

A car passed and Gary was talking again.

Four cars passed.

Gary was well into the stories at the statues.

At a pause Mike remarked, "Hank should be here."

Gary said a line.

Chester replied, "Hank's already been here."

I was taking pictures and left the recorder sitting on a bench that went around the statues.

Gary came back with a story.

At a break Chester pointed out, "But his kids are there."

Three cars pass with Gary telling the story.

After the third car Chester asked, "Did you look for Hank everywhere?"

Another car passed with Gary back on the story.

At the next short pause Chester asked, "Check everywhere?"

Gary continued the story even with another car passing. As he began the next story he asked, "Do you guys live here?"

Mike claimed, "Both of us live here."

The TV people answered, "Yes."

Gary went back to the story about the streets of Lake Havasu City.

At the next pause Mike announced, "Hank is here."

Gary went on with the story and a car passed. He finished that story with more cars passing. He told another story with so many cars going by there was never a break.

When Gary stopped Chester admitted, "I would not be here. Except what I'm doing with him. You might get a crossover."

A truck went by.

Chester asked, "Can anyone hear what I'm saying?"

Mike replied, "I can hear you."

Gary and the tour group talked as we started walking the bridge with the cars passing. Gary began a story before the first set of cars went by.

At a pause Chester figured, "I should have Hank put on the bridge."

Mike asked, "You can do that to him?"

Another car passed.

Gary started talking as the car passed, but paused when it passed.

Mike asked, "Hank did you eat anything?"

Gary talked again and a car went by.

After the car passed Gary paused and Mike finished, "It's my favorite food."

Gary continued with a motorcycle and a car going by.

Mike stated, "The garbage should be checked already."

Two cars passed and Gary was into a story.

At a pause Chester commented, "I don't believe this."

Gary continued and a car passed.

Coming out of the car noise Mike pointed out, "He won't touch. Any Mexican food either."

Chester related, "Blossom wouldn't touch that either. I'll go with Hank." My camera beeped.

Mike offered, "I'll just take those pencils."

Chester ordered, "Before you say that turn to me."

The tour group talked and Gary joined in.

Gary went back to a story.

Two cars passed and a siren approached. Only Gary was talking.

A third car passed and Chester demanded, "Get out of my fucking chair," with the siren going.

Mike said timidly, "That wasn't me," which was hard to hear over the siren.

Chester reassured Mike, "I'm not mad at you."

The siren went by.

Gary and the host were talking and more cars went by.

Coming out of the car noise Mike asked, "What's been bugging you?"

Chester answered, "I can't expect the Hank to know the true reason. About what's going on here." This was with the sound breaking up a couple of times. "Go on as you've been. What he really went through." The sound broke up three times. "The Judge of the Angels is over here."

Christine admitted, "That is what we've been doing here."

Mike asked, "Do they tell me what to do?"

Chester answered, "They won't give us an answer. So they're stripping me because of what Hank is doing."

Mike announced, "Hank's over here."

Two cars passed.

Chester declared, "He won't get to live here," with the sound breaking up between his words. "Maybe he'll have an answer for Jesus. I hope Hank knows what he is doing."

A car passed.

Chester mentioned, "Cosworth will be here."

Gary came in and a car passed. Gary paused after the car.

Chester stated, "I don't understand."

Gary talked as more cars pass by.

Between two cars Chester guessed, "I don't think Hank can do it."

Mike reminded him, "It takes a long time to quit."

More cars passed with Gary talking.

Gary paused after a car passed and Mike remarked, "It doesn't seem like he'd miss it."

Gary gave a line.

Mike offered, "I have a pencil here."

More cars passed and Gary continued. When the cars passed Gary was still telling the story then he paused.

Chester asked, "Does everybody have a seat?"

Gary went on with four cars passing by.

At a pause between the cars Chester suggested, "I wouldn't take that."

Gary continued with two cars passing.

Coming out of the car noise Mike bragged, "I've actually been through that door."

Chester asked, "Did you ever remember?"

Gary said a short line.

Chester remarked, "It's like you've been everywhere."

Gary was telling the story with more cars passing.

Gary and the cars stopped.

Chester commented, "Hank's out of business. Into the store he worked with me and Christine. Tattoos right here for sale."

Gary came back with the cars.

I started going ahead of the tour.

When all the cars passed Christine mentioned, "He's nice when he's in his bedroom."

Mike asked, "What's he do for fun?"

One of the TV people called out.

Chester said quietly, "He really doesn't do anything."

Christine asked, "Is he the hero today? You know he's not like that in business. Don't you get it? It's all Michael's fault. Hank never does anything."

She sang, "Everything is loose."

Mike replied, "I don't think it's too loose."

Christine ordered, "Me first to get in there. Are you retarded now?" She sang, "No you don't."

Chester asked, "What's Hank doing here?"

Christine added, "In the middle of the neighbor..."

I cut her off with, "I'd like to know if there is some healthy food for me."

Christine asked, "Did you hear what happened? You know that I'm talking. They meant it." She sang, "Playing everywhere. Can't even hear a word. I can't see your order."

I asked, "Is there someone with me?"

A male spirit answered, "Not if it's Hank."

Mike asked, "What queer was that?"

Chester asked, "Was he here today?"

Christine sang, "I don't even know if he even had a mother. What order Jack would be. Everywhere."

I said, "Now I went over there and I was trying to explain what happened."

Chester asked, "So what you thought you were fine?"

Christine asked, "Do you believe he's here?" She then half sang, "Standing over your head. Should it be different? Can we be the same?"

Chester complained, "I've had enough of this."

Christine warned, "Careful Hank knows."

Chester replied, "I don't see Hank."

Christine declared, "He loves you." She then asked, "You wanna try?"

I said, "An interesting thing we know."

Chester confirmed, "I see him."

Trying to stay on the energy topic but still trying to find out about Mr. McCullough I said, "There's nothing to call it except energy. What's his name?"

Christine asked, "Don't you even know your name?"

Chester directed, "We already went through that."

Christine sang, "Don't answer. Is Hank gonna push us here? The main thing is not to..."

I cut her off with, "If not then anyone know where he is?"

Mike answered, "Nostradam know."

Chester added, "I'd say happy for it."

Christine advised, "That's you, wait and see."

Chester told her, "But you bump ass, you go away."

Christine replied, "Not like you said it before."

I said, "But."

Christine asked, "Did you hear that?"

Chester suggested, "You were dreaming it all. I am building..."

I cut him off with, "Thank you for talking to me."

Chester joked, "He's gonna screw that mop of yours."

Christine asked, "Does Hank know?"

Chester explained, "Pretty soon we will see about going. Maybe they will change their mind and take me. The finality of Hank is still over. Do we have to do that on Thursday?"

The "queer" spirit from before confirmed, "Everything we marked down here is on Thursday."

Chester stated, "And we have the right to live alone. All of us get to go home."

Christine observed, "That's what juries do."

The camera was man the first to arrive at the passage door and asked, "What's happening man?"

Chester mentioned, "They sold my favorite thing. Get out of here."

Gary came in talking.

At the first pause Christine directed, "Come back tomorrow."

The TV host spoke.

Christine asked, "Did you hear that they were coming?"

Chester answered, "Yeah, that's right."

Christine pointed out, "There's Mike over there."

Chester replied, "They don't know that Mike's here anyway. So maybe they went somewhere. Put your bag right here. What does he look like?"

Christine answered, "I'll tell you later. Can you come by my place later? I miss Hank," with my camera beeping in the middle of it. She asked, "Can you ever believe us?"

Chester suggested, "I guess we need a tape recorder. Hank is busy. I wish Hank was here."

Christine declared, "Our Castle would play us on there."

Chester commented, "Guess we better turn around."

Christine reminded him, "Don't forget me when I'm at home. Do you have the eight ball? If I was you."

Gary asked a question of the cameraman and he answered.

Chester related, "Only bees like that."

Christine remarked, "Hank went to the bathroom. I can't hear any better."

Chester advised, "It's about time we started talking neighbor. Hank is off doing something. Yo Hank!"

Micah came over and told me something.

Chester stated, "I never had such a good line. Yeah that's what I thought."

I talked to Micah.

Gary and the TV people talked.

Micah talked back to me.

Christine began singing in the background, "I want it better."

Chester acknowledged, "You want it."

Christine exclaimed, "Y'all love me." She sang, "Get happy. Or else you'll get hotter."

Gary started telling a story.

At a break Christine asked, "Do you know what they've been having?"

Gary went on with the story.

At the next pause Christine remarked, "They don't know."

Gary said a line.

Christine blurted out, "Suck my titty."

Gary talked to the end of the story.

Christine warned, "Wait till Hank hears rock and roll. I can't do all of this."

Gary gave another line.

Christine refused, "I don't want to get a picture with Hank."

Gary continued talking.

At the next pause Christine guessed, "I think you're wrong."

Gary ended another story and we head downstairs.

Christine stated, "I'm ready to go back in here. Do you already have someone like me? You will have to take him there."

Chester added, "Take him to a secure place."

Gary and the tour group talked.

At a pause Christine started, "When Jesus was Master all he ever had to do..."

Gary interrupted with a short line.

Chester replied, "That's your opinion."

Gary spoke but behind him Christine asked, "Did you see what the angel did?"

Gary and the tour group talked again.

At the next pause Christine asked, "Are you gonna help me?"

Chester answered, "Catherine's still got money."

Gary talked some more.

Christine started singing, "They do it all the time." She then spoke, "Hope you believe that."

Chester replied, "You can't tell from here."

Gary talked again.

The TV people talked a little.

At a short pause Christine ordered, "Get Hank out."

Gary began the Jack the Ripper story.

At the first pause Christine insisted, "He's not on the bridge."

Gary went on.

At the next pause Chester added, "Not in the bathroom."

Christine complained, "Aw, I already have company."

Gary said a word.

Christine announced, "They're coming. Let your mind get set."

Gary went on with the story.

At the next pause Chester asked, "What are you doing?"

Christine answered, "Getting together with Hank."

Gary continued with most of the pauses having noise from the Heat.

At another pause with no noise from the Heat, Chester suggested, "There's always the weekend."

Gary asked a question.

Chester confessed, "And that's all we know."

The TV host answered Gary.

Christine asked, "So what will Hank do?"

Chester commented, "Maybe we could shampoo him. Maybe he wouldn't stink so much."

Gary closed out the story with a few facts.

At a pause Chester told Christine, "He dances for you."

Gary began another story as we move towards the stairs.

When Gary paused Chester announced, "Hank is here."

Gary told the "me" EVP story real quick as we went by the passage door.

Christine proclaimed, "That was me."

The tour group remarked on the story.

Chester worried, "They're going to take me."

Gary started another story.

At a pause Chester asked, "Can you hear Hank?"

While we were on the stairs with Gary telling the story there was another pause.

Chester ordered, "Pig clean your room."

Gary said a few words.

A female spirit asked, "Is he clean?"

The TV host remarked about the story.

Christine pointed out, "She had you."

Gary went on with the story but being so close to street level the traffic noise came in. Near the end of the story there was a pause.

Chester asked, "Does this story have an end?"

The TV host asked a question and Gary answered.

Gary explained another thing on the bridge.

Christine asked, "Are they going to?"

Chester answered,""They're talking."

Christine replied, "I see that."

Gary continued with the TV host commenting.

At a pause Christine admitted, "I'm just kidding."

The TV people talked about the next shot.

Gary made a comment about it.

Christine predicted, "Hank could really be big here."

Chester related, "He found it."

Christine asked, "Have you ever Mike?"

Chester asked, "Is that what they're aiming for? Touch me right there when Hank moves on."

Mike answered, "Nostrum might know."

Chester announced, "Hank's coming."

Christine confessed, "I've been everywhere."

Chester asked, "Did they finish yet?"

Gary and the tour group talked.

At a pause Chester advised, "Don't be a folly."

Gary and the tour group continued.

We climbed the stairs to street level and as we got there a car passed.

Gary spoke to the tour group when we got to the street.

Chester admitted, "I don't see Hank anywhere. I was sure he was right here."

One of the staff of the TV show talked to me.

Chester stated, "Hank can't save her."

Gary remarked at what the TV people were saying to him.

Chester claimed, "I was hoping that the dare was not good. Anyway something bit me."

Gary gave a line.

Christine started, "Hank won't let anybody."

Chester picked it up, "Anybody would probably choke that."

While Christine stated, "Hank is also a man," at the same time.

Chester then asked, "You think he's going to remember? I wouldn't trust Hank. He wasn't smart anywhere. If I could mix it."

Gary said another line.

Christine started, "And naturally that would be."

Chester finished, "That would be what Hank needs to feel better. Did you like that?"

Gary spoke and a car passed.

Chester stated, "Hank was working on it."

Gary continued.

At the next pause Chester asked, "Did anybody see where he went? Now that his case is in order. I could teach him better. Bring him to me right now. Get your fucking booty movin'."

A car passed.

Christine reported, "I couldn't see him."

Chester replied, "The mark of experience. I know Hank never."

Gary called for his jacket.

Chester finished, "Make your mind about that. After tea and see we'll go somewhere. I could make some rain out here. I swear to God I'm gonna make her fuck Hank."

Another car passed.

Chester explained, "He likes to move. I can't move us with Hank. We got him now so what does it matter?"

Again a car passed.

Chester admitted, "I would rope it. I miss him already. I could send you something."

Gary began a story and two cars passed.

After the cars passed Chester proclaimed, "That one went right through me."

Christine replied, "I never seen it."

Another car went by.

Chester suggested, "Maybe you could help look for him. You won't miss the spirit of Hank. Then you'll feel like you've known somebody."

Two more cars passed.

Gary talked again.

At a pause Chester pointed out, "There is Hank over there. Go send Hank over here."

Gary came back in and a car went by.

At a pause Christine commented, "There is something there."

Chester confirmed, "See you later."

Christine guessed, "Maybe Hank will come at seven thirty."
A car passed.
Chester decided, "I will play with Hank. Can you make it any longer? We ought to put Hank up there."
Two cars passed and Gary came back telling a story.
At a pause Chester admitted, "That hurt him."
The host of the show said a line.
Chester remarked, "That made him screwed."
Gary went on as two more cars passed.
At another pause Chester instructed, "So now to work."
Gary continued the story.
The recorder got full and shut itself off.

CHAPTER SIXTEEN

THE DOWN ON HANK TOUR

The judge was listening to the lamp post story
behind the man's shoulder with Mike by the phone booth

I knew I dreaded writing this chapter. The first time I listened to it the EVP's I filed, they were not that bad but most were from Christine. My decision to drag this thing out had left me feeling like I was now in big time trouble with Chester. It was a feeling it was named after rather than the EVP's I got from it. This is the Down on Hank Tour.

When I turned the recorder on there was a rustling against it. Through that I could hear, "Whatcha doin' Hank?" from Chester.

He also commented, "I wish Hank would help us," a little clearer but through the same noise.

He then claimed, "We got the bridge Hank." Through a heavier rustling he asked, "Can you get your fingers around it?"

I decided to leave the recorder in the phone booth for the first part of the tour.

Mike suggested, "Hank could go crazy," very quietly.

Chester insisted, "Not crazy from me. He wanted to get this."

Christine added, "He wanted the bridge too. What do you know Hank?"

Mike warned, "You might have to take it. You might have to take us through here."

Chester stated, "They said I'm coming back. Hank you're in trouble. And yes. You are in trouble for what you're doing. You told us yourself about the main frame."

Mike added, "You haven't asked a favor. From him once in a while."

Chester ordered, "But now we'll take you on the tour. Then you can sit by yourself. Especially after the tour's finished. Then wait till the sun shines the next day. Hank you're not supposed to be..."

Gary and a lady going on the tour started talking.

Chester remarked, "I just think they're ready. What the heck are they doing? We can do this later. What will Gary think of this? You won't have any favors. Except the ones Mike can do. All I know is you need a trash can. For what the conference is like. You forgot to sign up for asshole Hank. I don't think Hank realizes what we're doing. You better quit your smoking anyway. Maybe you should help Hank. You just do the best that you can. Hank has been waiting for you. Can you feel that? I knew you guys were together. Are you going to talk to Henry?"

Christine admitted, "I can't go through with this."

Chester related, "I told you that we have to. Maybe you should tell him. Maybe Hank will listen. You've always got the plan. You could take the plan to Hank. Only the three of us would know. Then we could get this thing started. Brother has to see what Hank's doing. Hank wants to go through that thing with you again. All you really have to do is look out for Henry. Don't you think Henry deserves time? Hank could meet us upstairs if that's cool. Even Mike could meet us there. Ghosts who go stay with me. Watch out for the new scene."

Christine replied, "I'll remain here."

Mike added, "I'm coming."

Chester mentioned, "That would make us feel better. Hank will be so glad you're here. I could say that you're with him. I will respect your decision."

Mike suggested, "You should take her with you."

Gary and the lady on the tour gave a line each.

Chester pointed out, "There he is right there. Why don't you go over to him?"

Christine answered, "Don't want to be with him anymore."

Mike asked, "Is that what I hear?"

Chester commented, "You look like you're mad at me. Who's the guy that made him talk to you? Maybe the tour will do something good. What will Mike say to his crew? Maybe you shouldn't quit now. Want me to give you his number? I know you don't have his number."

Christine confessed, "I like Hank."

Gary said a line.

Chester told her, "He's your hero for today. You know we've got our duty. I know that you like him. Maybe you should see what it's all going to be."

Christine remarked, "I know you're going somewhere."

Mike asked, "Don't you want to see Hank? Thought you didn't know who he was. I'm ready for Hank. You want to hear something? You don't feel sorry for him do you?"

Christine answered, "I refuse to be hurt though."

Mike admitted, "First I thought it would be a little different for you."

Chester ordered, "You're going somewhere cause I need you. Take him back with you on Thursday."

Mike asked, "Didn't you say you wanted Hank to win?"

Chester decided, "I shouldn't leave her here. I just wanted you to try her. He'll be dragging if you don't."

Christine asked, "Miss your father? Hank didn't do shit."

Chester insisted, "Let me at him. I thought Hank would have told you. Did you hear who came through?"

The clock tower chimed.

Chester asked, "Are you going anywhere?"

Mike guessed, "I know what he's doing here. He came back for her."

Chester mentioned, "We can't just take him anywhere."

Mike offered, "I'll go bring him here. I can't take her."

Chester directed, "Give Hank the first winner. Now what am I supposed to do with Henry? Wonder what he's doing here."

Christine commented, "There's nothing else for him to do."

Chester suggested, "Let's put the paper on Hank."

Christine replied, "It wouldn't matter. I'm not used to being without him."

Chester remarked, "That must really screw it up. Maybe Mike already has it. Isn't T.J. his nephew?"

Christine answered, "No that's his son."

Chester confessed, "I think we better get out. It made my plans fucked up. You can all answer him. Now we're ready. For a grandpa he sure fucked up."

Christine reprimanded him, "That's not a very nice thing to say to him."

Chester reminded her, "Remember Hank is coming. The bridge is up already. I could just say you're coming. They started here last time."

Christine asked, "What did the angels do to him?"

Chester admitted, "They stripped him of everything. Chris was off his mind. Where the hell is Mike? They're ready to start the tour without Henry. If he was right he'd need a different lawyer. They should talk to him like a neighbor."

Mike cursed, "God dammit anyway."

Chester complained, "Don't tell me Hank's not coming. Now we can't have the best tour. Guess Hank screwed up anyway."

Mike stated, "Hank is back there."

Chester told him, "The tour is starting. Ask Hank to do you a favor."

Mike explained, "I asked Gary 'cause I thought he was hungry. This place is really scary."

Christine blurted out, "I'm not talking to you."

Chester remarked, "Put it back on you right now. This way it'll be there when you need it. Maybe Hank could get it together."

Mike added, "Maybe he likes Christine."

Chester replied, "Maybe you two should get together."

Mike commented, "I'm hungry different."

Chester instructed, "You should help Christine. This was you're biggest fish catch you told me. I just wanted Hank to come back for his thing. Did you have any problems?"

Mike related, "I was talking to a moron."

Chester asked, "Who would that be Henry?"

Mike mentioned, "He had a sticker put on him."

Christine asked, "What did he say to you?"

Mike answered, "He started to mention you. Maybe Hank would like to hear some music. Maybe it's you that expects."

Christine demanded, "Mark is through with this here."

Mike guessed, "That should make you feel better."

Christine stated, "That's who sent me."

Mike worried, "You might kill somebody."

Chester suggested, "Let the Hank fly out of you."

Mike asked, "Doesn't Hank still live here?"

Chester declared, "Only you can feel it. I would put Hank on the bridge right now. Do you think Hank would be happy here? Did he ask about that picture? Of you and Henry."

Mike announced, "It's like they already started. Yes I can."

Chester explained, "That's what censors do. I just want to give Henry something that he needs. There's a plan that I have to find. That dress is too tight for him. Time is wiser. Grandpas like to eat up their girls."

Christine mentioned, "I already had an occasion. You told me a different story."

Chester asked, "I think he's a big boy don't you? His mother said it's good for him. Here's the new plan now. I don't know what it taste like. You all should be like I am. Don't say it's for nothing. I think we should really go on the tour. I don't think we should make the spirits suffer. Besides we're all here for the tour. Molly's got her racquet going. There is something you need to do on the tour. Tell all the spirits about Henry. There's a couple that you know. Besides there's coffee brewin'. Can't you help your own family?Now you got the same long hair. Think that's a joke? Not with Hank. He already told me he misses you."

Christine replied, "No he didn't. Slow down," with a short whistle. "Thank you all for coming."

Chester asked, "Did you call them?"

Mike answered, "Yes I did. It's a tsunami. They all got here."

Chester complimented him, "Very good helping with what we need. Maybe you would like to do something on the tour."

Mike admitted, "Make you live here."

Chester commented, "I can't do that. Bull will stay here. Bull will make sure Hank stays in line. And there's a sink hole in the plan. If Hank gets any bigger."

Mike asked, "When is the River Dance coming up?"

Chester warned, "He wants the dance to destroy you."

Christine remarked, "Maybe you should take those dimples out."

Chester asked, "Don't you want Hank up here? He's also a modulator."

Christine started, "Bad day for a headache. The last fucking shower..."

Chester interrupted, "Get all the dope he can find."

Christine asked, "When do they get here?"

Chester sighed, "Never mind."

Christine confessed, "I didn't hear you."

Chester mentioned, "I thought in the morning you did. You gotta be careful who you like. What kind of dope does he like? Does he like green bud? Regular apologize from Hank. Don't forget what we got."

Christine agreed, "I can do it."

Chester stated, "Hank is not at home. Cathy is the secretary for what we got."

Mike announced, "Cathy is my new favorite girl. Can I tell you something?"

Chester pointed out, "Hank is the bearded man. You've got him smoking right now you know. I'll tell you a secret. That's not a very nice Henry. You will have to tell him so. It's nicer than in prison though. There's small stuff like that he has to move. Do you think he'll know what you're talking about? Last year in Washington. My cadaver went after the ice cream truck. Now the museum's got him. What did you think of that story?"

Mike complained, "That was sickening."

Chester asked, "How many EVP's does he have?"

Christine replied, "I don't know."

Chester leaned over the recorder and demanded, "No TV." Then back to normal for, "That'll get him. There's justice in the universe."

Gary laughed.

Chester informed them, "They're waiting for Henry."

Christine commented, "I'm draining."

Gary gave a line.

Mike asked, "Did Hank even buy a ticket?"

Chester answered, "They comp Hank's ticket."

Christine remarked, "I'm not MacGyver."

Chester asked, "You know who made that? Dustin Weaver."

Mike decided, "I should just support what you guys are doing. There he is. Now he went there."

Christine mentioned, "My favorite song."

Chester asked, "Is that all you got? Stop her like that."

Gary laughed again.

Chester guessed, "I don't think they care if even he does it."

People on the tour talked.

Chester asked, "What are you doing with Jessie?"

Gary laughed and said a line.

Mike admitted, "I think you'll do it."

Chester advised, "Doug fits with him on his head. Probably down in that hole is pressure. What's his problem again?"

Mike spoke into the recorder, "I loved it."

Chester directed, "In the first half we'll be together. Tear me a pinch off."

Christine replied, "I don't get it."

Chester remarked, "Here we go, not again."

Mike suggested, "Just leave your things up here. Get your own bed."

Chester instructed, "I think they're supposed to be on foot. Where's the film lady? Did I tell you Hank's at fifty three eight? He bumped her the first week over. He represents me. Listen to my tune I think. Did you finish it and get Phillip's reaction to it?"

Gary gave another line.

Chester stated, "Dublin was right here. And stuff like that would go good. Just bring her. And you'll object to anything. Wait for him to get his jacket."

Gary said a few words.

A male spirit asked, "Does he bring his vehicle in here?"

Chester ordered, "Michael there's something wrong with Cassie. That's how you get started Mike."

The male spirit asked, "Does he eat or drink anything?"

Chester predicted, "Hank will get to be a monster."

Gary came back in with a line.

The male spirit asked, "What else do you think he's doing?"

Mike directed, "You take a spot."

Chester suggested, "Appreciate yourself. I used to be comfortable in Dublin."

Mike confessed, "I've never been through here."

Chester mentioned, "At the Heat."

Gary gave another line.

Chester told Mike, "Watch this."

Gary said a line.

Chester started, "I can tell that you're afraid. They had to separate for destruction. Miss the TNT. Made your heater go boom. I'll try not to work this hard on his book again."

Christine commented, "You can't destroy the bridge."

Chester continued, "Maybe they told you it's been set. I'm not joking. Not what you think we were doing? Have any of the answers brought? I'm teasing you. Now it sucks we got to get them back in."

Gary gave another line.

Mike suggested, "There needs to be a bathroom on it."

Chester practiced, "Dublin had streets with their name on them. Which helps to differate yours and mine. These are the features I'm thinking about doing."

A female spirit ordered, "And make mine with a heater on it."

Mike agreed, "You'll get your heater."

Chester asked, "Have you ever been kissed by anybody? I knew you could get you some."

Mike added, "It's not the only one I issued."

Chester suggested, "Maybe you shouldn't be tasting so good."

While someone was whistling he said, "I'm sure you're bothering Henry."

Mike remarked, "There's not much that gets by Hank."

Chester asked, "Did you see a strange look upon him?"

Mike asked, "Can you see P.J.?"

Chester offered, "I just want to give you this. Those were happy years."

Mike asked, "And do you think his Goddess will save him?"

Chester answered, "Not if he turns his back. On everything we did up to this moment. I think they already started. I have only one decent question. Can Hank only hear what Christine's been saying? Does that mean he does not need me? It seems strange to me."

Gary said a line.

Chester announced, "Welcome to Christine and Hank's world. Those who do wrong get what they want. If you could just magazine me. Now he's changing his mind again. He changes his mind every time."

Mike advised, "Doug will have to seam it right there."

Chester admitted, "There's something wrong with it. It helps to differate when yours is gone. Maybe Hank's not moving."

One of the judges from the Judge of the Angels assured them, "Hank will answer for all his screwin' around. Do you need me to stand by?"

Chester offered, "If you need anything grab Mike."

The judge suggested, "There's more that Mike could handle here. Did you take him through the rules again?"

Chester answered, "There's not a refrigerator where he can go and eat. Don't you think that's strange with all the refrigerators they got?"

The judge remarked, "I just don't believe that this is a compulator."

Chester explained, "You don't think a compulator. Runs through the chopper. Take it back to where Jesus wants it. I don't think there's a handle on it. If you have to push on it. If you talk on it, it will seem better. If everybody could wait right here. And he's married to her. Interactive drive-by elope. And he's thinking serious. But what were you saying to me? Maybe Hank would like some. Has he said anything in response to you?"

The judge asked, "Did I mention I was in a hurry? He asked for a two four zero."

Chester asked, "Were you able to perceive that?"

The judge commented, "Looks like you got your kids in line."

Chester informed him, "If Hank is ready to go through we could put him right here."

The judge asked, "But can he really stand the move?"

Chester answered, "I should take him through this again. Doctor doctor what is this? Cancer would be what the doctor says to him. When we did the conference we discussed this. We have here everything is by the phone that he can do."

A person walked by saying something.

Chester directed, "You could stand over here for a minute."

Gary came in talking about the inside of the pub. He then moved on to the lamppost story.

At a pause Chester confessed, "I think Gary has better stories."

Gary said the next line in the story.

The judge stated, "I like this story."

Gary told the tour group, "It still has the gas regulator."

Chester confirmed, "I knew that."

Christine greeted, "Hey there."

Gary said, "And."

Christine remarked, "Be like that."

Chester directed, "You first. Never could go there."

The judge replied, "I hope you liked it."

Gary added a comment to the lamppost story.

The judge admitted, "I don't like it here."

Gary asked, "Wouldn't you?"

The judge answered, "Yes I would."

Gary asked another question.

Chester suggested, "Just come on."

Gary said, "You know."

The judge asked, "What's he doing?"

Gary said, "Amazing." Then he got the tour to come over to the phone booth.

Chester guessed, "I know what he's doing."

Gary gave the first line of the story.

Chester yelled, "Hank!" loud and clear and then, "is an asshole," he said softly.

In the opening of the story Gary said, "It's not that old."

Chester replied, "It's older than you. Hank is coming."

The judge asked, "Does he have a motorcycle club?" A motorcycle passes by on London Bridge Road.

Chester answered, "No but Hank is streetwise."

Gary and the tour group talked about the phone booth before getting fully into the story.

At a pause Chester asked, "Got the recipe?"

Gary and the tour group kept talking.

At the next pause the judge asked, "Hank was here before him wasn't he?"

Chester commented, "Across the street from the bridge is where we got him. For the last time."

The judge acknowledged, "Alrighty then."

While Gary and the tour group talked, I went into the phone booth and got the recorder.

They paused and Chester reminded, "I told you he was coming."

Gary and each person in the tour group said a line at the same time.

The judge remarked, "That's telling them."

Gary got into the phone booth stories with the tour talking occasionally. When he reached the paranormal stories connected with the phone booth the tour group got quiet and there was a short pause.

The judge stated, "I see that."

Gary told the Marsha and Cheryl story.

At a pause near the end of the story the judge mentioned, "That was pretty."

Gary told about some of his EVP's.

At the end Chester ordered, "Don't tell Hank about this."

We moved away and Gary started telling about the bridge in London.

At a pause Chester asked, "Have you got him?"

Gary went on about the bridge.

At the next pause Chester suggested, "Let's go see what Hank is doing."

Gary worked his way into the selling of the bridge.

At a pause the judge asked, "What's he doing?"

Gary said a line.

Chester answered, "I don't know what he's doing."

Gary said another line.

Christine remarked, "Betcha he can't move."

Gary came in with another line.

The judge asked, "Will he have answers?"

Gary asked the tour group, "You know the problem with the push-up bra?"

The judge questioned, "What did he just ask?"

Chester replied, "Those are probable what Mike misses a lot. I'm not ready."

Gary continued, "God was sorry."

Mike added, "He gave that to Christine."

Christine said, "Beautiful people," over, "Christine."

Chester stated, "This might be the first problem we have."

Mike reminded him, "Don't forget about her."

Christine interjected, "Especially when Hank's here."

Chester instructed, "That's what you could do, hand out pictures. As long as we gotta try to make this."

Gary finished, "God was trying to invite everyone he knew to look at what he created."

A lady on the tour laughed and commented.

Christine remarked, "He tells a pretty rotten story."

The judge mentioned, "Only in name apparently."

Mike ordered, "Pull down the first gear real quick."

Gary got back to the story of how the bridge was built. A minute went by with Gary talking about paranormal investigation and even me talking to some people on the tour about it.

At the end of the conversation Chester asked, "I haven't been talking much have I?That's broken."

The judge asked, "Does Hank go to work?"

Chester answered, "He's only got this right here."

Someone said, "Hamburg, Germany."

Chester directed, "Watch the difference in us right here."

Mike asked from a distance, "Now is everybody back in here?"

Chester explained, "We're just waiting on you."

The judge requested, "I would like some Mexican lighter fluid."

Chester replied, "That's a problem. They have a future as light as..."

Mike interrupted, "Thank you very much for coming down here. Both of you like this?"

We heard Gary say, "Blackbeard's ghost."

Chester asked, "Beards like his did that for you didn't they?"

Gary said, "This is actually called Dead Man's Hole across here."

Mike complained, "Spirits are not after me."

Chester pointed out, "Mandy's still here."

Gary returned with the story.

At a pause Mike remarked, "There's a new man here."

Gary went on with the story.

At the next pause Christine guessed, "They must be mad at Mike."

Gary said a line with a pause.

Mike asked, "You want me to disappear?"

Gary continued the story.

At the next short pause Mike announced, "I'm here."

Gary finished the story.

Christine claimed, "Somehow he called. It was nice of you to ask for her. I just want to hurry."

Chester added, "That's what you get when Hank is here."

Christine stated, "Hank doesn't matter."

Chester replied, "I just don't believe you."

Gary went into the stories on the stairs.

At the first pause Chester asked, "You see Hank anywhere?"

Gary said a few words.

Mike announced, "Hank was here."

Gary finished the first story.

The judge asked, "Whatcha got for Hank there?"

Chester answered, "A lawn chair."

Gary began the next story. He paused after the first line.

Mike guessed, "There must be some time gone."

Gary said, "Now."

Chester ordered, "Try Hank again."

Gary got back to the story.

At a long pause the judge requested, "Tell me more about Hank." At the same time Chester predicted, "He gets sued first."

Gary went on with the story about hitting the bridge with a hammer before a pause.

At the pause the judge asked, "Who's the man. Under the bridge?"

Gary said a few more lines and I turned the recorder off to avoid the traffic noise.

I turned the recorder back on at the passage door after I crossed the bridge.

Christine asked, "Should we talk to him?"

I said, "Okay I'm in."

Christine stated, "It's not the main frame." Then, "No time for Hank though," came from behind me as I was trying to get situated with the recorder and everything else I was carrying.

She remarked, "He's not my favorite project. And now he's in danger of doing this."

A female spirit confessed, "He's too big for us to take him."

I said, "I already ruined the other one."

Christine asked, "What's your name?" at the same time.

By herself Christine mentioned, "Now that we got him."

I answered, "It's Hank."

Christine replied, "Really."

I said, "It's stupid food," while Christine asked, "Now what's the problem?"

Christine came back with, "I wish I had some answers."

I said, "I'm starting to feel like milk," while Christine asked, "How are you going to deal with this?"

Christine reminded, "I asked you a question Hank."

Chester asked, "Did the angels hear?"

I said, "Like a substitute," while Christine stated, "Now we're getting it."

Christine directed, "Go ahead."

I said, "That's what they figure." Christine screamed, "Let's go back!"

A spirit asked, "Can you get a Master?"

Christine yelled, "Now!"

Chester started, "When he's asleep." The judge asked, "You check it?" and Chester finished, "I check his heart."

Mike joked, "Give me a Hank's in there. Hank's in there chopping."

Gary came in with a few lines at the top of the stairs.

Chester asked, "What was Hank doing in here?"

Gary gave a name.

Christine asked, "Can we stay with Hank?"

Chester stated, "Guess who's next to go to his bedroom." Then, "You did last March okay," while Christine replied, "I suppose."

Gary said a line.

Christine announced, "He's in there."

Chester related, "It's actually your tombstone Hank."

Christine asked, "You got the buses?"

Chester confirmed, "Check."

Gary said another line.

Christine asked, "Did you hear my scream? We got you."

Chester answered, "That's more of what I'm talking about."

Christine told him, "They used to be all over me."

Chester confessed, "I don't know what to do about that."

Christine let it out, "You mean you never had a joke favor."

Chester admitted, "I was curious about where you were gonna go back."

Christine stated, "It made you laugh."

Gary said a line to a story.

Christine remarked, "Now that he has something from me."

Gary said a line about me standing at the passage door. I laughed.

Chester informed me, "They wish you were gone."

Mike replied, "I'll wish you back."

Christine announced, "Anywhere I go to I'm everywhere."

Chester started, "Gary and you could..."

Gary interrupted, "Not take food."

Christine corrected, "Hank did not take food."

Gary said, "I got five thirteen year olds to adjust."

Chester replied, "I hope he doesn't mean Hank."

Gary faded out saying a line to his story.

Christine asked, "You haven't been taking their food have you?"

I said, "I never stood by his."

Chester reassured, "That's alright Hank. Baldini's they knew how to treat Hank good."

I was saying, "I couldn't cook to do this."

Chester guessed, "They might do a different loss on Hank. It could be that he knew the first family."

Baldini's was a casino in Reno that comped a meal for me once a week.

Gary came in with a story but behind him Christine requested, "Talk to Hank for me."

A spirit asked, "You want the pass?"

The next line Gary gave Christine ordered, "No reading allowed."

Chester replied, "I already know." He added, "Everybody's programmed to be like that," with Christine saying, "Here we go with some answers that are right."

Christine sang, "Now I'm a head long," with Chester saying, "I don't think you should be doing that."

Chester stated, "They tried to pick up the pieces. It's a tour tour tonight."

Christine sang, "We still love you though Hank."

Chester instructed, "Go agree."

Mike mentioned, "I do."

Gary came in with a story.

I asked, "Christine was it you that's been at the house and talking to Gary?"

Christine answered, "Yeah that was me." She then confirmed, "And I will get on it." Chester asked, "What'd you do Christine?" at the same time.

By herself she admitted, "Right now I'm kind of steamin'."

I said, "And now I'm only on one. And then one decision."

Gary came back in with the story.

I said, "I guess I'll have to at the house so I can feel what's going on."

Gary was still telling the story.

I said, "It's hard for me to have proof of the afterlife."

Christine announced, "We're waiting."

Chester commented, "There's truth after all."

I continued, "When this fine asshole."

Christine asked, "Hank what's the problem?"

I finished, "Always afraid to cut with their food so."

Christine suggested, "You don't have to take it no more."

I added, "I don't like to begin this way."

Christine asked, "You're mad at us?"

Chester replied, "I don't know who he's calling an asshole," with Christine saying, "I don't know at all."

Christine admitted, "I don't know what he's doing here."

Chester pointed out, "All the lies are on Hank right now."

Christine claimed, "He won't make them feel good or bad. I know that he's in love with me," while Chester asked, "Now fight with what?"

With the tour noise in the background I said, "Here comes the tour again."

Christine announced, "Hank's havin' a breakdown."

Chester was saying, "So the story here is," at the same time.

Chester finished, "You listened to a green monster. All the spirits have wide eyes."

Christine asked, "Hank are you going?" I hurriedly said, "Thank you for talking to me." She replied, "You won't get Gary to come around. You might as well just stay down here."

Gary came back in as I caught up to the tour.

Three seconds later Chester stated, "Hank has seen the very first light. And there's no way to pay for that."

Christine disagreed, "There is a way he could pay for that."

Chester admitted, "I don't know what Hank would do."

In a high screechy voice Christine declared, "I have a plan for him. He's still my favorite now. And he and I will screw tomorrow."

Chester asked, "You'll be with that monster? I've got to be there for this."

Christine agreed, "If you have to."

Chester remarked, "That will be my next big project."

Gary said a line.

Chester announced, "There's Gary."

Then the song in the background sounded like Christine singing, "Since we ring a bell. And we sing about it. But we're not rocking too much."

Gary came back in with a story. He finished that story then went on to the Jack the Ripper story.

Behind Gary, sounding like the public address system at the Heat, Chester asked, "Can you hear what I'm saying? Two of my favorites are back here. We'll be stopping soon. There was someone here yesterday is that true or untrue? Okay Hank, take a picture if you know what I said. I'm tired of this. All the angels roaming they've seen what you're doing Hank. Everything you've done has put you in that situation."

Gary paused and Mike stated, "You turned him down."

Gary continued the story without Chester in the background.

At the next pause Christine asked, "Who you blaming?"

Gary gave a line.

Christine asked, "What are you doing?"

Gary said, "A sailor."

Christine remarked, "That's your problem."

Chester announced, "They are through with that."

A lady on the tour said, "Wow."

Christine confessed, "They all know what you're doing."

Chester defended himself, "I'm just playing with Mike."

Christine replied, "You're a man."

Chester changed the subject with, "Hank's around here somewhere. Now Hank will take a picture."

I told our friend on the tour I was going to take a picture.

Gary said a line.

Our friend offered me his camera and I told him, "I like my camera."

Chester stated, "Now he'll do it."

Next came the click of the shutter but not the electronic beep. I said, "Weird stuff happens like that."

I kept talking about pictures with the friend.

As I was describing a picture Christine remarked, "He knows about us."

I finished talking about the picture.

Gary went into another story.

At a pause Chester predicted, "There'll be a grave."

Christine was saying, "He wants to be cremated," at the same time.

The tour group talked a little.

Christine suggested, "They won't let you."

Gary continued the story.

At the next pause Chester guessed, "A heart attack will do."

Gary went on with the story.

At the next pause Christine asked, "Can you see over there?"

Gary gave a line.

Chester pointed out, "That must be Hank over there."

Gary continued to the next pause.

Christine remarked, "It's like he never did."

There was some talking from the tour group as we climbed the stairs.

I turned the recorder off before we got to street level. We crossed the bridge again. As the tour reached the top of the stairs I went down to the lion spot and turned the recorder on.

Chester stated, "He's not the Jesus of men."

Gary started talking and I said, "There's a spirit behind us."

Gary went on talking.

After the story Chester directed, "Rest tonight Hank."

Gary went into the lion story.

At a pause Christine mentioned, "He is an asshole."

Gary went on until he talked about the two lion pictures he had and paused.

Chester reminded me, "So do you."

Gary said he's taken thousands of pictures of the same spot and never got a lion.

Chester asked, "What about Hank's picture?"

Gary stressed, "Nothing," with a reaction from the tour group.

Chester figured, "So Hank doesn't count."

A lady on the tour laughed.

Christine exclaimed, "What the heck!"

Chester replied, "The gift that was brought to Hank doesn't count."

I asked softly, "What the hell was that? Was that good of him?"

Gary finished that story.

Chester reassured, "Don't worry."

Gary asked a question to start the last story.

Chester advised, "You're listening to Hank too much."

The tour group answered Gary.

Chester confessed, "I don't see a problem with it Hank."

I stayed at the lion spot when the tour moved on and sighed, "That was it."

Chester asked, "What's your problem?"

I asked, "Why did he do that?"

Chester answered, "I don't know."

Gary called out for my camera.

I acknowledged, "Okay."

Christine commented, "Hank sounds better."

Chester replied, "Dope."

Christine added, "Hank's still trying."

As I joined the tour they spoke to me.

Chester stated, "But he's still the same as he was."

Christine remarked, "He didn't ask any questions."

Chester advised, "Wait till we get home. Wait till you see what's coming here. That's your savior."

The judge asked, "He is emotional isn't he?"

Chester said softly, "I didn't want Fred to notice. Get a picture of this."

Gary started talking about the picture.

As I showed the picture to the tour group Chester denied, "I didn't do it."

Gary continued the last story.

At a pause near the end of the story Chester announced, "We got Hank performing here. Not while I'm thinking."

Gary went on with the story.

At the next slow down in the story Chester complimented me, "That looks a lot better Hank," with Gary saying, "Okay."

Gary went on.

At the next short pause Mike asked, "Should we go home?"

Gary continued with the last lines.

At the end Chester warned, "Hank better be careful going home."

On the way to leave through Dead Man's Hole Gary paused.

Chester stated, "I know what they're doing."

Gary said a line.

Chester rallied, "Now we can do this."

Some spirit said, "I'm not a liar."

Chester asked, "Who was he?"

A male spirit answered.

Gary said, "Olaf the Viking," in Dead Man's Hole.

I shut the recorder off.

CHAPTER SEVENTEEN

THE WINDY NIGHT TOUR

Some orbs could be dust particles, others are not

Everything happened that week. Christine and I were together a couple of times at the beginning of the week. Thursday Chester took me out of my body when I was asleep. I woke up four feet above my body with Chester pulling on me. I said, "I'm not finished, I have to write the book." I broke free to get back into my body.

It felt like my connection to life was very loose for the next day. I felt I would die if I fell down or bumped into something too hard. I was doing better by the weekend for this tour. It was a windy night and I was wondering how the spirits were going to react to it. This is the Windy Night Tour.

I went to leave the recorder on top of the phone in the phone booth and when I turned it on Chester asked through the wind noise, "Hank what are you doing there? I brought the council with me."

Christine remarked, "Now you're talking to Hank."

Chester explained, "I just want to talk to Hank. Can you get Hank to move? Hank will you move over? Thank you. Can you get over here? There will be a space here. Just be careful you don't bump into that. Did Hank tell you anything? I know what he's doing with Mike."

Christine asked, "Now that Hank's here are you gonna do it?"

Chester replied, "Now you want to stay with him. And you'll change about the bathroom. You don't think Hank knows what he's doing?"

Christine asked, "You don't think Hank cares?"

Chester answered, "I don't think he knows that. I'll tell you what he's gonna do. He will fuck you later. Probably tonight again. But here I'm gonna fuck with Henry."

Mike asked, "Is that okay so far?"

Chester came back with, "As long as that makes you happy. I'll talk to you about it later. According to what Hank says. We've all been talking. Hank will go to the bathroom. If you want to be with Hank. Then you could smash the shit out of him. Now he's a monster for sure I think. That will match up better. Go to the bathroom. You're all up for it anyway right?"

Mike confessed, "I would have been earlier."

Chester instructed, "I will see you later. Now that Hank is here. We're gonna take what Hanky said. And that's not what the inventory said. That Hank was told. Hank won't be able to get away with that. But Hank will feel good later. Right here I'm gonna tell him like it is. Did you ask him why he did that? Go to the bathroom like that. I can't believe he accomplished that. He is a psychic."

Mike volunteered, "I can vouch for him."

Christine replied broken up, "You don't have to there Mike."

Chester asked, "You know what you're doing there right? Hank will be back here later. You stay put. While I pick this up. And hear the stories that Hank has told me."

Christine suggested, "You should turn it down just a little."

Chester mentioned, "Hank can do that."

Christine announced, "Hank is here."

Chester ordered, "Now you'll be with Hank later."

Mike asked, "How much later would that be?"

Chester insisted, "You're not supposed to be doing anything."

Mike claimed, "I was just getting started."

Chester asked, "Do you think Hank would mind him doing that? You know what Mike is doing."

Christine asked, "Is he making Hank horny?"

Chester directed, "No you would have to do that."

Mike stated, "Hank is just getting started. If you want to get started on it. Bring Hank over."

Chester asked, "Are you going to do that to him? There's too many out there. You'll have to do that to Hank later. We will have a chance to talk to Hank."

Mike asked, "Can I talk to him later?"

A female spirit requested, "Can I step right through here?"

Mike answered, "If you would like to."

Chester remarked, "You have the hots for her."

Christine added, "She just might take him out of here."

Mike came back with, "That's not it, I'm talking to Hank."

Chester commented, "You don't think anymore."

Mike remembered, "Hank went right through here before you guys."

Chester replied, "That's okay we'll talk to him later. Take good care of our friend Mike. That's our friend over there Mike. You're going with Mike to do that. I didn't think Mike would take that on. Can you tell me what you think? So I don't have to tell Hank this story. And now we'll have to talk to him after all of this. I didn't know you cared. He's constantly been over here. Did you think that Hank might be over here? I've been with Hank a million times. If you like Hank then say something. Didn't you hear those conferences?"

Christine answered, "If you need whatever then I have to. Hank..."

Chester finished, "Doesn't even know. He has to quit smoking. You've been smoking Hank. I gave him a simple task. He got the best of everything I gave him. I might as well not given it to Hank. I guess it doesn't matter right now. Talk to Hank for a minute. That's who I'm talking to."

Mike asked, "Hey Hank are you doing something? Remember all the things I've done for you? You have the best thing on Earth right now. All the spirits that know her. Think that you're a lucky man. It's okay if I stay right here. I got to go with her to the bathroom. I hope I get to talk to you again."

Chester returned with, "Okay Hank I'm back."

Christine pointed out, "That's his car right there."

Chester asked, "You want me to give some assistance?"

Mike admitted, "I think we can get it done right here by ourselves."

Chester offered, "Then I'll go on talking. I've been talking a lot more than usual. That's what Hank wanted us to do. And all we want him to do is quit smoking. Hopefully that will get to him. That is all I have to do. Get Hank to stop smoking. I wish you would smoke a pack to accomplishment. Over accomplishment of each of us. That's what you get when I am on it. Give me that room right next to Henry."

Mike asked, "You won't mind if Hank lives here?"

Chester declared, "Hank will always do whatever."

Mike added, "Hank's been down there."

Chester asked, "Does he tell you where he wants to live?"

Christine replied, "As long as it's not the bathroom."

Chester advised, "People do have to go in there. That's your sweetheart."

Christine countered with, "You don't have to trust people."

Chester stated, "Hank was long before that. A different version of Hank. That's the one we saw," with a siren going by. "That was his maintenance man. That sure was Henry. Nice of you to ruin that man," with the siren again. "Why did he have to lose it? He won't be smoking here anyway. I don't want the rest to be like Henry. They will laugh when he's living here."

A male spirit exclaimed, "Get the fuck out of my room!"

Chester asked, "I can't go in there? What if Hank comes with me in there?"

The male spirit answered, "I'd like to see you make that happen," with the siren still going.

Chester admitted, "That was a very good answer. Let's get the fuck out of here. I'm through with Hank. Did you see what happened?"

Mike asked, "With the siren?"

Chester told him, "Hank was welcome. But I would have to go with Hank."

Mike replied, "I don't see why Hank could do it. Maybe 'cause of Christine."

Chester complained, "All the spirits like Hank. What a guy. Hank is so popular. This is not the only thing I've ever done. You can ask anybody that's here. He's got some pussy right now. And he has some money. And I think he has some meals. Hank couldn't be more happy. Should I take him to dinner and a movie? I just might have to do that. If they agree to push it. I love these days even more. Until Hank sees everything. He ever does doesn't matter to me."

Christine ordered, "You can't say that to Henry."

Chester pleaded, "If you really like him. Then you'll know why I did that. Maybe if you really like Hank."

Christine remarked, "It doesn't matter what I say. Nobody can hear us."

I went by and said, "I did good."

Chester asked, "Did I just hear your husband Hank? Now that is his true form. Do you have a message you want me to give Hank?"

Christine answered, "Tell him I asked for therapy. And it's not because of him."

Chester asked, "Can I ask what you mean?"

Mike suggested, "Maybe he damaged her."

Chester replied, "No I don't think." Then Christine said, "Hank," and Chester finished, "Would do that."

Christine stated, "Hank would be a good philosopher."

Chester asked, "Are you serious? Hank isn't smart enough to do that."

Christine related, "He has to do nappers like I do."

Chester admitted, "You're alright. I have all the proof I need. Do you think he's satisfied? Do you know what he's doing? He is smoking whatever he can get his hands on. Didn't I try to tell you? Hank is such an asshole. Are you going to his place tonight?"

Christine sighed, "I can't even if I wanted to."

Chester offered, "Then I'll do it. You won't mind if I do that?"

Mike added, "He knows you."

Chester mentioned, "It's not like we have an inventory."

Mike suggested, "Maybe he's accomplished to do everything."

Chester confessed, "Hank is all the inventory we have."

Mike guessed, "You'd think Hank would come in here."

Chester informed him, "Hank likes the wind. He's excited."

Mike stated, "We're not going anywhere."

Chester explained, "It's not like he's on a magick bus. It's more like he's got magick time. All it took was his life. There's the dose we need. I need the bathroom."

Mike announced, "Hank is coming."

Chester remarked, "It's about time. Come to dinner Hank. Downstairs Mike has something for you Hank. There's nothing for you to do Hank. He still likes to come in here."

Mike asked, "Did you know he has the hiccups?" He hiccuped when he said it.

Chester replied, "No wonder he won't talk. That just makes matters worse. And I've been waiting. I'm tired of talking."

Christine asked, "Is Hank up here yet?"

Mike figured, "Whatever we cover up. I suppose you can't afford everything."

Christine guessed, "I don't think Hank would be coming back here."

Chester ordered, "Let's go do magick work."

Mike confessed, "I forgot your cousin was going to be here."

Christine asked, "Why won't you give Hank the chance to try something different?"

Mike answered, "There are only so many things he can handle."

Christine asked, "Got any smooth tape? Dustin just answer."

Mike asked, "You think Hank will remember us after he dies?"

Chester declared, "I don't care if he remembers me anyway. If Hank makes it up here we're good."

Mike asked, "So what would be your answer?"

Chester replied, "Maybe if he hurts you."

Christine warned, "Now you're gonna stress out Mike."

Chester asked, "Did the world treat him fair? It's his blind side. Don't you think we should trust him?"

Christine commented, "Yeah but we should try to be nice."

Chester claimed, "I was being nice."

Christine pointed out, "When you talk to Hank you're not very nice."

Gary came through with a line.

Chester stated, "They're going to miss the party tonight. Wait for Hank and then we can get started. Hank's in trouble with the Judge of Angels. Give Hank the compulator."

Mike suggested, "Let's try to get out of here."

Chester asked, "Did you ask Hank about doing that? You were also gonna ask about doing something to Hank. Hank's the most blind person I've ever seen. Can you move through there? Let's go see what Hank is doing. We don't have to move from here. Now Hank is ready to get started. Did you ask about doing that to Hank?"

Mike answered, "I don't see Hank though. Hank is still back there."

Chester replied, "I said he could be ready. Will you look after Sharon?"

Mike asked, "You won't fight with me will you? When will Hank be ready?"

Chester asked, "Do you know what you're doing?"

Mike confirmed, "When we get started."

Chester admitted, "You will know about it when I get started. Just be ready for Hank then."

Mike mentioned, "Hank is the one that really matters."

Chester instructed, "Back on the girl Mike."

Mike complained, "Hank is busy doing that. Hank will never get to this side over here. Hank better do something real soon."

Chester ordered, "We'll be right here when he does. Maybe you should sit down and think a bit."

Mike assured him, "It'll be okay once I speak to Hank."

Chester asked, "Ready to go meet him there?"

Mike asked, "Can we even do that anymore?"

Chester answered, "Nothing they can do about it."

Christine interjected, "Hank will be larger."

Chester added, "Hank will be larger than all of us put together. That's the truth even if you don't believe Hank invented the compulator."

Christine asked, "So what has Hank been doing here?"

Chester proclaimed, "I'll be damned if he's gonna mess that up," with someone saying, "Buy cat food." He then figured, "I know that Hank will do that. Like he built the compulator. I'm surprised you didn't marry him. Let Mike do the compulator."

Mike asked, "Did you see him in the newspaper?"

Christine remarked, "I don't know what you're talking about. Don't be so careless."

Chester insisted, "You'll do that. Doctor, I think Hank will be saying that."

Mike asked, "How many chances does he get?"

Chester guessed, "I think he has three or more."

Mike replied, "I'd marry him."

Chester suggested, "Maybe you two should get together."

Mike remarked, "Hank would rather be married to Christine."

Chester declared, "I don't think he knows he's gonna be the author of our book."

Mike confessed, "I don't have any idea what Hank's gonna do."

Christine confirmed, "He already said what Hank did."

Mike agrued, "You all want me to be a computer."

Chester stated, "I heard that."

Christine exclaimed, "Thought he said that. Are you lying for me when you say that to me?What was that? I haven't heard that before."

Chester commented, "Hank wouldn't say that. Now you're gonna say that to us when Hank is present?"

Mike related, "When I say something it shouldn't make a difference."

Chester asked, "And that's it?"

Christine admitted, "Yes that's what Hank would say."

Chester added, "Except Hank would have done that much later. That's the way we've been doing this Mike."

Mike complained, "Still feel like I'm in the middle of what you're trying to do with Henry," with Chester saying, "You're closer," before he could finish.

Chester suggested, "Though you need to move faster Mike."

Mike replied, "I'll be going right now."

Chester agreed, "Okay don't come back until you've cleared it up."

A new male voice asked, "What was that about?"

Chester answered, "Mike got his panties twisted."

The new male asked, "Was it something Hank said?"

Chester confessed, "He just got twisted on me."

The new male asked, "But wasn't he talking to Hank?"

Chester explained, "He was talking to Hank's machine."

The new male voice asked, "Well has Mike been helping?"

Chester came back with, "That's funny, I had to train him to help me."

The new male asked, "And he has a computer?"

Chester told him, "But Hank knows how to doctor those things on a computer. You'll meet Hank when we go the last time through."

Christine claimed, "That'll make him happy."

Chester declared, "Jesus came to see what Hank was doing. Hank will never hear of this. I will bring Hank home with this. But he's never gonna believe it. That computer is not worth it. Do you hear what I'm saying? Are you and Mike going somewhere?"

Mike admitted, "We're not going where Hank is at."

Chester remarked, "I still can't believe Hank recorded Jesus. Even after the problems he had."

Christine stated, "You're grandmother's here."

Chester replied, "I haven't seen her yet."

Christine added, "She is as close to family that Hank's got."

Mike commented, "Looks like you know what we're doing."

Christine mentioned, "And Hank's got a new bed."

Mike suggested, "Let me smell the new bed for him first. Is that the best that Gary could do?"

Christine answered, "You gotta give Gary credit."

Mike asked, "Can I stay in the bathroom with Hank?"

Christine pointed out, "He has an apartment here."

Chester confessed, "I thought you already went there first."

Christine told him, "He was in the bathroom first. Have you asked where the spirits have gone?"

Chester related, "They took Jesus back home. Hank must not matter to him."

Christine asked, "Is he leaving that tour for us?"

Chester instructed, "Whatever you give to him doesn't matter."

Mike stated, "He's a good man."

Chester confirmed, "John left Saturday."

Mike remarked, "That was good for here. Can you leave on Saturday?"

Chester announced, "I just want to say Mike's the captain of my little tour."

Mike asked, "Hank, have you even found her?"

Christine asked, "What did he look back for?"

Chester asked, "Has he looked for you?"

Mike requested, "I wanted to visit with Hank. Do you know where Hank went? I was gonna get that order of medicine."

Chester guessed, "I don't think Hank is coming."

Mike asked, "What if the council hadn't been here? Would Hank been here?"

Chester answered, "I'm angry about Jesus."

Mike replied, "That was a beautiful man it shouldn't matter."

Chester confessed, "That was just true Mike. I guess you're better as a magickal being than I am."

Mike acknowledged, "Now you're thinking better."

Chester announced, "Baseball is at nine-thirty. Are you looking across the infield now?"

Mike added, "Then maybe Jack has been here."

Chester suggested, "You better go get Christine back here. What are you supposed to be doing?"

Mike asked, "Is that a vest you're wearing?"

Chester asked, "What happened to the compulator?"

Mike answered, "They dropped it a couple of times."

Chester remarked, "It looks pretty beat up."

Mike admitted, "It's just mancipated. They already made arrangements. A long time ago they started."

Chester asked, "Have you ever used one?"

Mike claimed, "No I haven't had the chance to use one."

Chester stated, "The inventor of that was Henry. He carefully stored it for us to find it. Now look what they've done to it. I think that Hank would like his compulator. Can you move it to our place?"

Mike insisted, "I'd rather let Christine do it."

Chester asked, "Did you remember what happened before?"

Mike commented, "I just think it would make Hank feel better."

Chester replied, "I will talk to her in a little bit for you."

Mike asked, "Can you say I'm scared?"

Chester confirmed, "Yes Mike I'll say you're scared. What did you say to Hank over there?"

Mike confessed, "I was trying to get Hank to move."

Chester declared, "You won't get that man up outta there. You should hear him in his bedroom. I can't think of a better disaster on TV. He has so many problems that he can't remember."

Mike recalled, "I can remember that he felt much better. After he had gotten better. It's pretty windy down here."

Chester asked, "Does it make you feel a lot better? If you have to we can talk upstairs. There's nothing left that I do."

Mike asked, "Have you figured anything out?"

Chester announced, "No man does like I do."

Mike remarked, "I'd rather try anyway."

Chester asked, "Have you talked to Hank?"

Mike answered, "Around the corner from the famous London Bridge. I hear all the peeps got corners. Did you want me to do any better?"

Chester instructed, "Those are fine, whatever you get to work. Goth said what you say doesn't matter."

Mike asked, "You want me to talk to him?"

Chester directed, "You might as well stay on the subject of corners. Hank won't mind what type of corners."

Mike added, "That's amazing how nice he is."

Chester admitted, "I could say it doesn't matter. I don't think Hank would get mad. Talk to the stupid machine."

Mike explained, "If I was in the military I would. Give Hank a Sargent. Over him. I'll be by in a couple of minutes to heal you. You know you've got a shoulder injury. And a bad memory. I can't help you with that. Whatever you say. Puts a bounce in me."

A female spirit boasted, "I can fix just about everybody."

Mike asked, "Do you know who said that? Did you say you know her?"

Chester asked, "Did you know her Mike?"

Mike continued, "Everything in my heart says you're hungry. You've got to get something to eat."

Chester related, "Hank you can't go without eating. I can have you turn this over. And you won't have us on there."

Mike remarked, "Hank wouldn't know what happened."

Chester mentioned, "Then you could turn it on. Exactly to where it's supposed to be. That's gonna be my next idea."

Mike commented, "That's not fair to Henry."

Chester replied, "Like Hank's been unfair to us. Remember we don't have much time left. Remember what Hank just told you."

Mike asked, "Can Hank do that?"

Chester answered, "Hank doesn't know what he's doing."

Mike added, "I still got things for Hank."

Chester stated, "He got Jesus on that thing."

Mike asked, "What was Hank doing there?"

Chester declared, "He came to see what Hank was gonna do. And me I was up in here. But then Jesus left because he was tired. But Hank never answered."

Mike replied, "I can't believe that."

Chester agreed, "I couldn't believe it either."

Mike asked, "What else do you think he did?"

Chester related, "He made a surprise visit. He had to see more people. I got the computer so he won't work. On it when he's being good. Can you pin this here? I don't like doing this anymore."

Mike confessed, "I don't think I can keep that straight."

Chester asked, "Did he bring anything in here so far? And now it looks like Hank is coming."

Mike mentioned, "Well I've seen Hank over here."

Chester asked, "Why don't you break that thing? Leave that for him on. That's exactly what I'm looking for. That's the road that goes through here. Hank will never get this done. Mike will get Hank done. Hank will never come through here again."

Mike added, "I don't know where he was."

Chester asked, "Jack, do you know where Hank has gone?"

Jack answered, "I haven't seen Hank for quite some time."

Chester asked, "Mike, have you seen Hank anywhere? Where has Henry gone? He's been walking around here smoking already. Maybe he won't favor us with coming. I know he's fascinated by what we're saying. Even though some of it's not true. You'd think he'd have to believe us. But he said now he wasn't sure. I had to bring his mother to him. And she said that she told him. That if he wasn't good forever. That he would probably not see her. But since he's old it probably doesn't matter. He just has to get busy to get started."

Mike asked, "Did he have much to do today?"

Chester informed them, "He has been killed. But he wanted to live. He doesn't have it calculated. How much time he has. But once he gets started. He should have gotten started last night. But I feel better. I never really thought he wanted to be an asshole. But he always tends to act that way with me. He's coming. Hank has a different volume than Hank had. I hope that's not a problem with what he had. After Saturday then nothing matters. I'd like to be proud of him."

Christine remarked, "I just think it takes Hank a long time."

Mike replied, "You came down here."

Chester figured, "That's worth the time it took for examining Henry. What is it Hank?"

Mike confessed, "I was comfortable in here."

Chester suggested, "It's time we started pickin' up the asshole."

After some people walked by talking Christine asked, "Can you guys tell what Hank is saying?"

Chester related, "That would have been our present."

Christine stated, "Hank is a computer."

Chester added, "That's when the journey is nothing. Did you ever get started? No matter who you are."

Christine asked, "Can you wait out here with Hank?"

Chester asked, "Does it matter to you? Do you like it longer? Hundreds of miles to pick up shampoo for him. Got a stupid answer?"

Mike tried, "Midnight at Boomtown."

Chester continued, "That's not too smart. That's not too hot apple for you. That would be cool if I had a camera."

Mike asked, "Did he last all night?"

Chester answered, "That's not a good question Mike. I guess I should keep it secret I suppose. Now we can move out."

Mike asked, "Do you like blonde hair?"

Chester replied, "Just when we're getting ready to go."

Mike added, "But we have to smoke their tires."

Chester stated, "I think the party's over."

Mike asked, "Did you want to type this out?"

Chester ordered, "We'll let Hank do that."

Mike asked, "You don't have the fire to wake up do you?"

Chester explained, "No I've never experienced that."

Mike announced, "Hank isn't wearing any underwear."

Chester informed him, "Hank never does and neither does Christine."

Mike admitted, "Damn if I had only known that."

Chester finished, "You would have peeked at her."

Mike confessed, "It's the shocking truth. Especially before Christine and Hank were together. Are you a family man?"

From there it was so broken up it couldn't be understood. I got the recorder out of the phone booth and we started the tour. It was most clear by the phone booth with no important EVP's. Gary canceled the tour by the time we got to the stairs as sand was blowing in everyone's eyes.

This book was meant as a guide to the recordings. Each sentence spoken by a spirit is a sound file.

I feel that Wicca is more correct with the equality of male and female matching the pairings of Chester and Christine, Sherry and Brad doing the everyday workings of the bridge, the Gopie Gary and Misty settling disputes and leading the bridge residents. The energy working of Wicca exactly matched the way spirits will lien, give energy and heal. Even when Chester said, "You start the balling right here," he was making an energy ball just like you can learn in Wicca.

In this book we saw the spirits refer to each other as family. Can't we learn to do that in this world? They also showed us there is nothing to fear on the other side. Can we learn to accept the journey that our souls take?

I can't say what Christine actually is. I would define spirits as those who have to lien. Angels do not have to lien. Christine never openly liened but never admitted to being an angel. Chester told Gary and me he was an angel over the ghost box. Christine will always seem like an angel to me. We are still in contact two years later.

I tried to write this book without a lot of my opinions so that you might get your own impressions of what they were saying. My opinions are affected by other conversations I've had with these spirits and other spirits without recording them.

Lightning Source UK Ltd.
Milton Keynes UK
UKOW04f2000050815

256466UK00001B/121/P